Women in Science, Engineering and Technology

Women in Science, Engineering and Technology

S Thakur

MD Publications Pvt Ltd
New Delhi
www.mdppl.com

Published by :

MD Publications Pvt Ltd
"MD House", 11, Darya Ganj,
New Delhi - 110 002
Phone : +91-11-45355555
E-mail : contact@mdppl.com
Website: www.mdppl.com

ISBN: 978-81-7533-356-7

Published and Printed by Mr. Pranav Gupta on behalf of **MD Publications Pvt Ltd** at Mohit Enterprises, Delhi.

Preface

Women have contributed to science from its earliest days, but as contributors they have generally not been acknowledged. Historians with an interest in gender and science have illuminated the contributions women have made, the barriers they have faced, and the strategies implemented to have their work accepted.

The Age of Enlightenment saw an expanded role for women in the sciences. The rise of salon culture in France in the period brought philosophers and their conversation about contemporary political, social, and scientific topics into the homes of the wealthy and powerful. These salons were mostly orchestrated by women, as the home was traditionally female space, and several well-known women emerged as figureheads in salon culture for both their hostess skills, bringing together the enlightened intellectuals of the day, and their own intellectual contributions to the conversation.

Three decades ago women's movements around the globe were rigorously questioning the exclusion of women, their interests, and visions of the good life, from policy debates, including those of science. What underlying assumptions and processes had led to the noticeable underrepresentation of women scientists and engineers, and what was responsible for their even lower numbers at higher levels in scientific and technological institutions?

In the last 30 years, great progress has been made in analyzing and responding to these concerns. Despite the roadblocks, women have made headway, if unevenly, as they enter the fields of science and technology. Greater opportunity in these fields has allowed more women to share good wages, interesting work, and high social status associated with these occupations. It appears that improving women's opportunities in science has benefited both the sciences and the cause of women in general, for the example of women's successes in fields thought to be most resistant to them has provided powerful encouragement to women seeking equality in other endeavors.

Advancing scientific careers for women has led to other benefits for science, the most obvious being an enlarged pool of smart, well-trained, and highly motivated individuals from which to staff its projects. Whatever the social, political, or psychological benefits that men may have gained by discriminating against women in the past, the intellectual loss has never been justified. Invoking gender criteria when recruiting and advancing the best scientists and engineers works against their interests. Moreover, these days the presence of significant numbers of women in a field often increases its legitimacy and the value of its work in the public perception.

I am very grateful to Mr. Pranav Gupta, Director of MD Publications Pvt Ltd, New Delhi, for his kind cooperation and support for this book.

S Thakur

CONTENTS

1

Women in Science, Engineering and Technology

An Introduction

Young girls do not start out with low achievement in science. Early in the high school years, however, many girls experience the beginning of a departure from science typified by enrollment in fewer science courses, lowered achievement and increasingly negative attitudes. The significant loss of talented young women from science education and occupations is the focus of this.

Even though women have been entering the formal workplace in record numbers since the middle of the twentieth century, they have not entered jobs in science at a similar rate. Women represent 46 percent of the U.S. labour force, but they hold only 22 percent of the jobs in maths, science, and engineering. Somewhere along the way, between the earliest training and entry into the labour market, gender stratification occurs. Science jobs are among the highest paying, highest status jobs in the labour market. The shortage of women in this area helps maintain gender inequalities and represents a significant amount of lost talent.

GENDER AND SCIENCE

There is considerable agreement among researchers, educators, and policy makers that the last few decades have seen progress for women in science. Young women are now as likely as young men to take certain high school math and science courses. The gender gap in average math proficiency scores has disappeared at ages 9 and 13 and has nearly disappeared at age 17. The number of women earning advanced degrees in math and science is increasing, as is the number employed in math and science occupations. In spite of these gains, however, the gender gap in science has not disappeared. Recent reports using information on students and workers in the 1990s provide alarming evidence of the persistance of the gender gap in science:

- In elementary school, young girls are less confident of their abilities in science and math and less interested in careers in science and engineering than are young boys. This is true in spite of similar exposure to courses and similar achievement (National Science Foundation, 1994).
- Surveys of 17-year-olds show that young women take fewer advanced courses in math and are less likely to take chemistry and physics courses than are young men.
- Surveys of 17-year-olds also show that gender differences persist in math proficiency scores at the highest levels (e.g., algebra and multistep problem solving) and in math achievement test scores. Beginning at age 9, there are gender differences favoring males in both science proficiency (what the student knows and can do) and science achievement (what the student should know and should be able to do) test scores.
- In their last year of high school, young men are more than three times as likely as young women to expect to pursue a career in science, math, or engineering.
- In many areas of science at the secondary and postsecondary level, teachers are overwhelmingly male. Teachers at all levels of education and of both sexes discriminate in the classroom and have lower expectations in science and math for females than for males.
- Parents also discriminate against daughters. A majority of parents believe that their sons are better in mechanics

and math than their daughters, and they fail to give their daughters the most elementary training in the use of tools to build or repair mechanical objects.

- Although women have earned the majority of bachelor's degrees in all fields combined since 1982, they earn a smaller portion of bachelor's degrees in science and engineering (44%). Women are especially underrepresented in engineering, where they earn only 15 percent of the undergraduate degrees. Although the proportion of master's degrees and doctorates earned by women in science and engineering has increased, women are still underrepresented here as well. They receive 45 percent of the master's degrees in science and engineering fields and 29 percent of the doctorates. In engineering, women account for only 14 percent of the master's degrees and 9 percent of the doctoral degrees. At all post-secondary levels, women are more likely to drop out of science and engineering programs than are men. A vast majority of women in science programs are in life sciences, psychology, and social sciences. Recent evidence suggests that the 20-year trend toward less sex segregation in fields of study has slowed down considerably.
- Women make up 42 percent of the labour force but only 22 percent of the science and engineering labour force. Within this labour force, they hold lower status positions, receive smaller salaries, and are more likely to be unemployed or underemployed compared to their male counterparts. Many of these differences persist when qualifications are taken into account. Despite initiatives on the part of industry to recruit and retain women, women scientists are less likely than men scientists to be employed in the industrial sector of the market.
- Institutional practices that begin in graduate school and continue in the workplace function to keep women out of science. In a recent survey of engineers, 56 percent of the women said that they were aware of cases where females had been overlooked with regard to career opportunities. Another survey of women scientists showed that large

numbers had experienced or witnessed sex discrimination or harassment. There is considerable evidence that the culture of science in the workplace continues to be a male culture.

THE SCIENCE PIPELINE AND LIMITATIONS OF PAST RESEARCH

Many researchers and policymakers use the imagery of a science pipeline to think about the relative access of women and men to the fields of science, math, and engineering. The image is one of a training pipeline running from early training in primary and secondary school through advanced training in the university to the hiring of qualified scientists in the labour market. Berryman was one of the first to introduce the notion of the science pipeline and the formation of a scientific talent pool from which science professionals could be drawn. Aptitude, course taking, and achievement are often used to determine whether a student is in or out of the pipeline.

When visualizing the pipeline, it is perhaps more accurate to think of it as a funnel, since all elementary school students are in the pipeline but many drop out along the way. Research on women's participation in this pipeline shows a pattern of declining course taking and achievement along with increasingly negative attitudes about science. Most researchers have suggested that this decline begins in high school and worsens in the undergraduate and graduate years. Sells considers advanced high school math classes the "critical filter" that keeps many women from entering the male-dominated math and science professions.

Although the pipeline imagery is becoming pervasive in the literature and descriptive information on the number and characteristics of men and women in math courses or with high math scores is available, the research in this area has a number of limitations. These limitations go beyond the well-known problems of unrepresentative samples and inconsistent measures that have led to conflicting findings. There is surprisingly little research that provides insight into the complexities of the process by which so many women opt out of science. A good example of the lack of attention to these complexities in past research is the tendency of many analysts to focus on single dimensions of the science experience or single dimensions of factors affecting science experiences.

For example, Oakes has noted that much attention has been given to women's math experiences, but that very little attention has been aimed at their science experiences. In a similar fashion, researchers often focus on a particular dimension of experience, such as achievement, course taking, or attitudes. The implicit assumption has been that the different areas of experience are related in such a way that knowledge of the experience in one area reveals insights into the experience in other areas.

There is, however, evidence that the different dimensions of experience in math and science are not so perfectly correlated. In fact, young girls' attitudes about math and science may turn from the positive long before they stop taking the classes. And even after many girls stop taking the math and science classes, those who stay in the classes do not get lower grades than their male counterparts, although their standardized scores are usually lower.

In a research four aspects of experience in both math and science explored: achievement (e.g., grades and standardized test scores), access (e.g., course taking), attitudes, and activities (e.g., use of calculators, microscopes, computers and the like). The first three of these have been given some attention in the literature, but we know less about young women's activities in math and science. Researchers and the federal agencies that monitor science achievement in the United States have suggested that these areas of science are important dimensions of students' science experience.

In general, we know much more about women's experiences than we know about the causes of these experiences. When researchers do look at causes, they often follow the same unidimensional approach that they use to describe science experiences. Some researchers have focused on schools and teachers, some on personality characteristics and choices, and some on family characteristics. Although these studies are important, they do not provide a view of the entire process leading to success in science or of the complexities in that process. For example, when researchers focus on personality characteristics, explanations for the original source of the personality differences are often not attended to.

In one of study four sets of causal factors: gender, family resources, school resources, and individual resources. I describe women's science experiences as being at the end of a complex path of causal influences. That is, the influence of gender is not necessarily just. A direct influence, but rather it might also work indirectly through family experiences that affect school experiences and that ultimately affect individual characteristics and experiences.

Additionally, researchers have been slow to realize the ways in which the individual and social factors that are typically seen as causes of science experiences might interact with each other to affect those experiences. Likewise, these individual and social factors might interact with experiences in one area of science (e.g., attitudes) to in turn affect experiences in another area of science (e.g., achievement). This research acknowledges the fact that women's resources in one area of life might interact in a unique way with resources in other areas by carefully examining interactions between multiple causes of science experiences.

A set of interactions that are particularly important for understanding the complexities of women's science experiences are those involving gender, race, and social class. Special attention is thus given to these interactions in this research. Although some researchers have used multidimensional models to examine women's science experiences, these experiences have typically been addressed in a relatively static way.

Some researchers use cross-sectional data to infer causal relationships. Even when longitudinal data are used, science experiences are often seen as a one-time outcome, with early science experiences included as independent variables predicting later experiences. Some researchers use longitudinal data to present "snapshots" of students' experiences in the different time periods.

In effect, they are using longitudinal data in nearly a cross-sectional fashion. This is especially problematic given evidence that the science pipeline is very fluid, with many students entering and exiting. It cannot be assumed that snapshots of students at various points in time (even snapshots using longitudinal data) represent the same pool of students. In addition, longitudinal studies examining the pipeline from high school into careers are rare. A long-term approach does not stop with the end of education, is important given the evidence showing a considerable exiting from the sciences after college and graduate school and before young people enter occupations.

In this research, the fluidity and long-term nature of experiences are recognized by following young people and developing patterns of experiences' over time science trajectories. These trajectories begin with early training in high school and extend to postsecondary school and occupations. For example, some individuals will have early success and interest in science but will drop out at critical decision points (e.g., after their sophomore year in high school, after their senior year, after college) while others will drop out later or stay in the pipeline.

In other words, this research describes distinct patterns or trajectories that women experience in science and the school, family, and personal/psychological experiences as well as resources that are associated with the trajectories. Few researchers have looked at multiple sets of experiences in the sciences over time as outcomes to be predicted. The research reported here follows the life course perspective in acknowledging the fact that science experiences, like other individual experiences, are not onetime events but rather are dynamic and constantly changing, with much variation between individuals in the way they are encountered.

Another limitation of the literature on women in science is its atheoretical nature. The typical approach to the problem is to create a long list of independent variables and test them for statistical significance. The emphasis is on statistical sophistication, not on theoretical development. Thus when statistical relationships are found, there is no broader conceptual context within which the findings can be interpreted and understood. In the research presented here, a conceptual framework involving the creation of lost talent through selection processes and unequal resources is used to look at the role gender plays. Both differential treatment on the basis of gender and differences in family, school, and individual resources are seen as critical factors in understanding why so many talented women leave the sciences.

Another critical shortcoming of much of the research on gender differences in science is the tendency to make conclusions about "boys" and "girls" without paying attention to important statuses other than gender, mainly race and class. We know that low-SES (socioeconomic status) and non-Asian minority youth have lower achievement in science than do their upper-SES white counterparts. But some have found that African American youth hold more positive attitudes about science than any other subgroup. Thus we cannot assume that some or all of the science experiences of African American women will be more negative than those of white women.

Interestingly, some have found African American girls to be more positive about math and science than their white counterparts. Can we conclude that the gender pattern among white youth is duplicated amongst nonwhite youth? The limited research which is available suggests that we cannot. For example, athough overall gender contrasts show boys in more advanced high school math courses than girls, among African American youth, the opposite pattern prevails.

A final limitation of past research on women in science involves the emphasis on the individual actions and decisions of women in the science education realm as separate from larger structural processes involving education and occupation systems. That is, the link between the reproduction of power and status at the macro level and the individual expectations and attitudes of young men and women is seldom acknowledged. Work by Kerckhoff, Bourdieu, and others that show how culture is reproduced and how personal education and occupational choices draw on real structures and opportunities is essential for understanding the loss of talented young women from science.

Fox's work on women in science occupations provides further support for the importance of structural factors over individual factors in understanding women's success in science. When different school, family, and individual experiences of young women are examined in this research, they are viewed as reflections of gender differences in power at the macro level. Recent work showing how advances for women in science training have not been equally matched by their increased entrance into scientific occupations sheds more light on the need for a structural approach to women in the sciences.

In spite of these findings, the majority of work on women's access to science professions assumes that training is the key to occupational equality and focuses solely on the factors that would enhance that training (e.g., teachers, curriculum, nonbiased books, etc.).

These limitations leave many unanswered questions about women's experiences in science. Do young women lose interest in science at the same rate as they lose interest in math? Is this true for all women, regardless of their social class and race? Do they experience a decline in all aspects of math and science, including achievement, course taking, attitudes, and activities? Does gender have a direct influence on science experiences, such that equally qualified girls and boys end up with different experiences, or does it indirectly affect science experiences through the unique family, school, and individual characteristics of women? What are the characteristics of women who stay in science? Are their families different? Their schools? Are these characteristics causes of perseverance or just correlates?

In sum, although the alarm has been rung on the shortage of women in science, we have not come very far in our understanding of the complexities of women's experiences in science nor of the complexities of the explanations for these experiences. In this research, groups of young women are followed over time in an attempt to begin to understand these complexities. Using large, national samples of young people and a conceptual framework that suggests that deficits in resources are a key in understanding the loss of scientifically talented young women from the sciences, the research seeks to discover the complicated patterns of women's experiences in diverse areas of science.

It also presents a picture of the successful woman scientist-what her family is like, what her school provided her, and what personal strengths she had that made the difference in beating the odds. Before describing these women and their experiences, it is important to consider the larger social and economic context of science in the United States.

THE STATE OF SCIENCE AND THE ECONOMY

We are living in a society that is increasingly reliant on science and technology. With the Soviet launching of Sputnik in 1957, a push to produce more and better U.S. physicists, chemists, mathematicians, engineers, and medical researchers began. Since then, the United States has been an international leader in research and technology. But whether the United States can retain that lead is far from certain. Noted scientist Carl Sagan has concluded that we "live in a society dependent on science and technology in which hardly anyone knows anything about science and technology." Changes in the economy have not resulted in larger numbers of students going into science and engineering. The percent of college students majoring in science and engineering has remained constant over the past 30-some years.

Others suggest that interest in these fields may actually be waning. In 1988 less than 1 percent of college freshmen said that they would major in mathematics, down from 4 percent two decades ago. Physics and chemistry majors fell from 3 percent to 1.5 percent. The late 1980s saw a similar decline in interest in engineering, although in 1990 and 1991 enrollment in engineering programs increased slightly after a 9-year decline.

International comparisons of students provide additional cause for concern. The best American students are not competitive with their peers in other countries when it comes to math and science. The Second International Math Study (SIMS) and the Second International Science Study (SISS) look at students from 20 countries, including the United States. They show that students from many other countries, including Japan, Hong Kong, England and Wales, and Sweden, know much more math and science than do even the best students in the United States. One of the findings from the science study is that U.S. students were tied in science with students in Singapore and Thailand for fourteenth place in a group of 20 countries.

Concern about U.S. competitiveness in science and technology is rampant. It is fueled not only by the state of science education in the United States but by the consequences of weakening competitiveness for America's economy, standard of living, and national security. It is in the nation's interest to have high-quality education in science and engineering. Well-educated workers are increasingly seen as the "human resources" or "human capital" that is required for a competitive advantage. The state of science education is not the only problem looming in the country's science future, however. Demographics add a further complication.

Demographers, labour economists, and concerned government and business leaders recognize a potential problem in the nation's labour pool. Projected retirements in the science and engineering sector during the 1990s will reduce this segment of the work force by about half. According to the National Science Foundation, 60 to 70 percent of current faculty members in engineering and natural sciences will be retiring or leaving their positions in the next two decades. Regardless of whether the number of exiting scientists is as large as this, the documented stable or declining interest in science and engineering majors in recent decades does not suggest a labour pool rising to fill these openings.

Future work cohorts will include increasing numbers from two groups-women and racial minorities. Most of the college freshmen of 2005 were born by 1987. Demographers tell us that because of the low birth rates of the 1960s and 1970s and the resultant "baby bust" generation, the number of 18-year-olds is declining and will not stop doing so until the mid-1990s. At the same time the number of women getting college degrees and the number of minority youth are increasing. Women and non-Asian minorities have not historically held degrees or jobs in mathematics, science, or technology.

Although women have been entering the work force at an increased rate since the end of the Second World War, they often occupy lower status, nontechnical jobs in the service sector of the economy. One of the major labour supply challenges for the United States over the next two decades is to develop a balanced work force possessing the technical skills necessary for jobs in science and engineering. To do this, women will have to be integrated into the technical and scientific sectors of the labour force to a far greater extent than at the present.

Education, family, and occupation systems in the United States have consistently turned a majority of females away from science education. Many young girls who start out doing well in science end up with little scientific interest and knowledge. It is this training and education that provide the critical link between labour force needs and supply. What happens to the talented young women in this educational process? Recent work on educational systems suggests that gender is one of the major classifying characteristics in determining who will succeed and fill high-level positions. This assumption is at the core of the conceptual framework used here.

THE CONCEPTUAL FRAMEWORK

Beginning with the work of Blau and Duncan and continuing in the "Wisconsin" model of status attainment, the research on educational and occupational attainment in the United States has primarily relied on a functionalist, socialization model. That is, the research assumes that differences in attainment can best be understood by differences in learned skills and motives, and thus that the attainment system offers a fair system of rewards to the most talented. Prior to the introduction of Blau and Duncan's status attainment model, theoretical work in the United States and Europe focused more heavily on the structural factors that affected attainment, irrespective of individual merit.

The inability of the status attainment model to explain equally well the achievements of blacks and whites, men and women, and upper class and lower class brought about a renewed interest in the structural impediments to achievement. Theories focusing on class, allocation, sponsored mobility, the regulation of ambition, cultural capital, and segmented labour markets all questioned the ability to understand achievement without considering social structures.

These arguments about the import of nonindividual factors in social mobility systems suggest that there will be a considerable number of youth who are talented and motivated but who do not achieve because of their placement in the stratification system. In this research we are interested in exploring this "lost talent" among young women in science. The conceptual framework that is used here to approach the problem of talented young women exiting the sciences is one that stresses structural barriers or selection processes that directly affect science achievement through gender discrimination but that also indirectly affect science achievement through the transmission of "gendered" socialization and unequal allocation of resources in family and school environments.

Kerckhoff and others have questioned the socialization model of achievement and argued that young people's expectations are not so much developed through the socialization process as through knowledge of the real world. Although everyone may want to succeed, people in different strata have different expectations as to their chances of success. For youth in more disadvantaged social positions, these expectations may start out high but tend to be lowered over time as they observe the successes and failures of others like themselves.

The link between position in the social structure and individual attitudes is discussed in a number of theoretical works on the achievement process. Bourdieu suggests that societies reproduce themselves and maintain a system of power by means of the transmission of culture. The reproduction of culture through education plays an important role in the reproduction of the whole system, and culture is arbitrarily imposed by dominant groups. Bourdieu suggests that education systems control mobility by selecting out the students who will achieve.

The selection process is one that assures the continuation of the status quo of the system and is based on categories such as gender, race, and class. Those who are not in favour then begin to develop more negative attitudes toward school in anticipation of the barriers that confront them. Other work on the role of status effects in educational systems is remarkably similar in noting the selection process and the anticipation of success reflected in students' attitudes. Kerckhoff discusses an allocation process whereby individuals are not free to achieve according to their talents but rather are subject to social forces that "identify select, process, classify, and assign individuals according to externally imposed criteria". Students' expectations for their future are then affected by these observed constraints.

Further insights into the notion of lost talent come from Turner and Hopper. Turner made important contributions to our understanding of the role of structural factors in educational systems by distinguishing systems that allow free competition (contest mobility) from those that stratify early on (sponsorship mobility). Hopper added to this notion by stressing that societies need to be assured that high-level positions will be filled. They must, then, develop ambition in all youth. Through the process of selection by external criteria, some but not all will succeed. Hopper suggests that societies must then "cool out" the ambition of the unsuccessful in order to avoid social conflicts. Education is a major vehicle in both the selection and the "cooling out" processes.

Little empirical work has been done on the intersection between status in the stratification system and loss of talent. Although there is research that shows that the status attainment model works less well for women, blacks, and individuals from lower SES backgrounds, it often does not explicitly look at stratification status and the selection process. In my recent examination of lost talent among U.S. youths I found considerable loss of talent through mismatched aspirations and expectations and through reduced educational expectations. This loss varied with gender, race, and class.

One way to examine the selection process is to look at changes in expectations over time. Much of the evidence on women's educational expectations suggests that women are more likely than men to adjust their educational expectations downward over time, especially with the advent of marriage and children. Research has shown that boys' educational aspirations and expectations exceed those of girls, and that there is a greater consistency between the aspirations (hopes) and expectations among young men than among young women. One of the few researchers who have not found gender differences in educational expectations and aspirations is Mickelson. Her unique sample and measures may be a partial explanation for her findings.

In Gaskell's study of working class females, she found that young women believed that they were making personal educational choices but that those choices drew on real structures, and opportunities. The choices tended to reproduce class and gender structures, with the working class girls choosing nonacademic courses of study that would prepare them for clerical jobs. In sum, research on the general educational aspirations, expectations, and achievement of young people suggests that gender is an important factor in creating lost talent. What does the research show about science education?

Although it is clear that women are underrepresented in science, longitudinal examinations of the extent of lost talent and the process leading to it are rare. The first goal of this research is to describe carefully women's and men's experiences in the sciences in order to assess the nature and extent of talent loss, especially among young women. But how does the lost talent process work? How are talented young women "cooled out"? Evidence from science research grounded in feminist theory and focusing on power and status in science occupations and from the structural theories reviewed above suggests that inequalities based on gender are maintained by differential treatment based on gender alone as well as by differential access to resources that favor young men over young women.

The assumption is that different ties to the power structure create gender stratification but that differential access to resources is necessary in maintaining the stratification. Although economic structure at the macro level will not be measured in this research, the conceptual framework used here assumes that the differences in resources flow not from natural individual differences between the sexes but from gender differences in these ties. As the discussion below suggests, the family and school play a major role in redistributing resources that are potentially important for success in science from the larger system to individuals. How does this process work?

LITERATURE ON RESOURCES AND SCIENCE

FAMILY RESOURCES

Family socialization and resource allocation are key ingredients in maintaining the sex stereotypes and norms that keep the gender stratification system intact. Beginning with birth, parents give children cues about appropriate gender-linked behaviors. These cues act as resources for children's later educational activities and interests. For example, mothers' communications with sons contains more of the verbal stimulation thought to foster cognitive development (e.g., explicit speech, and teaching and questioning that contain numbers and action verbs) than does their communication with daughters. Boys and girls are given toys, clothing, physical environments, and rewards for two distinct types of behaviour.

Boys are encouraged to be outgoing, aggressive, independent, and analytic, while girls are encouraged to be passive, dependent, and nurturent. Likewise, parents encourage mathematical achievement more in boys than girls and accept lower mathematics achievement in girls than boys. Parents hold different educational and career expectations for sons and daughters, and these expectations influence those of their children. Even parents of mathematically gifted students have been found to view careers in mathematics as less appropriate for daughters than sons. These data are complemented by children's perspectives. Boys perceive their parents as being more positive about their mathematics achievement than girls do.

Research on women who succeed in science education and occupations shows that these women often had family backgrounds that allowed them to develop independence in an environment with diverse role models. They tended to have families characterized by well-educated, parents, family stability, parental encouragement of androgyny and of achievement in science, and maternal employment. These women were also more likely than others to be first born.

Experiences in their family of procreation have also been found to be associated with women's entry into and success in science. Women with husbands and with young children fare less well than do other women. These family experiences do not appear to work to the disadvantage of men in science.

SCHOOL RESOURCES

Three areas of school influence have been stressed in the science achievement literature - the "hidden curriculum," course taking, and peer influence. This literature shows how teachers, courses, and peers act as resources for achievement in science. They stress gender differences in treatment and access that limit women's resources and accomplishments. Advocates of the "hidden curriculum" thesis propose that teachers hold different expectations for the two sexes, which they communicate in subtle but pervasive ways. It has been shown, for example, that teachers give more attention to boys than to girls, invest more cognitive time with boys than with girls in mathematics and science classes, and hold higher expectations of mathematics achievement for boys than for girls even before actual differences in achievement appear.

Girls also receive less encouragement and information about courses and careers in math and science from high school guidance counselors. And these teachers and counselors have effects on decisions that last well beyond the high school years. Teacher influence during the high school years also comes in the form of role modeling, for having women science teachers in high school increases chances that a young girl will choose a science major in college and do better in college science courses.

The gender gap in science course taking has been well documented. On average, girls and boys perform equally well in mathematics up to about grades 6 to 8; however, the number of females who continue to take mathematics courses drops precipitously during high school years, and this differential course taking in mathematics is found even when achievement and ability are controlled. Further declines in science course taking among women occur in college. Women choose science majors at a much lower rate than do men. One obvious implication, then, is that as early as junior high school females choose not to undertake the advanced training in math and science that leads to careers in the science and technical fields.

An additional loss occurs through lack of exposure to scientific thinking and, perhaps, leads to a lack of appreciation for the kinds of understanding scientific knowledge can provide. Women's knowledge and course taking in math are important resources for access to high-status occupations. Their lack of knowledge and course taking in math acts as a critical filter that keeps women out of a host of occupations, including chemistry, physics, engineering, computer science, and occupations in the social sciences and business that require an understanding of statistics. Numerous studies show the importance of gender differences in attitudes and achievement in math and science during high school for determining persistence in the scientific pipeline in the college, postsecondary, and early work years. For example, interests and performance in college math and science courses are strongly linked to math course taking and achievement test scores in high school.

Finally, we can think of the school peer group as a resource for young women's science achievement. Studies have shown the importance of support from female friends for young women's continuation in science. Peer group norms are at least part of the explanation for the success of single-sex girls schools in recruiting young women into math and science courses and, in general, in preparing women for nontraditional occupations. Finally, a recent ethnographic study of college women showed that the peer group was a major factor in shifting young women's goals away from careers and interests in science and toward romance and heterosexual relationships.

INDIVIDUAL RESOURCES

How do individual characteristics of young men and women affect their science experiences, and to what extent are they a product of the different resources allocated to men and women in school and the family? At the center of the research addressing these questions are the notions that institutions define gender roles and that these definitions become forged into a diffuse "gender belief system" that shapes the day-to-day behaviors and attitudes of men and women, boys and girls.

Although boys and girls are equally likely to report that they like math, math comes to be defined as a male preserve. Girls often fear that success in this male domain will make them less popular among peers. The content of courses may be important in conveying messages about girls' ability in mathematics. Early research showed that girls do more poorly on word problems based on male activities (e.g., woodworking and guns) than they do on the same problems put in the context of femaletyped activities (e.g., cooking and gardening). It is also interesting that girls' math skills improve when they are examined by other women.

There is ample evidence of the effect of cultural norms on women's perceptions of their abilities. For example, a number of studies have shown that students' achievement in math depends on its perceived usefulness to their future careers. Thus if girls do less well in math, it may be due to their implicit understanding that math skills will not be useful to them in their future family and work roles, and, in fact, that the pursuit of professions that use these skills will conflict with their future family roles. In both high school and college, women's identification with traditional sex roles and their perception of the incompatibility between science careers and family pursuits keep them from entering and persisting in the sciences.

Men, on the other hand, do not see the pursuit of math and science as being in conflict with their family roles. In fact, women's perceptions of the career/family conflicts for women in science careers are probably accurate given the pressure for early productivity in these careers. Others cite the motive to avoid success as an explanation for women's lack of achievement in math and other areas of intellectual ability. According to Homer's research, women want to succeed but are ambivalent about success in the context of social proscriptions concerning bright, successful women. However, replications of Horner's work have not reproduced her results.

There is no reason to believe, then, that men and women differ in their basic motivations for success, but the research stimulated by the fear-of-success concept has shown that individuals are sensitive to the social consequences of their achievement behaviour and that these consequences are perceived as different for men and women in particular situations. Related to these social costs are the strong stereotypes held by young women. Many believe that math and science are more useful and important for and better understood by boys. This stereotyping begins as early as the primary grades. Other personality characteristics that vary by sex and that have been shown to act as resources for achievement in science include confidence and self-esteem; sex role attitudes; educational/occupational expectations; and locus of control. These personal resources persist in their importance after the high school years. DeBoer found that one's perceptions of one's ability in science and one's attribution of success in science to ability were important predictors of participation and performance in science during college. Men have the advantage on both of these.

GENDER AND LOST TALENT

In sum, it is argued here that young talented women are more likely to leave the sciences than are young men because of structural barriers and selection processes. To some extent, the larger power structure is reproduced in the cultural milieus of families and schools that offer different experiences and resources to young women and men. But structural theories also argue that these experiences and resources cannot fully explain the differences in women's and men's achievements - in this case, persistence in the science pipeline. Gender status in and of itself is an explanatory variable to the extent that equally qualified young women and men will not have equal opportunities in science. Discrimination based on gender alone is part of the reason for young women's lack of success in science.

Recent work by Stockard, Charles, Hanson et al. and others documents the fact that women's advances in education (including science education) have not been met by similar advances in occupations. When Stockard looks at variation over time in the disparities between men's and women's education and income in the United States, she finds that income variations are much larger and virtually unrelated to variations in education. Stockard concludes that the ultimate explanation for the continuing disparities in the occupational world cannot, then, be attributed to women's lesser training but instead must be assigned to cultural beliefs and practices that give preference to males.

Charles's examination of data on occupational segregation in the United States between 1950 and 1970 confirms Stockard's analysis. In the same years that the economy was developing and entering a postindustrial stage in which women obtained more education, Charles finds that occupational segregation increased. Fox provides further evidence for the importance of structural rather than individual factors in determining science achievement. She finds that individual characteristics involving training and family experiences have little explanatory power in understanding the gender gap in status and earnings in science occupations.

There is a long history of research on women in science that suggests that structural impediments are a major factor in marginalizing women scientists. Thus well-trained women continue to experience barriers in the science occupations. The loose link between women's access to education and occupations suggests that although education systems have been opening up to women, gender discrimination in the work arena continues to consign them to low-status, low-paying occupations.

In sum, the research presented here utilizes a structuralist framework that suggests that gender will have both a direct and an indirect effect on science achievement. The direct effect will occur through discriminatory actions and policies of key institutions that are based solely on gender, regardless of qualifications. The indirect effect will occur vis-à-vis the unequal resources offered to young women and men. Thus both insufficient resources as well as gender discrimination are explanations for the exiting of bright, talented women from the sciences.

DATA AND METHODS

It borrows from the above literature on lost talent, status and resources, and the science pipeline. In general, the model shows the different ways in which gender can affect science experiences and the relationships between key variables in the science achievement process. The time order of the key factors in the model is suggested by the left to right placement of the blocks of variables, with causation moving from left to right. All blocks of variables are assumed to have direct effects on science experiences. In addition, earlier variables can work through variables that occur between them and science experiences to affect these experiences.

Gender is exogenous in the model. It is the status variable, which comes first in the process. Family and school resources and ultimately individual resources are endogenous variables, which come next. Finally, the model shows the outcome of interest - experiences in the sciences. The model reflects several important characteristics of the science outcome. First, these experiences are multidimensional. To understand the totality of science experiences fully, four dimensions must be considered: achievement, access, attitudes, and activities. Students may be high on some of these dimensions and low on others.

Hence, focusing on a single dimension denies the multiple ways in which young people can experience science. A second important characteristic of the science pipeline is its longitudinal nature. Over time information on students in different stages in the pipeline is provided to describe these experiences. In addition, this causal model operationalizes experiences in each area of the science pipeline with trajectories that represent typical paths in an area over time.

The model also reflects a number of characteristics of the causal process leading to experiences in the sciences. Most important is an acknowledgment of the different ways in which gender can affect science experiences. First, gender can have direct effects on these experiences, regardless of the family, school, and individual resources a student might have. Another important aspect of the effect of gender on science achievement is that the effect of resources might be different for girls and boys. (Both interactions and separate analyses for males and females are used to address this issue.)

That is, girls may be less able to convert their family, school, and individual resources into science success than their male peers. Thus gender interacts with resources such that resources have different effects for girls and boys. This effect, together with the direct effect of gender on science outcomes, can be classified as the cost of being in the female status. These effects represent gender inequality and discrimination since they involve differences in outcomes that are dependent only on the gender status, regardless of individual qualifications. Gender can also indirectly affect experiences in the sciences by influencing important determinants of science experiences - resources on the family, school, and individual level. Gender differences in status and power are legitimatized by cultural beliefs and sex-role socialization that define science as a male realm and contribute to the unequal channeling of key resources. Young women then come to agree with these beliefs and develop individual and personality characteristics that conform to them. Thus the model shows family and school resources preceding individual resources.

In sum, the model reflects two ways in which gender per se can affect experiences in the sciences - a direct effect and an effect vis-à-vis its interaction with resources. Both are effects of gender status that occur in spite of individual talents and resources. The model also shows how gender can indirectly affect science experiences by affecting the level of resources allocated to young girls and boys - resources that are critical for science achievement.

A variety of statistical techniques will be used to assess the model. Descriptive statistics will be used to show levels of resources and types of science experiences for young women and men. Multivariate statistical models (including Analysis of Variance and logistic regression) for the total sample and for subsamples of women and men will be used to show the effect of gender and resources on science experiences.

The empirical analysis in this research will focus on available longitudinal data sets involving large nationally representative samples. These data sets allow assessment of the factors in our lost talent model and cover the years from grade 7 through early adulthood, during which youths might travel through critical education and early occupation segments of the science pipeline. The longitudinal nature of the data allows for clear assumptions about time ordering of life events and the straightforward creation of trajectories, or over-time patterns of experience. The data sets are ideal for testing the model of gender and lost talent in the sciences.

Three data sets are used. The first, High School and Beyond (HSB) contains data that were first collected in 1980 under the auspices of the National Center for Educational Statistics. Base-year data collected in the spring of 1980 from approximately 58,000 high school sophomores and seniors were obtained from a multistage stratified cluster sample from 1,015 high schools. They were interviewed again two, four, and six years later, providing information on high school experiences as well as early postsecondary and work experiences. HSB offers excellent measures of resource variables as well as science experiences.

The sophomore cohort is of special interest since it is at this time that women begin falling out of the sciences. Given this and a need for parsimony, the causal model will be applied only to the HSB sophomore cohort. Only those individuals who participated in all phases of the study were included in these analyses (N = 11,683). Note that those who dropped out of high school between grades 10 and 12 are not included in the sample. However, all analyses include weights that control for sample attrition and nonresponse. Important descriptive information on the nature of young women's and men's experiences in the sciences will be provided for all data sets.

The High School and Beyond data also include information from the teachers and principals at the students' high schools. We use data from the supplemental 1984 "Administrator and

Teacher Survey" to provide information on teachers (gender, training, ratings, time spent on instruction, and influence on curriculum, content, and teaching technique) and schools (number of years of math and science required). Although the respondents were no longer in high school in 1984, the NCES argues that these data are still valuable since these school characteristics are fairly stable over time.

The data come from a probability sample of 532 of the original 1,015 schools in the High School and Beyond survey. One principal from each school and up to 30 randomly selected teachers from each school were surveyed. The final samples included 402 principals and 10,370 teachers. Given the subsample of schools represented, we restrict our study of these data to descriptive analyses. Important information on teachers and schools is also included in the student component of the High School and beyond survey.

The second data set, the National Educational Longitudinal Study (NELS), was begun in 1987-88 with a nationally representative sample of 26,200 eighth graders from 1,000 schools. They were interviewed again two years later. Like the HSB, the NELS was collected under the auspices of the National Center for Educational Statistics. Its design is similar to that used for the HSB. The NELS data are valuable for studying transitions from middle school to high school.

The HSB and NELS data represent the best large-scale, nationally representative information on the high school and post-high school years in the United States. They are two of the chief policy instruments of the U.S. Department of Education. The third data set used in this research is the Longitudinal Study of American Youth (LSAY), conducted by the Public Opinion Laboratory of Northern Illinois University and funded by the National Science Foundation. Beginning in 1987 information was collected yearly from 60 seventh grades and 60 tenth grades in a national probability sample of 52 middle schools and 52 high schools.

The survey has a special focus on students' attitudes toward science and math. In this research, only the seventh-grade cohort is analyzed (given the tenth-grade HSB cohort analysis).

The data used here include the years 1987 through 1990, which represent grades 7 through 10 for this seventh-grade cohort. The LSAY data set will provide important information on experiences in the science pipeline during the middle school years and the first year of high school. It provides more detail on math and science experiences than any other data set.

The three nationally representative longitudinal data sets provide excellent measures of multiple science experiences and resources for critical years in the formation of young scientists. Descriptive and causal information gleaned from these data sets are used to provide insights into the complexities of these science experiences for women and explanations for the exiting of female talent from the sciences.

2

Gender and Resources

Of critical importance in an understanding of young women's experiences in the sciences is the causal process. Of special import in this causal process is a discovery of the role that gender per se plays in affecting science experiences. That is, when other important predictors of science experiences (family, school, and individual resources) are taken into account, does the fact of being a female or a male still have an impact on what happens in the science arena? A second important question about the role of gender has to do with the interaction between gender and resources. Do resources have different effects on the science experiences of young men and young women? That is, do some resources make more of a difference for one gender than the other? Do they sometimes work in opposite directions?

A third important issue in trying to understand the role of gender in affecting science experiences involves connecting our earlier descriptive findings with our causal findings. For example, we found that young men have more of certain family resources than do young women. If our causal analyses show that these resources have an important causal impact on science experiences for young men and young women, we have acquired an important insight into why young men have more positive science experiences: they have more of the critical resources. To answer these questions we turn to the results from multivariate models that predict science trajectories and that include gender, family resources, school resources, and individual resources.

First we look at ANOVA models, which reveal how well the gender and resource variables are able to predict variation between the different types of science trajectories. Interaction terms from ANOVA models will also show whether resources have significantly different consequences for the science experiences of young men and women. Second we turn to logistic regression models, which provide information on the effect of gender and resources on the chances of being in one trajectory or another. Special reduced form models will offer details on the extent to which the effects of gender are direct or indirect (through its impact on family, school, and individual resources). Separate logistic models for males and females and subsets of females will provide information on the difference in these effects for young men and women and for women in different SES and ethnic groups.

GENDER, RESOURCES, AND VARIATIONS IN SCIENCE EXPERIENCES

The findings show that the independent variables explain a significant amount of variation in each of the three sets of trajectories. Gender significantly predicts variation in the type of achievement and access trajectory a young person will experience, even when important differences in family, school, and individual resources are taken into account. Thus at least some of the differences between young women and men in science achievement and science access are not due to different qualifications or levels of resources, but to the pure and simple fact that one is female and one is male. In the area of science attitudes, gender per se does not affect science experiences.

The ANOVA results also show that the effect of resources on experiences in the three areas of science vary for young women and men. Several interaction terms involving gender and resources are significant in each of the equations. These results confirm our earlier prediction that the same level of resources will sometimes have different consequences for the success experienced by young women and young men in science. Resources that have different effects for males and females include SES, mother's work status, mother's and father's involvement in monitoring homework, mother's occupation, and respondent's marital status. Later examination of separate logistic regression models for young women and young men will reveal the specific ways in which the effects of these and other variables not included in the ANOVA model vary by gender.

THE ODDS OF BEING IN DIFFERENT SCIENCE TRAJECTORIES

Once again, the results reveal that even with the larger number of resources included in these models, gender per se often plays a role in determining which science pathway a young person will follow. Consider the effect of gender on the odds of staying in the sciences for longer periods as opposed to staying out of each area when variations in other resources are taken into account. For two of the three areas of science, the effect of gender is as predicted - being female reduces the odds of staying in the science access and science attitude pipelines, even when variations in resources are taken into account. That is, young women with the same qualifications as young men continue to be less likely to maintain high access to science and positive attitudes toward science.

Note that in the area of science access, although the effect of gender is not significant in the equation comparing the "in throughout" and the "out throughout" trajectories, it is significant in most of the other equations. Moreover, the direction of the effect is consistent - young women are less likely then young men to stay in the science access pipeline. There is, then, a cost of being female when it comes to science access and attitudes. In the area of science achievement, however, being female is not a detriment. It is, in fact, an advantage. When variations in resources are taken into account, being female actually increases the odds of staying in the science achievement pipeline (as opposed to staying out). In fact, the odds are increased by a factor of 6.98. When resources are taken into account, females also have higher odds of exiting and of having a series of ins and outs. Thus, although young women have a greater chance of staying in the science achievement pipeline than do equally qualified young men; they also have a greater chance of showing some sign of talent in science achievement but of dropping out regardless of that talent.

This examination of young people's experiences in science has focused on a description and prediction of the over-time experiences that we have referred to as science trajectories. Our earlier discussion of past research suggested that the conventional approach is to describe and predict a single indicator of experience at one particular point in time. Even though these descriptions and predictions might be performed separately at several points, the model still focuses on describing and predicting science experience at one point in time (e.g., a researcher might use a model to predict tenth-grade science grades and then use it to predict twelfth-grade science grades).

The argument presented here is that a more dynamic approach to experiences in science that looks at the paths of those experiences is needed. We also argue for multiple measures of each type of science experience. The pipeline model and the creation of science trajectories are critical to this approach. In fact, the argument has been that the two approaches will lead to very different conclusions and insights about gender and science. We have just presented some results from models predicting trajectories. What would a more traditional model have found?

It is much like the models that are typically used, in which family, school, and individual factors as well as earlier math and science scores (from the sophomore year) are taken into account. As the R2 suggests, the models are quite effective, explaining over 50 percent of the variation in these scores. Our earlier analysis of science achievement trajectories (which included these math and science scores as well as other achievement information for this and other years) showed that gender has an unexpected effect here. Although, as predicted, there is more lost talent among young women than young men in the science achievement pipeline, when resources are equalized, young women have a greater chance than young men of following a trajectory that involves staying in this pipeline throughout the survey period contrast these findings with those from the OLS regression. Here we see that the traditional model yields the traditional findings - being female creates a disadvantage.In their senior year of high school,young women are significantly less likely then young men to score high on the standardized math and science exam when resource are equalized.

Thuse depending on weather science experiences are seen as statics events that can be viewed at a single point in time with a single mesure, or wheather they are viewed as complex dynamic events that occur over time, one's conclusions about the effect of gender would very widly.

THE INFLUENCE OF GENDER

What is the precise nature of the causual mechanism through which gender affects science experiences? Here, we first consider the effect of gender along on the odds of following various science trajectories. Then each of subsets of resources is added to the questions. This series of equations allow us to look at the total effect of gender (when gender alone is in the equation), and, through comparison of these effect, the indirect effect of gender. In the area of science achievement, we discovered above that the direct effect of gender on the odds of having a science trajectory that involved staying in the sciences was positive, involving a female advantage.

When gender alone is considered, females are less likely to stay in the science achievement pipeline. How can we understand a total effect that is negative and a direct effect that is positive? The paths through which gender can indirectly affect science experiences are the key here. Thus, even though young women in general are less likely to stay in the science achievement pipeline than are young men, young women who have the same resources as young men are actually morelikely to stay in the area of science achievement.

Part of the reason that females in general do not follow the science achievement trajectory is that they have fewer of the important resources that affect science achievement experiences. The resources that appear to be critical here are individual resources, since the effect of gender does not become significant in a direction favoring females until these resources are equalized. Some of the most important individual resources are standardized math and science scores and science attitudes, those that we discovered earlier are often highly skewed to the advantage of males.

Causal mechanisms in the area of science access are different than for science achievement. Consider the odds of having access to science throughout the study period versus being out throughout. When only gender is in the equation, females are significantly less likely than males to be "in throughout." This trend continues even when different levels of family and school resources are taken into account. However, when variation in individual resources is controlled, there is no longer a difference between males and females in the odds of maintaining access.

Why is this true? It is neither discrimination nor the effect of gender per se that keeps women out of the science access pipeline, but rather inequalities in individual (not family or school) resources. Once these different levels of resources are taken into account and one essentially compares equally qualified young women and men, they are equally likely to stay in the sciences throughout the study period. Women's deficits in key individual resources involving standardized science scores, occupational expectations, and science attitudes and achievement are the main explanations for gender differences in the odds of maintaining science access.

It is the case, however, that when less extreme sets of science access experiences are considered, females often have lower odds of spending time in the access pipeline as compared to males, even when their different resources are accounted for. Regardless of resources, females have lower odds than do males of being in three of the five remaining science access trajectories. That is, they are more likely than their equally qualified male counterparts to remain out of science access than to have experiences in science access. In the case of the popular "in-and-out" pattern, which ends by exiting, when only gender is considered females are less likely than males to be in this trajectory.

And taking into account the family, school, and individual resources of the young men and women does not change this likelihood. A consideration of each of the sets of resources does lower the difference in male and female odds a bit, but the difference remains significant when all are considered. Thus when young women have similar family resources (e.g., mothers with high educational expectations), school resources (e.g., being in an academic programme and having interested teachers), and individual resources (e.g., high science scores, high educational expectations, and high levels of science achievement and attitudes), their odds of having at least some experiences in the science access pipeline are increased, but they are still not as high as those of equally qualified young men.

These gender differences in science access trajectories suggest that the unequal treatment that disadvantages females is often a factor in differential access to science (as in the gender effects that remain significant regardless of equal resources). At other times it is not differential treatment but different resources (as in the "in throughout" equation, where gender was not significant when individual resources were controlled). This situation is in contrast to the science achievement process, where differential treatment sometimes works to the advantage of females and where much of the effect of gender is indirect through different levels of resources.

In addition, a comparison of the two causal processes suggests greater losses of talented young women in the area of science achievement (where young women are more likely than young men to have participated and then left) than in the area of science access (where young women are less likely than young men to have had any kind of experience). An examination of the causal process leading to experiences in science attitudes illuminates a third kind of interplay between gender, resources, and science trajectories. The process suggests that gender is less important as a causal explanation for variation in science attitudes than for science achievement and access.

Although being female does decrease the odds of staying in the science attitude pipeline throughout the study period (even when resources are considered), it is significant in only one of the other science attitude trajectory equations. And in this equation (looking at the odds of leaving after 1980 as opposed to never having been in), it is females who have the higher odds. This suggests that young women are more likely than young men to have shown an early interest in science but then left (as opposed to staying out altogether). Although this gives women an edge in science exposure, it also shows more lost talent on their part (even when resources are equalized).

Returning to the critical role of gender in affecting odds of maintaining positive science attitudes. Gender is significant in this equation when no other resources are considered. Odds for females are significantly lower than odds for males by a factor of .66. Gender loses significance when family and school resources are controlled, but regain significance (although the size of the effect is diminished) when individual resources are controlled. Thus it appears that young men and women with equal family and school resources do equally well on science attitudes. But this may be because of women's higher level of some individual resources, because once these are equalized, women have a lower odds than men of staying in the science pipeline.

GENDER VARIATION IN THE EFFECT OF RESOURCES ON SCIENCE EXPERIENCES

We have observed that gender sometimes interacts with resources to affect science experiences. Thus the process leading to positive science experiences varies for young women and young men. Results from separate logistic regression models presented give insight into this variation. (In the interest of parsimony, we restrict our examination here to three trajectory comparisons in the areas of achievement and access.) A careful look at the patterns of significance shown suggests that there are considerable gender differences in the process leading to positive science achievement and access experiences.

For example, when levels of other resources are taken into account, a number of resources have a significant effect on the science experiences of young women but not young men - especially in the area of access to science. One of the most interesting findings is that when variation in important family, school, and individual resources is taken into account (or controlled), young African American women are more likely than other women to have experiences in science achievement and access (including being more likely to be in the area of achievement throughout the survey period). There is no race effect for young men.

Another resource that affects the science achievement experiences of young women but not young men is school program - young women who are in academic programs increase their chances of spending at least some time in the area of science achievement. The same is not true for young men. With regard to access, other resources that affect young women's experiences but not young men's include: father's occupation, mother's and father's monitoring of homework, marital status, type of school, locus of control, sex-role attitudes about men's and women's home and work roles, and math score.

An important trend to note here is that family resources have a significant impact on the science access experiences of young women but not of young men. And, in some situations, these are negative effects. For example, having a father with a higher status occupation reduces the chances of a young woman having science access. Being married and having a father who monitors homework are each associated with early signs of promise that are not fulfilled.

Young women are also more likely than young men to experience the effects of individual factors on their access to science. Again, these individual factors often work to detract from science access. For example, women who have a greater internal locus of control (i.e., those who feel more in charge of their lives) and high math scores actually are less likely to stay in the science access pipeline. More time spent on homework and expectations to marry later are associated with both early access and early departure from the science access pipeline for young women but not for young men.

In the case of science achievement, this pattern is much more common that the reverse and it is often individual resources that have a consequence for young men but not young women. Young men but not young women are more likely to have experiences in the science achievement pipeline when they go to a private school, have a positive self-concept and a greater internal locus of control, and date less. In addition, sex-role attitudes affect the science achievement experiences of young men but not young women and it is young men with less progressive sex-role attitudes who are more likely to stay in this area.

In the area of access to science, young men but not young women are more likely to have experiences in the science access pipeline when they are in an academic program and score high on the 1980 science attitude factor. However, young men but not young women who have friends who value education are less likely to have experiences in the science achievement pipeline, and young men who are more progressive on their attitudes about working mothers are more likely than other men to have early access to science but also an early departure.

Considering the large number of resources included in these models, there are relatively few instances in which a resource has a significant effect going in the same direction for both young women and young men, especially in the area of access to science. Scores on the science exam and on the science achievement factor in 1980 and 1984 are the only resources that have similar significant effects on young women and young men in the equations predicting their experiences in science access.

For both groups, higher SES, friends with good grades, higher standardized math and science scores, and higher scores on the 1980 access and attitude factors have a significant and positive effect on science achievement. Early marriage detracts significantly from science achievement for young men and young women. It is interesting to note that for both young women and young men, high science scores detract from their chances of having access to science but contribute to their chances of being involved in the area of science achievement.

A final consideration in our examination of gender differences in the process leading to positive experiences in the sciences involves resources that have opposite effects for young women and young men. This is not a common occurrence. In fact, there are only two instances of opposite effects. Having a father with a higher status occupation makes young women more likely to leave the science achievement pipeline after 1980 (as opposed to staying out), but it makes young men less likely to follow this path. That is, these young men are more likely to have stayed out of the science achievement pipeline than to have entered it and left early.

Having a high self-concept increases the chances that a young man will experience a trajectory involving going in and out of the science access pipeline but ending up out (as opposed to staying out). This same high self-concept decreases the chance that a young woman will experience this in-and-out trajectory (as opposed to staying out). In sum, an examination of the ways in which resources affect science experiences for young women and young men suggests that a consideration of gender is often important for understanding how a resource will affect experiences in science.

This is especially true in the area of experiences in science access. In this area, a large majority of the resources that are important for success have an impact that varies by gender. In the case of science achievement, the resources that are important for success are almost as likely to have similar effects for young women and young men as they are to have different effects for young women and young men. The evidence presented in this chapter provides strong support for the notion that gender per se is often a critical factor in determining experiences in science.

When family, school, and individual resources are taken into account, gender still has a significant impact in many of the equations predicting experiences in science achievement, access, and attitudes. In the areas of access and attitudes, the gender effect often involves a disadvantage for young women. They are less likely than young men with equal resources to spend time in these areas. However, in the area of science achievement, when resources are equalized, it is the young woman who has the advantage of spending more time in the pipeline. Gender is also an important factor in predicting lost talent in science, especially in the area of science achievement. Thus although young women with equal resources are more likely than young men to stay in this area throughout the 6-year period examined, there is also a greater exiting of female talent than male talent.

The findings presented in this chapter also highlight the fact that the way in which resources affect science experiences varies by gender. Thus' gender can have a direct impact on science experiences, but it can also indirectly affect them through its association with family, school and individual resources. The comparisons of predictive models for young women and young men gave us some insight into the role that gender plays in affecting experiences in science. Now we shall limit our attention to young women. Given their greater amount of lost talent (in two of the three areas of science) and lesser chances of success (in two of the three areas of science) relative to young men, what are the important variables in predicting successful science experiences for young women?

Alternatively, which variables are important in predicting lost talent among young women? Thus, the first goal of this chapter is to use causal models to describe the kinds of resources (or resource deficits) that lead to the development of female science talent and to the loss of female science talent.

The second goal of this chapter is to provide insight into the science experiences of different groups of women. Gender is not the only social status that is related to science experiences. Access to important resources necessary for success in science varies by race and social class as well. It is impossible to talk about women's science experiences without recognizing these variations. Thus this chapter concludes with an examination of the science resources and science experiences (and the relation between them) of young women with different racial and social class characteristics.

Given the large number of resources that are taken into account, or controlled, in these models, we can conclude with considerable confidence that a causal relationship exits when a particular resource continues to be significant in predicting the odds of following one or another science trajectory. What can we conclude about the causal process behind the science experiences of young women?

Several general patterns are clear. First, as we noted in our comparison of male and female models, young African American women are more likely than other young women to have a number of experiences in the science achievement and access pipelines. Race has no effect on experiences in science attitudes. Thus, even though some of the African American women's experiences in the sciences are not continuous, the bottom line is that they are more likely than other women to have at least some science experiences.

A second general conclusion that can be made about the causal process behind women's science experiences is that the nature of the process varies with the area of science that is being examined. Of the many resources considered, only standardized science scores have a significant effect on science experiences in each of the areas, and even then, the nature of the effect varies. High science scores increase the odds of being in each of the three science achievement trajectories examined, but they reduce the chances of being in certain access and attitude trajectories that end up out of the sciences.

Another important trend shown is that in the area of science achievement, resources often have a significant - and usually similar - effect in more than one of the trajectory equations. However, for the science access and attitude trajectories, there is usually a distinct group of resources that significantly predict the odds of being in the various trajectories.

SCIENCE ACHIEVEMENT

Patterns of significance show that it is a mix of demographic, family, school, and individual variables that are important for science achievement experiences. It is no surprise that race and class are significant predictors of young women's persistence in science achievement. It is also no surprise that it is upper SES women who have an advantage over lower SES women. However, the surprising finding here (but one that was noted earlier) is that young African American women with equal resources are more likely than other women to stay in the science achievement pipeline (as opposed to staying out) throughout the six-year period.

Other than social class, none of the other resources in the young women's family of orientation has a significant impact on their chances of staying in the area of science achievement throughout the six-year period. However, young women who form their own families at an earlier age significantly reduce their chances of staying in science achievement. Three individual resources also have a significant causal impact on these chances: young women who score high on the standardized math and science exams and on the 1980 science attitude factor also have significantly higher chances of staying in the science achievement pipeline. Interestingly, the access factors are not related to these chances. Thus, for young women, course taking is not related to staying in the achievement pipeline.

Which young women are more likely to leave the science achievement pipeline after showing early signs of talent? Having a father with a higher status occupation and avoiding early marriage are associated with both an early exit from science achievement and an in-and-out pattern leading to an exit by 1986. In addition, African American women and those from higher SES families are more likely to follow this in-and-out trajectory than they are to stay out.

Interestingly, having friends at school who value education decreases the chance of having an early exit but increases the chance of the in-and-out pattern (as does being in an academic program). The only individual resources that significantly predict lost talent in science achievement include standardized math and science scores and science access and attitude factor scores. Young women who score higher on these measures are more likely than other young women to have spent some time (as opposed to no time) in the sciences, but they did not stay in.

SCIENCE ACCESS

Very few resources significantly predict whether a young woman will maintain access to science throughout the survey period (the same is true for the total sample and for young men). Surprisingly, having a father with a higher status occupation and having a greater internal locus of control significantly reduce the chances that a young woman will stay in (as opposed to out) of the access pipeline. Higher math/science achievement factor scores in 1982 increase the chances of staying in the access pipeline. Thus, science achievement affects later access, but not vice versa.

The popular notion has always been that it is course taking that brings about high achievement in science. These results question that notion. Here we find that when science trajectories are examined (as opposed to the traditional focus on achievement or course taking at one point in time), taking science courses does not guarantee that young women will have high achievement in science. However, when young women have high achievement, they increase their odds of staying in science courses. A larger number of resources are significant in the equations predicting exits from science access.

Fathers who monitor homework, higher expected age at marriage, an interest in school, and a greater amount of time spent on homework are all resources that increase young women's chances of being in science in 1980 but exiting after 1980. A higher math/science achievement factor score decreases these chances. It is interesting to look at the relation between resources and early exits because here we are predicting something that has an ambiguous value. That is, it is better to have been in the sciences for at least some time than not at all. On the other hand, it is unfortunate when young women show early promise in an area of science that remains unfulfilled.

Being African American having a mother who monitors homework, attending a private school, having progressive attitudes about women's place in the home, and high math/science achievement factor scores increase a young woman's chances of being in the in-and-out trajectory that ends up out of the science access pipeline. High self-concept, locus of control, and math and science scores reduce these chances.

SCIENCE ATTITUDES

The first finding of interest here is the fact that the resources that are important predictors are very different in the equation predicting odds of an in-and-out trajectory versus the equation predicting an early exit. It is disproportionately family resources that predict the former and individual resources that predict the latter. The resources that increase the odds of an in-and-out trajectory ending up out of the area of science attitude (as opposed to staying out) include a mother with more education, a father who monitors homework, and a high score on the 1980 math/science achievement factor.

Resources that decrease the odds of being in this trajectory include a father with more education, a mother who monitors homework, friends who place a high value on education, and a high self-concept. These patterns provide insight into the nature of the causal mechanisms at work when comparing young women who show signs of talent but eventually exit the sciences (in any area) and those who never show signs of talent and stay out. The "lost talent" group shows a mix of resources that do not always work in a positive way for them. In other words, they do not consistently have certain advantages over those who stay out. This is part of the explanation for their exit.

When comparing the group of women who stay in the sciences to those who stay out, these anomalies are much less likely to occur. That is, the reason they are able to stay in is that they consistently have resources that act to keep them in. When predicting early exits from the area of science attitude, it is mothers who monitor homework, a greater amount of dating, interest in school, high educational and occupational expectations, and higher math/science achievement and attitude factor scores in 1980 that increase the odds of being in this trajectory. Resources that decrease the odds include enrollment in a private school, high grades and standardized science scores, high educational aspirations, and a high math/science access factor score in 1980.

Remember the comparison groups here. Neither group had much experience with science attitudes. We are looking at the odds of an early exit as compared to never being in this area. Thus the fact that young girls in private schools or those with high grades have a lower chance of being in this area makes more sense in this light, for they are more likely to have never had positive attitudes about science than to have had them and then lowered them. Very few resources significantly predict the odds of a young woman staying in the science attitude area as opposed to staying out.

High occupational expectations and a high score on the math/science access factor score in 1984 increase these odds. Rural residence and a mother who monitors schoolwork decrease these odds. The findings give us some sense of the critical resources that predict young women's experiences in science. However, to understand this process fully, we must consider the possibility that unique causal processes exist for groups of women who vary on two key characteristics - race and class.

CLASS VARIATIONS IN SCIENCE RESOURCES AND SUCCESS

RESOURCES

Are some women better equipped than others for success in science by virtue of larger amounts of critical resources? Consider family resources, for example. There are significant differences between race and class subgroups on a majority of these resources. In the case of class contrasts, there are significant differences between upper SES and lower SES women on each of the family resources, and these invariably are in the direction of upper SES women having more family resources. (Some but not all of these resources will be higher, by definition, in the upper SES group given the items used to measure SES.)

Not only do the upper SES women have parents with more education and higher occupational status, but their parents have higher expectations for their children and are more involved in their academic and social lives. In addition, upper SES women are about half as likely as lower SES women to marry or have a child early. Although a majority of the race contrasts on family resources show an advantage for non-African American women, this is not the case in all situations.

Women who are not African American do come from higher SES families, and have fathers who have higher job status and who are more likely to be living in the home. Their fathers are also more likely to monitor their progress in school, and both their parents tend to know more about the student's whereabouts and activities. These women are also more likely to have a calculator in the home and to have fewer siblings, and are less likely to have a child early. However, African American woman do have the advantage on a number of family resources, and most of these have to do with their mothers.

Their mothers were more likely than other mothers to work when the daughter was in elementary school, thus perhaps providing a positive role model. In addition, these mothers have significantly higher educational expectations for their daughters and are more likely than other mothers to keep track of their children's progress in school. Finally, even though young African American women are more likely than other women to have a child at an early age, they are less likely to marry at an early age.

Earlier we discovered that gender often worked through individual resources to affect science experiences. Do women in different race and class groups vary in the extent to which they have these important individual resources? These data also give additional insight into how young African American women, but not lower SES women, sometimes beat the odds and succeed in the white male domain of science.

Consider class differences in individual resources among young women. Although lower SES women do have a significantly higher selfconcept than do upper SES women, they score lower on other personality scales (such as locus of control and work orientation), hold more conservative sex-role attitudes, expect to enter family roles earlier, are less interested in school, get poorer grades and standardized test scores, spend less time on homework, and have lower educational expectations. One of the most striking class differences involves these expectations. Over twice as many young women from upper SES homes (58%) as from lower SES homes (28%) expect to get a college degree or more.

Consider now the information on race differences in individual resources among young women. Here we see that, even more so than in other areas of resources, young African American women sometimes prevail over other women. It is true that non-African American women have a higher self-concept, locus of control, and work orientation. They also spend more time on homework and have higher grades and standardized math and science scores. However, young African American women have a lower orientation toward family and more liberal sex-role attitudes (recall their greater tendency to have working mothers).

They date less and expect to marry and have children at later ages (even though, as we observed above, they actually have children earlier). Finally, and perhaps most unexpectedly, they express a greater interest in school than do other young women. Note that a good number of the items on which African American women show deficits in individual resources involve behaviors (e.g., grades, time spent on homework, standardized test scores). When these young women have the advantage, it often involves attitudes. And there are no race differences on some attitudes (e.g., educational expectations).

The final set of resources that is compared across class and race groups is school resources. It is not surprising that the litany of deficits associated with being a young girl from a lower SES background continues here. Young women from upper SES backgrounds are over twice as likely as those from lower SES backgrounds to be attending a private school and to be in an academic program. They are also more likely to have teachers who are considered excellent, who are viewed as being interested in the students, and who have influence on curriculum, content, and teaching techniques in the classroom.

The upper SES women have an additional advantage at school that goes beyond programs and teachers. They are more likely than other young women to have school friends who get good grades, are interested in school, attend classes regularly, and plan to go to college. Lower SES women do, however, have one advantage over their upper SES counterparts. The sample of math and science teachers from their schools was more likely than the sample from the upper SES women's schools to include a female math or science teacher.

Differences by race in school resources provide some additional insights into our earlier finding that young African American women sometimes do better in science than other women. Non-African American women are more likely than African American women to be in private schools (almost three times more likely) and academic programs. Their teachers are more likely to have influence over what happens in the classroom and to spend a greater amount of class time on instruction. But this is where the clear advantage stops. Young African American women are more likely to have female teachers in their school sample, and their teachers in general tend to have more education.

In addition, the schools that they attend require more math and science for graduation. Some differences in school peer groups favor non-African American girls and some favor African American girls. In their sophomore year, non-African American girls are more likely to have friends who are interested in school, but African American girls are more likely to have friends who plan to go to college and who think well of students with good grades. In their senior year of high school, nonAfrican American girls are more likely to have friends who get good grades, but the young African American girls are more likely to have friends who are interested in school, attend classes regularly, and plan to go to college.

SCIENCE TRAJECTORIES

To what extent do women's experiences in science over time vary with their race and social class? A quick look at this suggests that - once again - class, but not race, is related to science experiences in a simple, straightforward manner. Regardless of the aspect of science, lower SES women are much more likely than upper SES women to stay out of the science pipeline throughout the six-year period. The most extreme contrast is in the area of science achievement, where almost three times as many lower SES (43%) as upper SES (15%) women never enter the science pipeline.

Conversely, upper SES women are more likely to be in each of the areas of science throughout the survey period. Again, the greatest contrasts are in the area of science achievement. Over three times as many upper SES women as lower SES women stay in the science achievement pipeline (7% versus 2%). It is this area that the upper SES women are least likely to stay out of and the most likely to be in. Lower SES women are also least likely to stay out of achievement than other areas, but they are almost equally unlikely to stay in any of the three areas.

Although upper SES women are more likely than lower SES women to be in the sciences, the loss of talented young women from the sciences is also greater in this group. Upper SES women are more likely than lower SES women to have entered science and left it - especially in the areas of achievement and access. Throughout this research, unexpected findings on the situation of young African American women in science have been revealed. Earlier, in a descriptive analysis of the science pipeline, we saw that young African American women are overrepresented in the "out throughout" trajectory of the science achievement pipeline but not in the science access and attitude pipelines.

In our causal analyses, we saw that, when other factors were controlled, African American women are more likely than other women to spend time in achievement and access. When other resources are not controlled, African American women are more likely than other women to be out of and less likely to be in the science achievement pipeline. Thirty-five percent of African American women but only 29 percent of other women remain out of this area. Less than 1 percent of African American women stay in this area, while over five times as many other women stay in (5%).

There is a different race pattern in access and attitudes. Here African American women are less likely than other women to remain out of these pipelines and as likely (if not slightly more likely) to remain in. There are minimal differences between the two racial groups in the amount of lost talent. However, in all areas of science, African American women are more likely than other women to go in and out of science and to end up out of it altogether.

The final question to be asked about the different groups of women is whether the causal process leading to success in science varies by subgroup. Unfortunately, because the subgroups are small (especially for African American women), logistic regression models could not be used. ANOVA models are more robust and will provide estimates on smaller samples, but they limit the number of resources included as independent variables and tell us nothing about the direction of effects. First consider differences by social class in the models predicting science experiences.

Certain resources have similar effects for lower and upper SES women in each of the areas of science. In the science achievement model, this includes resources such as early marriage, friends' value on education, and math and science scores. In the access model, this includes race, early marriage, and attitudes about math and science. Additional variables that have a similar effect in the science attitude model are school program (e.g., academic versus nonacademic) and access to math and science courses.

However, each model has a large number of resources that are significant for one SES group but not the other. For example, mother's work status when the young woman was in elementary school affects the science achievement and science attitude experiences of lower but not upper SES women. Having a mother who monitors schoolwork is associated with experiences in the area of science achievement only for upper SES women. Self-concept helps explain the science achievement and science access of upper SES women but not lower SES women.

The opposite is true when one is considering science attitudes. Thus these findings suggest that social class interacts with a considerable number of resources in affecting science experiences. Many resources have different effects on success in science depending on the social class of the young woman. Turning to the ANOVA models for the race subgroups, as with social class, the effect of resources on young women's experiences in the sciences often varies with race. Even fewer resources have similar effects for women in the two race subgroups than was the case for women in the class subgroups.

And the similarities in process are greatest in the area of science attitudes and smallest in the area of science achievement. Thus we find significant evidence that race and resources interact in their effect on success in science, especially science achievement. Although researchers typically speak in general about how resources affect young women's chances of success in science, our results suggest that these general statements may be misleading when so many of these effects are conditional on the racial identity of the young woman.

The single resource that significantly affects the science achievement trajectory of African American and non-African American women is the value that friends put on education. Marital status and attitudes about math and science significantly affect access trajectories of both groups of young women. Finally, mother's occupation, school program, and access to math and science significantly affect the attitude trajectory that both groups of young women follow.

One of the most intriguing findings presented is that when other resources are taken into account, social class (as measured by SES quartile) is significantly related to experiences in each area of science for non-African American women but not for African American women. From our earlier analyses we know that when SES has an effect on science experiences, it is invariably a dampening effect. Somehow, young African American women, but not other women, escape the yoke of class. For them, it is other family resources, in addition to school and individual resources, that help predict their success in science. It is the case that although overall SES is not significantly related to the science experiences of young African American women, one element of SES -mother's occupational status - does help predicts variations in science attitude trajectories.

Other resources that have a significant impact on the science experiences of non-African American but not African American women include father's occupational status, mother's monitoring of homework, school program, math and science scores, and math and science access and attitudes in the science achievement model. In the science access model, resources involving school type, school program, self-concept, dating, and achievement in math and science in addition to SES affect the trajectory experiences of non-African American but not African American women. Father's occupation, marital status, and locus of control are the resources that have a significant impact for the former but not for the later group of women in the area of science attitudes.

In this chapter results from a multivariate model that predicted science experiences for young women been presented. We found, first of all, that the important predictors of science experience vary with the area of science being considered. In general the findings show a mix of family, school, and individual resources that predict success in science. Some resources (e.g., sex-role attitudes, locus of control, and self-concept) that were expected to have consistently positive consequences were often not important when other resources were controlled.

Other resources such as experiences in other areas of science and scores on standardized math and science exams had the consistently positive consequences that were expected. A look at the resources and science experiences of groups of women who varied by race and class showed some unexpected findings. Although young women from lower SES families have consistent disadvantages in science resources and experiences, the same is not true for African American women. Sometimes these young women have resource advantages and end up with more positive experiences in science than do other young women.

3

Women's Perceptions of their Contributions to Science

Research and publication are the essentials in the production of knowledge. The extent to which research productivity affects status attainment continues to attract the attention of scholars of the sociology of knowledge. Whether research productivity affects directly status attainment of scientists has been examined by a number of scholars in the past. However, the direction of the relationship between productivity and status attainment continues to remain somewhat unclear. For example, Crane and Long maintain that institutional location is more important to productivity than is early productivity during the graduate school years.

On the other hand, Cole and Cole and Astin and Bayer argue that early productivity determines institutional placement, which in turn affects long-term productivity. Another area of interest is the relation of gender to both research productivity and status attainment. The present study will explore how environmental and contextual variables and experiences contribute to gender differences in research productivity. More specifically, this study will explore the ways in which often-cited women and men scientists plan, execute, and promote their significant published work.

Women in the aggregate publish less than men do; and this fact has generated numerous questions and hypotheses.

Do women produce less because they have fewer research resources at their disposal or because they allocate more time to other job tasks and requirements? Are they isolated from important collegial networks? Does their professed lower level of interest in research and publication erode their productivity? Or is it the tug of family obligations? Or gender discrimination, and other institutional barriers? Thus far, research has been able to provide only partial answers to some of these questions:

- In general, women are reported to have fewer institutional resources such as research funds and graduate students who serve as research assistants.

  In a study that examined facilitators and inhibitors to research productivity among highly productive scholars, men were much more likely to identify resources and graduate students as important facilitators to their productivity than were the women. Moreover, data from various national surveys have demonstrated differences among women and men with respect to financial support for their research activities and availability and use of research assistants. For example, Bayer in his normative report indicates that while 30 percent of men report financial support for their research activities, only 14 percent of women do so. More recent data from the Carnegie Survey of Faculty indicate that while 26 percent of men report having research assistants, only 11 percent of the faculty women says that they have such assistance (unpublished tabulations).
- Marriage does not appear to be a barrier to research and publication. As a matter of fact, in previous studies we have documented the positive effects of marriage on research productivity. Cole and Zuckerman in a recent study have concluded that marriage and family obligations do not account for differences observed with respect to women's lower publication rates.
- Women are reported to be somewhat more isolated from important collegial networks. Reskin, in her thoughtful

analysis of "Sex Differentiation and Social Organization of Science," suggests that "since the [collegial] role applies to relationships between scientific researchers of approximately equal status [and] because women's lower gender status is inconsistent with the implicit status equivalence of colleagues, sex stratification itself can block normal collegiality between male and female researchers". Furthermore, Helmreich and Spence and their colleagues in interpreting sex differences with respect to research productivity speculate that "women may be more isolated from the national 'old boy' network and thus out of touch with the 'invisible college' through which much exchange of scientific information takes place". However, these statements are speculations that call for further research on the issue.

While we are still exploring the hypothesized external or structural barriers to women's research productivity, we also realize that women's published research may not receive the same degree of recognition as similar research produced by men. A number of investigators have documented the fact that women's and men's work are not equally recognized by such usual academic rewards as salary, promotion, and professional recognition.

Furthermore, in an article entitled "The Productivity Puzzle," Cole and Zuckerman hypothesized that differential reinforcement, that is, more limited recognition and use of their research may account in part for women's lower productivity. Their research leads them to conclude that "women scientists in the 1970 cohort are slightly more responsive than men to the lack of reinforcement and considerably less responsive than men to positive reinforcement". In order to explore further how reinforcement may affect research productivity, we conducted the pilot study summarized in this chapter.

There is no question that perceived reputation- one's standing in the discipline or profession- influences a scientist's career progress, and that citations provide collegial recognition for one's scholarly contribution to the field. By looking at how highly cited published research by women and men scientists is conceived and by examining the reasons given by these scientists for its recognition, and to a greater understanding of gender differences in productivity. This analysis should also shed some light on how differential reinforcement affects women and men scientists. While citations represent an indicator of impact, they also provide reinforcement for a scientist's work. For example, in summer 1982, a sub-sample of 543 highly productive academic scholars was mailed a semi-structured survey questionnaire with questions about barriers and facilitators to research productivity. The survey also assessed what these scholars considered their most important piece of published work and why they considered it important. The two reasons given most often by both women and men were: that the piece broke new ground and explored a new area; that the piece was widely cited. In other words, they considered their own work important because colleagues often chose to cite it in their own publications.

Since the number of citations is considered a dimension of one's status in the field by both those who cite the piece as well as the scholar's own perceptions of its importance. The underlying assumption is that citations act as rewards that in turn provide incentives to further productivity in research. The study was designed to determine what types of scholarly work tend to be highly cited and in how such work was originally conceived. I also wanted to know whether there are gender and field differences with respect to how scholars conceive their best work and how they carry it out.

The study examines reasons why a piece might be highly cited because they represent a person's causal explanations for a success-oriented event such as published research that is highly cited. It was hypothesized that attributions have a direct effect on expectancies about future performance and subsequent achievement behaviour. Thus, any identified gender differences in attributions of success (i.e., reasons for high citation counts of their work) might give us some clue as to how women and men react to this form of reinforcement.

Citation "classics" and essays prepared by the authors of the classics were the primary sources of data for this study. A citation classic is a weekly feature in Current Contents. Publications labeled as citation classics are identified through the Science Citation Index (SCI) and The Social Sciences Citation Index (SSCI) data bases. A citation classic is described by the publishers of Current Contents as a publication that is "highly cited": "a large number of citations to a particular publication usually indicate that the cited work has made a significant contribution to the development of scientific knowledge in its field." The publishers of citation classics also believe that such publications have "a lasting effect on the whole of science." How does a publication become a citation classic? The publishers of Current Contents scan the citations in the various publications and select pieces that are highly cited. More specifically, certain areas of research are singled out by the publisher each year, and a search is made to identify the papers and books with the highest number of citations within these fields. The number of citations necessary to make a piece a citation classic depends on the size of the field, or the number of papers published in it. The authors of these highly cited publications are invited to prepare an essay about their publication in which they discuss (a) what prompted the research; (b) any obstacles they encountered in research and publication; and (c) why they think the publication has been so highly cited.

The present study is designed to examine gender and field differences with respect to the above three questions. A sample of 56 essays was used in this study. It was drawn from 589 essays which appeared in Current Contents published between March 1984 and July 1986. The areas covered among the sample of 56 essays included life sciences, physical, chemical, and earth sciences, agriculture, biology, and environmental sciences, and social and behavioral sciences.

The 56 essays selected for the present study included all 28 essays authored by women during the two-year span and a random sample of 28 essays authored by men and matched by field with the women's essays. Twenty-two of the essay contributors were from foreign universities, including Canada.

Descriptive information about the authors of each of the essays, as well as any other authors of the 56 citation classic publications, included academic field and sex. For the classic we also determined if it had single or multiple authorship, the number of authors, the type of publication (book, article, chapter, etc.), the year of publication, and the number of times cited. These were all treated as categorical variables in the analysis.

The response categories for coding the essays were developed by first reading the responses offered by the authors to the three questions: How was the research conceived? What obstacles, if any, did you encounter? Why do you think your work is so highly cited? Two analyses were undertaken. The first compared responses of men and women to the three questions asked of the authors. The second analysis compared responses by field of study.

Of the 56 scientists who wrote an essay about their citation classic over the two and one-half-year span, 56 percent were from the natural sciences (life sciences, physical, chemical, and earth sciences, agriculture, biology, and environmental sciences) and 44 percent from the social and behavioral sciences. The median year of publication of the citation classic was 1967 for men, with a range of 1946-1976; for women the median year was 1970 with a range of 1943-1979. Women's median citation count was 202 with a range of 40-2,125; men's median citation was 215 with a range of 65-1,850.

The citation count for each participant represents the number of publications in which it has been cited since the piece's publication date. Looking at the statistics about year of publication suggests that women in the sample tended to produce their highly cited articles during the more recent years. This is probably because the women's movement and affirmative action have increased women's overall productivity and thus their greater visibility. It may also be because more and more women are entering scientific fields. In an earlier study comparing the research performance of academics in 1972 and 1980, we found an increase in women's research activity.

Also, in a later study we failed to find any significant sex differences on four different citation indices among a recent cohort of academic scholars. These recent findings are consistent with earlier findings by Cole and Cole and Zuckerman, that when women and men are equal with respect to the quantity of research production, differences in citations cease to be significant. The issue of multiple versus single authorship was also examined. Previous research on the matter of collaboration and its effect on productivity found no evidence that women are less likely to collaborate than men. Thus, their lower productivity could not be explained on that basis.

The present study confirms their findings that women indeed collaborate as often as men do: 44 percent of the citation classic publications were single-authored by either sex; the remaining 56 percent that were coauthored tended to vary somewhat in the number of coauthors depending on whether the author of the essay was a man or a woman. Twelve percent of the women had five or more coauthors compared to none of the men. Also, more men tended to coauthor only with other men (77 percent); while only 10 percent of the women had coauthored with women only. This finding is not surprising since women, being a minority, have many more male than female colleagues, therefore more opportunities for coauthorship with men.

In research of gender and research productivity, journal articles have been studied more than other types of publications. However, it is important to examine other forms of publication as well. Thus, Davis and Astin examined the extent to which various forms of publication play a role in the scholar's professional standing, and chapters in books were found to be strong and consistent predictors of reputational standing.

Indeed, we do observe some sex differences with respect to type of publication that represents a citation classic. However, before we conclude that women's books are more highly cited than men's books, it would be necessary to ascertain whether the women in this sample are more likely to produce books, and whether the men are more likely to produce review articles.

It is important to note that both chapters and review articles are important vehicles for creating visibility. It will also be important in the future to explore further the gender differences with respect to books as a vehicle to collegial recognition. Questions to be addressed should include the following: Do women's books have a greater influence in the field? Are the topics women choose to write books about of greater general interest to other colleagues?

The first question was how was the research conceived? Five types of responses were coded.

1. Personal interest or experience. For example, "I was visiting my grandmother in a nursing home. I was struck by how little control she and other residents were permitted." Personal interest or experience was mentioned as an impetus by 12 women and 12 men.
2. To solve a problem was also a popular response to the question (14 men and 10 women listed this as an impetus to the research). "The work was done to answer a difficult clinical question [that] I didn't know ... embarrassed by my ignorance [I] decided to try to search for an answer." "Wigglesworth's findings prompted me to look for a function of the NC (neuro-secretory cells) of the brain of the adult female blow-fly."
3. Dissertation research was cited by five scholars (all women). For example, "This review paper was an outgrowth of my doctoral dissertation research," or "Our dissertation investigations ... led to an interest in cytotoxonomy and cytogeobotany."
4. Assisting graduate students was cited by just one man and one woman. The male participant reflected on the question and responded as follows: "The paper began as a handout to students in a graduate course in causal models." The woman scholar tells us that "when I completed work on the Family Problems Scale ... I did not intend to construct

another test. However, a graduate student ... decided to validate the Family Problems Scale's interpretation in terms of Ego Development, using a sentence completion test.... To complete her project, we needed a tentative scoring manual."

5. Invitations to prepare reviews on a topic were also perceived as the impetus to the preparation and publication of the citation classic. "When invited by the 'Annual Review' to write on this subject in 1978, I leaped at the chance." (One man and three women indicated invitations as a reason in undertaking the work.)

When look at these responses find that women tend to cite dissertation research and invitations somewhat more often, while more men indicate the need to solve a problem as the impetus to undertake the research that led to the citation classic. While only one of these sex differences- dissertation- is statistically significant ($p < .05$ using a one-tail binomial test), it is interesting to speculate on the larger pattern of sex differences. Are women's responses more "passive" and men's more "active"? Do men see themselves as being more actively engaged in problem solving? Do women see their work more as an outcome of circumstances (the need to complete a dissertation or a response to an external invitation)? Such an interpretation would be consistent with some of the research on attribution theory, which indicates a tendency for men to make internal attributions (internal locus of control) and women more likely to exhibit an external locus of control.

The essay contributors were also asked to report any obstacles or barriers they had encountered. Only women mentioned a lack of collegial support for their project or topic. Such an obstacle is represented in the comment: "Most of the work for this chapter was done at home on nights and weekends in order to minimize certain criticism for failing to be fully engaged in the 'right' kind of research, meaning physiology." Other comments include: "I discussed my idea with a number of senior colleagues.

One or two found it intriguing, but in general it was discounted." "The unpopularity of the subject was such that after I completed my thesis ... an eminent Oxford professor strongly advised me to change my field of study." It is significant that an earlier study of facilitators and barriers to research productivity also found that women were much more likely than were men to report colleague behaviour as a key factor in their scholarly work. Again, we have evidence here that women are more likely to make more external attributions, that is, focusing on the endorsement or lack of it by colleagues.

Four men and three women mentioned that their publication was initially turned down by publishers. For example, one author wrote that "we experienced considerable difficulty in getting it accepted for publication". Another one said, "Getting it published was not easy." Out of the seven participants who mentioned difficulties with publishing their work, five were from the social and behavioral sciences. This is not surprising given the high rates of rejection in the social sciences. However, the majority of both men and women did not respond to the inquiry about obstacles, and 7 of the 56 participants mentioned only facilitators. The last question- perhaps the most interesting one- deals with the participants' reasonings about the importance of their work. Participants were asked to indicate why they believed their piece was so frequently cited. Based on their responses, we developed nine categories that could absorb the various explanations that reflected their attributions for their work's high citation count.

This attribution "first of its kind" is not unlike the response given by a totally different sample of respondents to a survey in 1982. When a group of highly productive academics was asked to indicate why they chose a certain one of their publications as their most important one, they said that they chose it because they considered it a "ground-breaking" piece of work. In their words the "newness" of research is considered a critical part of its impact on the field.

Applicability and scope were also cited often by the participants. One essay author believes that the publication is cited often because "it provides a simple, highly reproducible technique for the determination of microgram amount of phosphate." Another suggests that many experimenters "can probably find a fact or statement within this publication that supports or appeals to them."

The third frequently cited reason for the publication's high citation is that the publication integrates knowledge and provides directions for further research. Usually this attribution is made by persons whose highly cited contribution was a review article. Two comments exemplify the nature of this type of attribution: "This frequently quoted review article probably provided [readers] with a convenient summary of the state of the art at a time of rapid expansion." Another one indicates, "Each chapter was an evaluative review of all existing research on that topic ... an integration of findings."

On examining gender differences it is found that women and men differ somewhat on their attributions. Men are somewhat more likely to believe that the high citation count was the result of timing of publication and its readability. For example, "Our paper was published at a time when the popularity of causal modeling via path analysis was at its peak in sociology." "The success of my review can be explained on the basis of being a thorough piece of work, much needed at the time." "It communicated the problem and the solution to researchers in a nontechnical, here's why-and-how-you-do-it style" (41 percent of the men compared to 24 percent of the women make such attributions).

These are attributions of circumstance rather than attributions about the significance or importance of the publication. Women are more likely to indicate that the piece was the first of its kind and that it had wide applicability. In part the attribution "first of its kind," often given by women, could be the result of recent changes in the scholarly enterprise, such as the emergence of the "new" scholarship (research on women). Indeed, women's contributions to this emerging area could rightfully be viewed by them as the "first of its kind."

Men have a propensity to attribute theoretical significance to their work; and they often tend to provide circumstantial rather than substantive reasons for the piece's high citation count.

Women, on the other hand, interpret the high citations as the result of their having produced work that facilitates others' efforts, by integrating knowledge, and providing further direction, by being widely applicable to the work of many other scholars.

What have we learned from these causal attributions by women and men scholars? When we examine their perceptions about what led them to undertake the highly cited research in the first place, women appear to be responding to others rather than being driven by their own quest. That is, they are less likely to undertake the work because they are interested in solving a problem, but rather that the work was the outcome of the dissertation or they were invited to prepare the piece.

Furthermore, when it comes to explaining why their work is so frequently cited, the women appear to be more interested in how their work can be useful to others (their research can help and the findings can be applied by others). They also make more positive attributions about the importance of their work than do the men. They see their research as integrating knowledge and providing direction for further work: "a useful procedure for calculating the affinity of the drugs for the receptor"; "the hope that this approach might lead to a new type of cancer immunotherapy."

It is interesting and somewhat surprising that women in this study make more positive attributions about the importance of their work than do the men- a finding that runs counter to scientists' characteristic "norm of humility," their insistence that their work builds on the work of others. How are we to interpret this observation? Do women- because they receive less recognition and validation- congratulate themselves more for their achievements? Is it that they are not as thoroughly socialized into the norms of science?

One should not forget however that many of their remarks also point out that their research has wide applicability, integrates knowledge, and provides direction for further research. In other words, it can be of assistance and help to other scholars and researchers. The findings summarized thus far underscore the importance of external reinforcement in women's participation in research and publication, as suggested earlier by Cole and Zuckerman.

The women in this study do not appear to take the frequent citation of their work for granted. On the contrary, they are more sensitive than men are to the environmental cues that suggest colleagues' acceptance and validation of their achievements. We might speculate here that women's past experiences of gender discrimination and differential treatment in education and the work place may sensitize them to external validation, which in turn can affect their motivation to engage in further research and publication efforts. However, the extent to which external validation or lack of it affects directly women's research productivity ought to be examined further by the use of longitudinal samples.

GENDER AND FIELD DIFFERENCES

Social scientists, independent of sex, are much more likely than natural scientists to indicate that the research was driven by a personal interest (15 vs. 9 indicate so). Both women and men natural scientists, on the other hand, indicate the need to solve a problem as a prime motivation (21 vs. 3 say so).

This could reflect something intrinsic to the fields (perhaps "problems" in the natural sciences are more easily and clearly defined), but it could also reflect differences in a person's initial motivation for pursuing "hard" vs. "soft" sciences as a career. While the analysis by field appears to mask the gender differences with respect to obstacles encountered during conception of research, two of the women natural scientists and one social scientist report lack of collegial support compared to none of the men. Problems with publishers tend to be mentioned more often by social scientists, women and men, than by natural scientists of both sexes (five social scientists and two natural scientists mentioned problems with publishers).

Again this finding is not surprising considering the fact that there is more room for debate about appropriate methods and about theoretical and interpretive statements in the social sciences than in the physical and biological sciences. Another interpretation is that social scientists are more likely to produce books that are harder to publish than are articles produced by natural scientists. Or, as mentioned earlier, rejection rates are higher in social journals than those in the natural sciences.

The results reported thus far suggest that overall; field may be more of a factor than gender in the experiences reported by scientists who produce highly cited research. It is possible that the norms of science within fields are a stronger determinant of the actual experiences scholars have with respect to the conduct of research and publication process than is gender. However, when we examine the attributions offered by these scientists about the high citation count of their research, gender differences persist. In other words, women more than men believe that their work is significant because it is the "first of its kind" and because it has wide applicability. Likewise males continue to indicate the "timeliness" and "readability" of their publications as crucial factors.

If indeed women in the aggregate are less productive than the men are, what accounts for it? Early research on gender differences in achievement indicated that such differences were the result of differences in needs for achievement and gratification. But recent theories on women's and men's approach to work argue that women and men are motivated by the same work needs (survival, pleasure, and contribution) and that differences in socialization and the structure of opportunity produce different expectations.

Even if both genders are motivated by the same needs, there is evidence that certain needs might be stronger in women than in men. In one study, college men and women were asked to give reasons for their future work interests. Women were more likely to answer that their future career would enable them to contribute to society, to work with people or ideas, to help others, and to have an opportunity for self expression. Men, on the other hand, were more interested in occupations that offered high pay, prestige, and rapid advancement.

More recently, Cunningham and Cunningham developed scales to measure the three needs hypothesized by Astin. In their study they were able to demonstrate that while both men and women express these needs in similar ways, women's contribution needs are slightly stronger than men's. Thus evidence from the study reported here showing that women feel their work is cited because it has wide applicability and is useful to others may reflect their greater contribution needs.

How to interpret another finding concerning why men and women pursued their research in the first place? While men look at their research efforts as a consciously motivated effort, women view theirs as happenstance: "it just happened," it was simply their dissertation, or they "were asked to do it."

Studies on locus of control and attributions for scholarly success indicate that the male has more of a sense of internal locus of control- a belief that he is responsible for his actions. This tendency has been attributed to differences in opportunities to control the results of one's behaviour. If men receive more reinforcement for high quality work than women do, then women may indeed begin to believe that they have less control over the consequences of their behaviour. Good work will not necessarily be rewarded.

Women's typical educational and career experiences may serve to reinforce their perception that they have less control over the outcomes. If this is so, it becomes easier to understand why women will be less likely to connect their behaviour to its consequences. Our data indicate that, even when they are as successful in their research as men (authoring "classics"), women exhibit less "ownership," that is, they are less likely to connect their behaviour with the outcomes.

Their work was conceived and undertaken because it was either suggested by the dissertation mentor or because someone invited them to do it. These findings suggest that differences in early socialization and in the structure of opportunity (as reflected in the differential reward structure) have produced differences in expectations about work. These different expectations, in turn, help explain why women and men scientists have different approaches to producing and publishing research.

Even so, more recent evidence suggests that the gap in research production is narrowing. After all, affirmative action and the women's movement have created more opportunities for women to enter scientific careers and to apply for and receive more research funding. While differentials in the reward structure still persist, they have somewhat diminished. Such changes in the structure of opportunity will continue to narrow the gap between women's and men's research productivity.

4

Motherhood and Research Performance in Science

Studies of scientists' research performance, as gauged by their published productivity, find that women generally publish fewer papers throughout their careers than male scientists matched for age, doctoral institutions, and field. Various explanations have been proposed to account for this disparity in scientific publication, ranging from systematic gender discrimination to biological differences in scientific aptitude. One frequent explanation holds that women, far more than men, bear the burdens of marriage and child care and that this fact of social life best accounts for gender differences in scientific publication.

Whether or not this is true, the belief that it is so affects women's career opportunities, their decisions, and the way they are actually treated. We decided (as part of a larger investigation of the careers of American men and women scientists) to test the counter claim, made in earlier studies, that marriage and motherhood have no effect on women's research performance. We did so by assessing the dynamic relation between family life and women's research throughout their careers- an approach not taken by earlier investigators, who simply correlated the number of papers published with current marital and parental status. Our study draws on interviews with 120 scientists: 73 women and 47 men.

We wanted to know whether scientists (both male and female) believe marriage and motherhood to be generally incompatible with a scientific career, whether this had been the case for them in particular, and what quantifiable effects (measured in numbers of publications) marriage and motherhood have actually had on the research performance of women scientists. Since men traditionally have not had primary responsibility for child care, we focused here almost entirely on women, comparing publication rates for those who are married and those who are single, those who are mothers with those who are childless.

Publication counts are, to be sure, an imperfect indicator of scientists' contributions. Yet such counts are highly correlated with better measures such as peer evaluations; moreover, the extent to which scientists publish is consequential for their careers. We therefore took the extent of publication as a rough but serviceable gauge of research performance. We recognized that women scientists are, in a sense, "survivors." They have passed through the rigors of graduate training, have earned doctorate degrees, and are employed in science.

We did not seek to examine the impact of cultural expectations on women's chances of running this gauntlet; that would have called for investigating the processes by which women are winnowed out of scientific careers. We chose subjects for this study by a stratified selection process that took into account gender, professional age, field of expertise, and scientific standing. To compare the effects of marriage and motherhood on women who took degrees in different historical periods, we divided the scientists into three age groups: those who received their doctorates between 1920 and 1959, before the advent of the women's movement; those during the decades from 1960 through 1969, and from 1970 through 1979, decades when the movement was getting under way and then becoming widespread.

Eighty percent of them were drawn from mathematics and the physical and biological sciences; the remainder from economics and psychology, with the same 4:1 ratio being applied in each age group. Scientists were further divided according to their peer recognition in relation to others of roughly the same professional age. The top tier of scientists (those we designated "eminent") in the oldest group were members of the National Academy of Sciences or the American Academy of Arts and Sciences or were full professors in departments ranked in the top ten in each field by national surveys of the quality of doctoral programmes.

In the intermediate age group, Guggenheim fellows or tenured professors in the top ten departments were classed as eminent. Younger scientists were considered eminent if they had held Guggenheim Fellowships or were assistant or associate professors in a top ten department. Scientists not meeting these exacting criteria were designated as rank and file. They were randomly selected from lists of the faculty and research staff at accredited four-year colleges and universities located in the same geographical regions as the eminent scientists. They were also matched to these scientists for professional age and scientific field.

Although these scientists were selected randomly, the criteria we used, their small numbers, and our exclusion of some important groups of scientists (such as those working in industry) mean that this is decidedly not a true random sample of all U.S. scientists. Our subjects were asked about their research and publication histories and for comments on graphs we prepared that showed the number of papers they had published each year along with important events in their careers and personal lives.

Both men and women scientists report having come up against the belief that marriage and motherhood cannot be meshed with demanding scientific careers. Not surprisingly, the oldest group of scientists encountered this belief most often. Before (and even shortly after) World War II, the proper priorities for women were widely held to be marriage and motherhood first and science, second, and good science was believed to be all-consuming. The notion that women could simultaneously be traditional wives, traditional mothers, and productive scientists seemed patently absurd.

These beliefs were articulated by a woman zoologist who reported that "if one had children and a working husband it was not part of the psychology to suppose that one's job was anything more than a secondary consideration." Many men and women scientists at the time shared these views. They believed most women could no longer be serious scientists once they were married. A distinguished woman biologist who is now in her seventies said her woman laboratory chief was appalled by the idea that her protege would marry: "She threw me out of the lab the minute she heard I was going to get married because that was treason against women."

For one male chemist, marriage meant that women scientists were "finished"; for a male physicist, "As soon as women got into domestic life that was the end of it for all of them." This climate of opinion meant that women determined to have serious research careers often did not marry. In the words of one biologist now in her seventies, "Marrying was not considered the thing to do [for women scientists]. In science, you're dedicated. You go into a shroud, you don't wear normal clothes ... you shouldn't get married; you shouldn't have children."

Not all women scientists accepted these views, of course, and some did marry, have children, and continue to work. Yet until the end of World War II at the earliest, women scientists were few in number and fewer than half were married. Married women with children were nearly invisible in American science. Such women were viewed, by many, as violating the prevailing family norms. Although social attitudes concerning the roles of wives and mothers have changed significantly, even the youngest women scientists report that many people still consider marriage and motherhood to be incompatible with a scientific career.

One young chemist said, "When I got pregnant I was written off as a serious scientist ... by lots of people." When those occupying positions of power and authority act in accord with these beliefs, they severely limit the opportunities and careers available to married women. To assess the actual impact of marriage and motherhood on women in science we needed answers to four questions: Are married women, as a group, less productive researchers than single women? Among married women, do those with children publish fewer papers than those who are childless? Is there a drop in women's published research performance after childbirth? Does the number of children women scientists have affect their research performance?

The publication and career histories of eminent scientists provided the first clues that marriage and children do not generally affect scientific productivity. On average, these eminent married women (and eminent women are just as apt to marry and have children as their rank-and-file counterparts) published slightly more over their careers- not less- than eminent single women: an average of 3.0 papers per year compared with 2.2. Among the eminent married women, those with children publish 2.9 papers annually and childless women publish 3.3.

Moreover, during the three-year period preceding and following the births of first children, the annual published productivity of eminent women rises from 1.5 to 2.7 papers annually. Finally, rate of publication of these scientists is unrelated to the number of children they have. These statistical findings are plainly counterintuitive, and yet they are consistent with earlier cross-sectional studies. How well do they correspond with the subjective reports of women in the interviews? Do they think that marrying and having children really is unrelated to the amount of research they publish, and if they do, how is one to account for this?

The publication histories of two older, eminent women scientists, one with four children and the other with three, illustrate one general pattern. Such scientists published less when they were young and had young children; there is a marked upward trend in the number of papers they published after the first decade of their careers. There are also year-to-year fluctuations- peaks and valleys- within the general upward trend. All these women do, to be sure, acknowledge that children take up a great deal of time. They are "a definite time commitment. That means that you are doing less with other things"- but not scientific research. The research continues.

How can it continue? These eminent women emphasize, first, that thinking about science goes on at home as well as at work. It does not end when they close the doors to their laboratories. "When the kids were small ... I had ideas when I was washing the dishes and nursing the babies. Scientifically speaking, I did my best work during the period when the kids were coming." Second, if they have a scientist husband (and that is the typical situation), they talk about their work during "so-called off-time." Third, professional obligations other than research are far more limited for younger than they are for older scientists. "I spent more time doing science then than I do now ... the calls on my time [then] were my job and my kids. Now it's so many other things."

Fourth, lower rates of publication in the early years are not necessarily attributable to the demands of motherhood but rather are characteristic of the beginning phase of a developing research program. As one physical scientist observed, "In the first years ... we were building those enormous instruments. Developing the theory and experiment [took up] a lot of time so there weren't that many papers." Another, commenting on the downturns in her own publication graph, "You are very busy in the valley."

According to these eminent scientists, marriage and motherhood did not reduce their published productivity. Should one believe their retrospective accounts? Perhaps their perceptions are not correct. After all, inspection of the graphs of these older eminent married women with children shows that they indeed were less productive scientifically when they were young and had young children. Did having young children in truth affect their rate of publication at least in the short run?

When thought of the publication patterns of two groups of scientists who should not be affected by marriage or parenthood- eminent single women and eminent men whose wives took responsibility for looking after children- would further illuminate these counterintuitive results. Do the presumably unencumbered scientists publish at a more rapid rate in the early years than women who had young children?

The answer appears to be no. Single women and married men are just as apt to show low levels of publication in the first decade of their careers. They are also as likely to show oscillations and an overall rising slope of publication with time. The fact that the early publication patterns of these two groups do not differ much from those of married women with children lends credibility to the married women's observations.

Another question comes up however. The eminent older women say that marriage and childbearing did not reduce their scientific productivity. If that is so, why do their publication rates increase as they pass beyond the child-care age- particularly in view of the additional distractions and responsibilities that they say come with professional maturity and a higher degree of recognition? Part of the answer is that the opportunities for collaborative research increase as one's career progresses.

Beginning scientists do most or all of the benchwork themselves; more established ones often assume major administrative roles and oversee the work that goes on in their laboratories. Their publication records reflect this upsurge in collaborative research. We should mention that the publication record of some eminent women scientists does not exhibit the typical rising slope with time. These women, too, say that marriage and motherhood had little bearing on their scientific productivity. Moreover, this pattern of comparatively constant productivity appears as often among married women as among single ones.

Our data seem to indicate then that older, eminent women with children generally published as much early in their careers as their unmarried counterparts. Could we have made a critical error, however, in compiling and interpreting the data? Could it be that women who have children and remain scientifically productive are "self-selected," that is, are simply more talented scientists than those who choose to remain childless?

Although strict comparisons of scientific ability cannot be made, we can compare the publication rates of older eminent scientists who did and did not have children, focusing on the years before motherhood. To this end, we matched the two groups of women roughly by their birth dates. The publication rate during the three years before women with children had their first child was compared with "equivalent years" in the life span for women without children. We found similar early histories; approximately 1.3 papers annually for women who subsequently had children and 1.6 for those who did not. In other words, older eminent women who eventually had children published inconsequentially fewer papers initially than women who never had children.

More important, might we be mistaken by concentrating on the histories of eminent women scientists instead of on those who might be more likely to experience the debilitating effects of marriage and motherhood on publication rates? The eminent women, after all, are successful scientists. If marriage and motherhood take a toll in their case, such women would presumably not have been able to achieve the recognition they actually did achieve. Do the publication histories of other women scientists, those designated as rank-and-file, testify to the negative impact of marriage and child care?

Rank-and-file men and women scientists do, of course, in general, publish less than their eminent colleagues. Within the rank and file in our sample, married women did publish slightly fewer papers than single ones (an average of 1.1 a year as compared with 1.7). But married women with children publish no fewer papers than married women without children; both groups average about one paper per year. As in the case of eminent women, their publication rates did not decline after children were born. Rank-and-file women averaged well under one paper per year (.2) in the three-year period prior to the birth of their first child and they averaged just under a paper per year (.8) in the three years following the birth.

Much the same impression is conveyed by these scientists' own testimony: having children did not significantly affect their records of research and publication. As one relatively unproductive behavioral scientist observed, "It didn't occur to me to stop working when I had (a child).... In fact, right after she was born I wrote one paper and started to work on the next one ... so if anything ... I seemed to work better," that is, more efficiently if under greater pressure.

Her account is consistent with accounts of other women, such as a young biochemist who asserted that her publication rate was unaffected by family obligations: "It's just fortuitous.... The kinetics of me as a parent and me as a researcher don't have a direct relationship.... One has not interfered with the other." Contrary to expectation then, such women are no more likely than older eminent ones to say that marriage and family responsibilities account for their rate of publication, and the statistical data we have in hand bear out what they say.

Would we find a similar pattern among younger women? Because marriage and childbearing usually come early in a woman's career, the records for younger scientists should show their effects on published productivity, at least in the short term. A behavioral scientist who is now a full professor in a high-ranking department and who had just had a child suggested that motherhood was unrelated to the pace of publication. "Having a child is draining in many ways, but not in terms of having affected my work, especially when I look at how much I've ... done this year. No, it's really movies, social life and things like that [that go].... I feel chronically slow and behind and this year I'm blaming it on the baby, but I realize that has nothing to do with it." In the past, it was "too many graduate students ... [a] grant reviewing committee, [an] editorship, [and now a] baby. So I have always had some kind of baby to blame it on."

Perhaps the limiting case is a woman scientist who has an endowed chair in a major department. She has been married four times and divorced three times, and she has had four children by three different husbands. If marriage and motherhood should bring a scientist's career to a halt, they should have done so here. Yet her published output has risen throughout this complex history. Ironically, the largest dip in her pattern came in 1979, one of the few years in which she did not get married, have a child, or get divorced. Asked about her publication pattern, she replied, "Suddenly you're ready to report on three different projects and therefore [the papers] roll off the presses. The ups and downs [have] nothing to do with the rest of my life."

Even so, pregnancy and its aftermath did interfere temporarily with research in the case of 3 of the 37 women in our sample who had children. A woman biologist told us "I was one of those women who said I'm so well organized, I'll just drop a child and that will be it- but I didn't realize that hormones could do such a job on a person." Asked to explain why her publication rate declined only temporarily and not by much, she said, "I was lucky because by then I had people in my lab. They were working [and] productive.... But I found that for a whole year my mind wasn't functioning. "

These longitudinal data indicate that marriage and children are not inimical to published productivity of women in the aggregate. Although a few people would question that marriage and motherhood impose formidable responsibilities, apparently many women scientists can manage a career and family obligations simultaneously. How do they do it? And how, when conflicts arise between home and career, do women scientists deal with them?

The answer can be found, in part, in how women scientists manage their "status set," that is, the array of social positions each of them occupies (such as professor, laboratory director, wife, mother, and citizen). We focused on three interconnected aspects of status sets: size (the number of positions held simultaneously), congruence (the extent to which various obligations are consistent rather than in conflict), and the timing of the addition and deletion of status obligations.

At the extreme, several women, convinced that marriage is incompatible with scientific work, chose not to marry, in effect, limiting their status sets. Yet three-fourths of the women in our sample did marry- a proportion that appears to be typical of women scientists in general now. For the majority of them, the fundamental question about marriage was one of timing. As a young, woman economist said, it "would also be a big career disadvantage for me [to get married]. Once I have tenure and am more settled down in a university, it would be a little bit easier."

Two-thirds of the married women had children. Timing their arrival, many women say, helps to maintain a research career. A renowned physical scientist delayed having her first child for nine years after marrying in order to prove herself as a valuable professional. Many younger women said they were delaying motherhood until they received tenure. Doubting that she could have a child and maintain the level of performance needed for tenure, a young biochemist noted, "My ideal scenario is to get a tenured position, and then have a child or two."

All told, eminent and rank-and-file women had about the same number of children: an average of two, with none exceeding four. Our data show that annual rates of publication are virtually the same for women with one child and for those with two or more. There are aspects of marriage and motherhood other than timing that can make for congruent status sets. Close to four-fifths of the married women we interviewed were married to scientists (again, a proportion typical of married women scientists generally). Such "assortative" or selective mating apparently gives these women (and men, too) a variety of benefits, including ready understanding of their professional obligations and way of life. A molecular biologist observed that her husband could scarcely be upset when she came home late because "he knew that no matter how well I had planned something, experiments do get delayed. I think that's made it a lot easier."

Women scientists married to scientists publish, on average, 40 percent more than women married to men in other occupations, and this is so both for eminent and for other women scientists. This difference in publication rates may result from self-selection, congruence of values, or the flexibilty of academic schedules. Women scientists may also achieve congruence of status obligations by compartmentalizing their lives. But compartmentalizing, they report, is not always feasible. In fact, many find it harder to keep their minds off work when at home than to keep their minds off children when at work. Moreover, every woman with children emphasized that they relied on some form of child care or household help-necessary arrangements but fragile at best. The illness of a spouse, child, or housekeeper can throw the entire scheme awry.

In view of these difficulties, is it possible that women and men scientists manage to continue research only by neglecting spouses and children? Our study was not designed to answer this question. This much we do know. The divorce rate for these women and men is unrelated to published productivity. Married women scientists with children do pay a price to remain scientifically productive. They report having had to eliminate almost everything but work and family, particularly when their children were young. As an eminent psychologist observed, what goes first is "discretionary time. I think I can only work effectively ... 50 hours a week.... If I didn't have children, I'd probably read more novels ... or go to more movies."

Loss of discretionary time not only affects leisure pursuits but also sometimes has serious consequences for women's research and careers, even if they have no significant effects on their rate of publication. Women scientists who adhered to rigid family schedules lost the flexibility to stay late in the laboratory to work on an interesting problem; they report not feeling part of "the club," not having time for informal discussions with colleagues.

Other investigators have shown that only some 12 percent of women scientists stop work after getting their Ph.D. Surely some of them do so because of the intense conflicts that arise between science and parenthood. One woman who had left a promising research career for a less demanding job said in a supplementary interview, "I was only in the lab the hours that the children were in school.... I was working with really bright people who ground out the publications at a rate I couldn't keep up with.... It was too frustrating." A small subset of women, then, finds that science and motherhood do not mix and alter their careers to give more time to their families. For some, science and motherhood do not mix.

Our study shows, however, that for most of these women, science and motherhood do mix. Women scientists who marry and have families publish as many papers each year, on the average, as single women. Managing the simultaneous demands of research careers, marriage, and motherhood is not easy; it requires organization and an elaborate set of personal adaptations.

The results of this study should not be interpreted as meaning that marriage and children have no effect on the careers of women scientists. They do, but they generally do not take their toll on women's research performance. How then can the disparity in rate of publication between men and women scientists be explained? Why do men publish substantially more papers on average over the course of their careers as women of comparable backgrounds? This difference remains a puzzle requiring further comparative inquiry into the research careers of both men and women scientists.

SEX DIFFERENCES IN CAREERS

In nearly all industrialized countries, men's and women's patterns of labour force participation are converging. Despite this trend, there has been little change in occupational segregation and earnings disparities by sex. In the United States, the work roles of men and women were about as differentiated in 1970 as they were in 1900, and there has been only a modest decline in the level of occupational segregation by sex over the past two decades.

When men and women do pursue similar occupational roles, they are often segregated across organizations or by job titles within organizations. Over the past several decades, women in the United States working full time, year round have earned about two-thirds as much as men and the discrepancy is almost as large when comparisons are made between men and women in the same occupation. Men and women bring different skills, aptitudes, interests, and work orientations to the workplace, and this accounts for some of the discrepancy in their career outcomes. Women's family responsibilities also affect the choices they make concerning work roles outside the home.

But these "supply-side" factors alone do not account for the persistence of sex segregation and earnings disparities. Structural factors include arrangements and practices in schools, workplaces, and other institutions that cause men and women to be treated differently even when they have the same qualifications and work orientations. Finally, there is a cognitive or social psychological basis to sex differences in the workplace; because of widely held cultural stereotypes about gender, the qualifications and performances of men and women are perceived differently.

These stereotypes affect the perceptions and actions of teachers, counselors, employers, co-workers, policymakers, and even the ways in which men and women perceive themselves. After two decades of empirical research by behavioral scientists, a consensus is emerging on how supply-side, structural, and social-psychological factors combine to produce different career outcomes for men and women.

The existence of cultural stereotypes, structural barriers, or differences in "human capital" investments is no longer at issue, although the relative contributions of these three factors are still debated. While some neoclassical economists argue that supply-side factors account for most occupational segregation and nearly all of the earnings disparity between men and women, most social scientists agree that structural barriers and cultural stereotypes are at least as important. Moreover, the debate has become less ideological and more scientific as the empirical research by economists, sociologists, and psychologists grows increasingly sophisticated.

In this chapter, I examine the implications of research on gender and work for the study of sex differences in the careers of scientists. At issue is whether the distinctive cognitive, normative, and institutional structure of science, attenuates the extent to which structural barriers and cultural stereotypes shape the careers of women scientists. Jonathan Cole, among others, has presented research results in support of the hypothesis that the reward system in science is essentially meritocratic and not biased against women. At the other extreme, the case has been made that the very content of science itself has been constructed from a masculine approach to the natural world.

SEX DIFFERENCES IN SCIENTISTS' CAREER OUTCOMES

Sex differences in career outcomes in science are strikingly similar to those in other institutional sectors. As in other occupations, the representation of women in science has increased markedly over the past three decades. At the same time, women remain segregated by academic field, by institution, by job, and by rank. In 1981, nearly half of the female Ph.D. recipients obtained their doctorates in the fields of psychology and education, compared to about a fourth of the men. Nearly a fourth of the men received PhDs in physical sciences and engineering, compared to less than 5 percent of the women.

The index of dissimilarity, a widely accepted measure of the extent of segregation, shows that the level of segregation across 24 fields for new PhDs actually increased slightly between 1971 and 1981. In the same period, however, the level of segregation by field at the baccalaureate level decreased substantially. Women faculty in the United States are also segregated by institution. They are more likely than men to find employment in two- and four-year colleges and less likely to be employed in universities. Female PhDs are also less likely than men to find jobs outside of academia. Female PhDs are also about twice as likely as men to be unemployed (National Science Foundation 1986, but unemployment rates are low for both).

Even when men and women scientists work in the same institutions, they are segregated by rank. In 1981, women constituted nearly half of non-tenure-track faculty but only 25 percent of full-time ladder faculty. Among cohorts of PhDs receiving degrees in the same year, men are more likely than women to be represented in the senior ranks of university faculty. Finally, salary discrepancies between men and women scientists are similar to earnings differences by sex in other institutional sectors. In 1984, women engineers and scientists earned about 71 percent as much as their male counterparts, roughly the same as within-occupation wage differentials estimated from national labour force data. Nearly all of the earnings differential can be attributed to segregation by field, institution, and rank.

In short, sex segregation is about as pervasive in science as it is outside of science, with predictable consequences for differences in men's and women's career outcomes. On the one hand, this might suggest that the structural barriers and cultural stereotypes that create inequities in other institutional realms also harm the careers of women scientists. On the other hand, science is a highly stratified institution, and even small differences between men and women in skills, training, or work orientation can lead to large differences in career trajectories.

The segregation described above may largely reflect individual choices men and women have made to specialize in different fields and in different kinds of careers. The debate over sex discrimination in science in large part centers on the extent to which differences in career outcomes of men and women are the product of structural barriers on the one hand versus achievement-related "supply-side" factors on the other, that is, factors or attributes of men and women relevant to job performance but which result from decisions they made long before entering the job market.

THE CASE FOR SCIENCE AS A SPECIAL CASE

More so than in other institutional sectors, scientists share a belief in an institutionally sanctioned goal and a normative principle governing actions in pursuit of that goal. The goal is the production of certified knowledge, and the normative principle is universalism. The norm of universalism prescribes that "rewards and resources are to be allocated on criteria of scientific merit and that judgements of scientific merit are to be made only in terms of contributions to knowledge". Sex, race, and other ascriptive criteria for allocating resources and rewards are functionally irrelevant and illegitimate within the normative structure of science.

Moreover, there is widespread agreement among scientists that the extent and quality of research publication is the most important measure of an individual's contribution to the production of knowledge. With such a visible and objective measure of productivity, deviation from the norm of universalism should be easily detected and negatively sanctioned. As in other institutional sectors, science as actually practiced does depart somewhat from its normative principles. But the meritocratic model is so widely accepted that it is the criterion by which scientists evaluate their own actions.

Most scientists who study discrimination in science also subscribe to the meritocratic model as an ideal type. Discrimination is measured as a departure from a base-line model that represents the distribution of rewards and resources as a function of the productivity of individual scientists. Functionally irrelevant criteria are presumed to operate when the meritocratic model fails to account fully for sex differences in the career outcomes of scientists.

However, structural, cultural, and other sources of discrimination are rarely studied directly, especially in quantitative studies of scientific careers. Instead, they are typically inferred from the residual net difference between men and women after controlling achievement-related variables in the meritocratic base-line model. As a result, we know much more about the extent to which "supply-side" factors do and do not account for reward and productivity differences between men and women scientists than we do about the impact of specific structural barriers and cultural stereotypes.

There is, of course, another view of gender issues in science, one that is less prone to treating science as a special case. Historical and organizational case studies are more likely to take a societal view of structural and cultural forces that shape women's careers and then examine how those same forces operate in the scientific community.

HUMAN CAPITAL INVESTMENTS AND DIFFERENTIAL PRODUCTIVITY

Neo-classical economists argue that differences in human capital investments account for much of the disparity between men and women in labour market outcomes. Because of intermittent labour force participation, women accumulate less experience and on-the-job training than men, which in turn leads to lower earnings. Occupational segregation comes about because women and men choose to specialize in different kinds of jobs. Unlike men, women tend to choose jobs that are easy to reconcile with family demands and do not impose a wage penalty on workers who drop out and re-enter the labour force.

Moreover, compared to men with similar labour market experience, women are argued to be less productive because they allocate more effort to household tasks and less to job tasks. Labour force studies show that differences in human capital investment account for at least some of the differences in men's and women's work experiences, although the extent to which the economists' hypotheses are supported by empirical data is the subject of vigorous debate. Nevertheless, the human capital model offers a comprehensive explanation for sex segregation and differences in the career trajectories of men and women- an explanation that might be especially applicable to careers in science.

PRODUCTIVITY OF SCIENTISTS AND FAMILY DEMANDS

In fact, research on men and women scientists provides mixed support for the human capital model. Productivity, as measured by number of publications, is lower for women than for men. However, sex differences in productivity fail to account completely for differences in the career outcomes of men and women scientists, especially with respect to academic rank.

Moreover, the impact of family demands implied by the human capital model is not supported by research on men and women scientists. Marriage and family status appear to have no impact on the research productivity of female scientists. Married female scientists with children appear as committed to their careers as their male counterparts. On the other hand, marriage and the problems of reconciling the constraints of dual careers do appear to limit the job mobility of women scientists.

As noted above, male and female scientists differ in their fields of specialization, but family demands probably do not explain segregation by field. Although little (if any) research has been done on the topic, it is probably no more difficult to reconcile work and family demands in the physical and mathematical sciences than it is in the social sciences. Since labour force participation of women scientists is much less intermittent than it is for women in other sectors, differences across specialties in rates of skill atrophy and wage penalties for dropping out are unlikely to explain segregation by field.

SPECIALIZATION IN QUANTITATIVE FIELDS

There is one obvious factor that is associated with sex differences in fields of specialization. Women are much less likely than men to earn advanced degrees and then to work in the more quantitative disciplines. Although not related to family roles, these are "supply-side" factors insofar as they reflect different kinds of choices made by men and women long before they begin their research careers. Sex differences in the extent of interest in science emerge prior to high school, and those interests have a strong impact on the propensity to obtain quantitative training in high school and college. Thus, perhaps because of early childhood socialization, many young women self-select out of the pool of individuals capable of pursuing research careers in highly quantitative fields.

Even if science were based on universalistic principles, the career outcomes of men and women could well be unequal if men and women differed in their human capital investments and other "supply-side" factors they bring to their jobs. Differences between men and women scientists in their household and family responsibilities appear not to affect the kind of investments they make in a scientific career. To the extent that family demands limit the mobility of women scientists, they may be less able than men to take advantage of opportunities that would enhance their careers.

Because of early socialization, girls express less interest in science than boys, and as a result they are less likely to get the kind of training that will prepare them for careers in science, especially in highly quantitative specializations. Differential childhood socialization is a "supply-side" factor insofar as it can generate sex differences in careers even when the allocation of resources and rewards in science itself are based solely on meritocratic criteria. On the other hand, sex differences in interest in science among children and adolescents may be shaped by structural barriers and cultural stereotypes similar to those discussed below.

Science, like other forms of work, is done in organizations. The careers of scientists are influenced by both the rules and procedures of the organizations in which they are employed and the decisions made about how to formulate and apply those rules and procedures. In addition, decision making in organizations is an inherently political process, influenced by the distribution of power among groups with differing and often conflicting interests. It is also shaped by the organization's history and by constraints imposed by its environment.

In short, the course of scientists' careers may be influenced as much or more so by the dynamics of the organization in which they work than by the "normative principles" or "goals" of science as an institution. The point is readily acknowledged in historical studies of the careers of men and women scientists. Historians have documented the impact of policies that kept women out of graduate programs of institutions like Harvard and Princeton, excluded them from faculty positions in coeducational institutions, and channeled them into subordinate staff roles in research laboratories.

Some quantitative studies note the impact of past structural barriers on the careers of women scientists who began their careers early in the century. However, blatantly exclusionary policies and practices have diminished; today's barriers are much more subtle. Unfortunately, studies of contemporary structural barriers and organizational dynamics are relatively rare. Nevertheless, the limited research that has been done suggests that structural factors in science affect women's careers in much the same way as they do in other realms.

Decisions on personnel matters in university settings are largely delegated to academic departments. This is perhaps the most distinctive feature of the organizational decision making which governs the careers of scientists. Of course, universities differ in the amount of autonomy they cede to departments, and decisions on the allocation of positions and resources across departments are usually made in centralized administrative units, often in consultation with a faculty legislative body.

As in any organization, individuals form informal alliances or coalitions based on common interests. Trying to influence the outcome of decisions is just one way that coalitions attempt to pursue their interests. They also attempt to shape the goals of the institutions and the agendas that determine which decisions are to be made. So far, research work on the politics of organizational decision making has been more theoretical than empirical, but anyone who has ever participated in an academic personnel case is well aware of how politics are played out in a university setting.

Although debates are often explicitly couched in terms of universalistic principles and the institutional goals of science, the participants typically include many individuals whose own contributions to the production of certified knowledge are marginal at best. The underlying issues can range from conflicts over methodological and substantive preferences, teaching versus research, and the interests of younger versus more established scholars, or social and personality issues even more remotely connected to the cognitive content of the scientific enterprise. Although the normative principles and goals of science are certainly relevant to personnel decisions, more proximate political factors can be just as decisive in shaping the careers of individual scientists.

EXTERNAL CONSTRAINTS ON DECISION MAKING

Universities, like other organizations, face external pressures as they attempt to maintain access to the material and symbolic resources necessary for their survival. Public universities depend on state support for financial resources; their fortunes are linked to general economic conditions and to the degree of public support for higher education. Increasingly, major research institutions rely on both government and private funding. It is particularly important that a university's external constituencies accept the legitimacy of the organization's goals and methods. A university's actions are likely to be especially subject to outside scrutiny-by public agencies, the mass media, alumni, professional groups, etc. during periods when that legitimacy is in question.

External pressures can produce inequities in the career prospects of men and women scientists. Direct pressure to improve the career prospects of women can be applied by government agencies and political constituencies, as can pressure to dismantle programs that are perceived to offer "preferential treatment" to disadvantaged groups. Policies aimed at supporting higher education for military veterans can indirectly place women at a disadvantage, as can financial aid programs that require full-time study. This seems subtle; but the impact of external constraints can be even more indirect.

For example, volatile economic conditions may lead universities to increase their use of part-time, temporary positions. Hiring women disproportionately for such positions would reinforce sex segregation between tenure-track and off-track positions. In short, a range of factors external to the organization can shape the way rules and procedures affecting scientists' careers are formulated and applied.

BEYOND THE MERITOCRATIC BASE-LINE MODEL

In sum, examining scientific careers from an organizational perspective provides an alternative to the conventional approach to studying gender inequities in science. The conventional view emphasizes the normative principles and goals of science as an institution, and it abstracts scientists' careers from the organizational settings in which they are accomplished. Research focused on individual scientists examines discrimination in terms of departures from a base-line meritocratic model. In contrast, organizational approaches directly examine the structures and processes that can create barriers to equity in the careers of men and women scientists.

Starting with the premise that decisions are the outcome of a political process and are subject to external constraints, an organizational approach suggests that the link between decision making regarding scientists' careers and the normative principles of science is almost certainly not nearly as strong as, say, those principles and editorial decisions regarding the publication of scientific research. As a result, there is considerable room for the emergence and persistence of the kinds of the structural and social psychological barriers suggested below.

The few existing organizational studies of scientists' careers consistently show greater sex stratification in elite institutions. For example, Cole found that disparities by sex in academic rank were greater at more prestigious institutions, even after controlling for differential productivity. Szafran's (1984) analyses of the 1969 Carnegie Commission data revealed similar patterns. In addition, he found a negative relationship between financial resources (measured as expenditures per student) and propensity to recruit female faculty. Szafran suggests that to protect their reputations, highly regarded institutions in the 1960s may have been using slack resources to attract and support eminent male scientists.

The association between institutional resources and segregation in universities is consistent with findings from Bielby and Baron's study of sex segregation in other institutional realms in the late 1960s and early 1970s. In a detailed examination of organizational arrangements and job segregation by sex in a cross-section of California firms, they found that large, bureaucratic organizations were among the most segregated. To the extent that segregation introduces inefficiencies in the allocation of human resources, those were the firms that could afford a segregated workforce.

In addition, highly structured firms have more dimensions along which to potentially segregate women from men- by department, division, geographic location, job title, and so on- and almost every large, bureaucratic firm in their study was virtually completely segregated by sex along one or more of those dimensions.

Research by Fox shows how sex segregation affected the careers of men and women scientists at one large, prestigious public university in the early 1970s. Her studies document the segregation of men and women by rank, administrative location, and field of specialization within the university and how that segregation sustained a dual reward structure. She found that for both men and women, achievement-related variables (rank, degrees, and experience) were the most important determinants of salary.

However, the payoff for specific kinds of achievements was consistently lower for women than for men. Moreover, her analyses show that both men and women earned less when they were employed in an administrative location dominated by the opposite sex. Fox argues that segregation by sex makes the dual reward system less visible. Given patterns of segregation at institutions similar to the one she studied, the most salient salary differentials perceived by any individual are likely to be among the same-sex colleagues employed in that individual's administrative location.

Since those salary differences are largely related to achievements, they are likely to be perceived as equitable. Much less salient (and visible) to an individual would be the salary differences among opposite sex employees in other administrative locations. Segregation therefore allows an achievement ideology to persist alongside a compensation system that rewards both men and women for their accomplishments but offers them different rates of return. Of course, we cannot tell from Fox's studies whether the same dual reward system operated at other universities in the early 1970s. However, patterns of segregation were probably similar at other large, prestigious universities, and the mechanisms she describes suggest a way that the inequities detected in aggregate studies such as Cole's and Szafran's may have come about. The studies of job segregation and structural barriers described above are limited in two ways. First, they are all based on data from the early 1960s and late 1970s, before the era of vigorous enforcement of equal employment opportunity laws and regulations. We do not know the extent to which the interventions of the 1970s changed patterns of segregation. Second, those kinds of organizational studies do not examine the decision making processes that lead to the implementation of the organizational arrangements that create structural barriers.

Evidence from Szafran's study suggests that a sizable female constituency within a university can affect its employment practices. In his data from 1969, universities with a greater percentage of women in administrative roles had a better record on recruiting women to faculty positions. Similarly, universities exhibited greater equity in assigning men and women to off-ladder positions when women were better represented in both administrative and faculty positions.

These results parallel findings from Bielby and Baron's study of segregation in a general sample of organizations in California, already noted. They found lower levels of job segregation by sex in firms with a sizable female workforce. In addition, the few organizations that exhibited significant reduction in levels of segregation over a four-to-seven-year period were ones that initially had a high percentage of female employees.

Evidence that universities have changed practices in response to pressure from federal and state agencies is mixed. Szafran found no relationship between level of government funding and measures of equity in faculty employment. However, his data are from 1969, and it was not until the mid-1970s that universities were subject to regulations on equal employment for government contractors. Szafran did find that public universities had a slightly better record in terms of parity between men and women in salary and rank, and this may be a function of the closer scrutiny of personnel practices in public institutions by outside agencies and political constituencies.

The formal procedures used in recruitment and promotion have certainly changed over the years since universities have been subject to Federal regulation of affirmative action. Most universities have an affirmative action office that monitors all personnel actions. Faculty openings at all levels are widely advertised through professional channels. Records are kept on applicant pools, candidates interviewed, and reasons why one candidate was chosen over another.Similarly, criteria for promotion and the procedures used to decide promotion cases have been formalized. While such efforts at reform by no means guarantee that personnel decisions are now made on universalistic criteria alone, there is considerable evidence that progress has been made since the early 1970s. Zuckerman and Cole (1985) cite recent research showing that women no longer face disadvantages in admission to graduate programs and are now no more likely than men to obtain first jobs in off-ladder positions. Overall, recent cohorts of female PhDs appear to begin their careers in positions comparable in quality to those obtained by men. On the other hand, the same studies cited by Zuckerman and Cole show that, even among recent cohorts, women are somewhat less likely than men to be promoted to tenure and move much more slowly through the more senior faculty ranks. In short, it appears easier to reduce and essentially eliminate biases in procedures used to recruit and screen candidates for new faculty positions than it is to remove the variety of structural and social psychological barriers women confront once their careers within the university are under way.

It is perhaps too early to tell whether the weakening in enforcement of equal employment opportunity laws and regulations in recent years is eroding the gains of the early 1970s. However, recent statistics on female enrollments in scientific fields show that the trends of the past decade are not irreversible. A recent report of the Commission on Professionals in Science and Technology shows that in 1984 the proportion of women declined in the cohort of first-year engineering students, among those obtaining undergraduate degrees in geology and earth sciences, and among those receiving advanced degrees in mathematics and biological sciences. These trends and the persistent sex segregation by rank among university faculty suggest that some of the barriers faced by women scientists are either so subtle or so deeply entrenched that they are difficult to dismantle, even when there is an organizational commitment to do so. Recent research on the social psychology of prejudice, summarized below, indicates that the biases that arise in day-to-day interpersonal interaction may be even more difficult to eradicate than the structural barriers built into the rules and procedures of organizations.

In 1936, physicist Robert A. Millikan advised the president of Duke University against hiring a woman for a faculty position in the university's physics department. In his letter to President Few, Millikan asserted; "I should, therefore, expect to go farther in influence and get more for my expenditure if in introducing young blood in a department of physics I picked one or two of the outstanding younger men, rather than if I filled one of my openings with a woman". He based his assertion on several assumptions about the competency of women physicists and the potential negative impact women faculty might have on a department's prestige.

In regard to teaching, he argued: "In a coeducational institution where there are many women students it is undoubtedly also desirable to have for pedagogical purposes women instructors, but only in very exceptional cases would I think that the advance of graduate work would be as well promoted by a woman as by a man". No doubt some male scientists still hold attitudes like these about the capabilities of women, but they are almost certainly in the minority today. Those who do, are at least more cautious about articulating them. Public attitudes about women's careers have become much more liberal over the past 50 years, and no doubt scientists' attitudes have moved in the same direction.

Few male scientists today would openly admit to being influenced by prejudice in their interactions with female scientists. On the other hand, narrative accounts by female scientists consistently report situations in which their careers have been affected by the prejudicial actions and attitudes of male teachers and colleagues. Recent social-psychological research seeks to explain how dominant and subordinate groups can have such different perceptions of their social interactions.

Both laboratory and field studies suggest that stereotypes and prejudices are more subtle and less visible today than they were in Millikan's era, that they influence the behaviour of both men and women, and that most of the time we are unaware of how they influence our behaviour. Social psychologists view stereotypes as an essential feature of human perception, a cognitive shorthand invoked to achieve economy in processing, storing, and retrieving information.

Gender stereotypes are constellations of traits and behaviors attributed to the categories "male" and "female." Research on the content of those stereotypes consistently finds two clusters: "instrumental" traits ascribed to men and "expressive" traits ascribed to women. Thus, traits and behaviors commonly associated with the scientist's role conform to cultural stereotypes of "maleness."

Stereotypes influence the attributions individuals make about the causes of their own behaviour and the behaviour of others. Laboratory studies show that men typically attribute success in performing "masculine" tasks to ability, whereas women tend to attribute their own success on the same tasks to luck or effort. Similarly, in evaluating others, performance consistent with stereotypical expectations tends to be attributed to stable, internal causes, whereas performance inconsistent with expectations is attributed to transient, contextual factors. Thus, a successful woman scientist might tend to minimize the extent to which her abilities contributed to an extraordinary research accomplishment. At the same time, her peers might attribute her performance to situational factors instead of talent. As a result, the "Matthew effect," the tendency for advantages to accumulate for visible and successful scientists, might be less strong for women than for men, especially in the most highly sex-typed fields.

Stereotypes affect actual behaviour, not just attributions about what causes behaviour. In a study of racial stereotypes, Ward, Zama and Cooper discovered that white subjects exhibited more "low immediacy" behaviours- less eye contact, shorter verbal interactions, less expressive nonverbal behaviour- when interviewing blacks than when interviewing whites. In another part of the same study, interviewers were trained to exhibit either low or high immediacy behaviour. Interviewees randomly assigned to the low immediacy interviewers were rated to have performed less effectively by naive raters. Similar processes may explain the "chilly" climate in classrooms and laboratories that is often invisible to men but widely perceived by women.

Research on "expectancy confirmation sequences" shows how stereotypes can lead to self-fulfilling prophecies: individuals subject to stereotypic expectations may eventually act in ways that play out the stereotype. In a laboratory study, Skrypnek and Snyder asked pairs of subjects, one male and one female, to decide how to allocate a list of tasks, some of which were male typed and others female-typed. Subjects were blind to the actual sex of their partner.

A male subject led to believe his partner was female typically allocated fewer feminine tasks to him than when he believed his partner to be male. The female subject was also more likely to choose feminine tasks if her partner assumed she was female, even though she was not given information about her partner's expectations. If the same processes operate in scientific settings, then women scientists might adapt their behaviours to the stereotyped expectations of colleagues without even being aware of the ways in which they are being influenced.

In scientific work contexts, women are likely to find themselves interacting in social groups that are predominantly male, especially among networks of the scientific elite. Unfortunately, gender stereotypes are especially difficult to undermine in groups with highly skewed sex ratios. Individuals tend to retain information that confirms stereotypes and to ignore information that fails to fit their expectations. One or two exceptional cases can either be ignored or categorized into subtypes. As a result, the social-psychological barriers faced by women scientists are likely to be greatest in the top ranks of scientific fields. Pettigrew and Martin review the social-psychological processes described above as they pertain to barriers facing minority groups in organizations and conclude that they constitute a new kind of "modern racial prejudice." On the one hand, majority group members eschew both gross global stereotypes and blatant discrimination. On the other hand, members of the majority group are unaware of the subtle ways stereotypes influence both perceptions and behaviour in newly integrated work settings.

Women scientists may be similarly affected by what might be called "modern social prejudice." Few male scientists, for example, believe that women are biologically less capable of contributing to science or favor policies that would exclude women from university faculties or scientific laboratories. At the same time, however, scientists, like the subjects in the social-psychological experiments described above, are largely unaware of the more subtle stereotypes that affect their perceptions, expectations, and behaviours when interacting with members of the opposite sex.

Social-psychological research therefore suggests that the disadvantages facing female scientists are not exclusively structural. They are also embedded in the subtle nuances of everyday interaction between the male majority and female minority. Structural interventions that change the rules and procedures used by universities and scientific laboratories to hire and promote scientists have little effect on subtle and largely invisible social-psychological processes. Moreover, scientists subscribe to an ideology of achievement which denies that bias and prejudice have any role in the pursuit of certified knowledge.

Many may appeal to that ideology in the face of any charge that their actions as scientists are implicitly sex- biased. As a result, identifying and eliminating social-psychological barriers are likely to be even more difficult than dismantling the exclusionary practices that have historically kept women from fully participating in science. A decade of "supply-side" research on stratification in science has provided some important insights into the links between gender, careers, and the productivity of scientists. That research tradition has also produced important findings that it cannot explain. We still do not know why it is that women move more slowly through the highest ranks in the profession than do equally productive men, nor do we understand why it is that women tend to publish less than men. An adequate understanding of sex differences in scientists' careers requires more than simply documenting the extent to which there is a net association between sex and career outcomes after controlling for productivity-related characteristics of individual scientists.

Regardless of "who owns the null" when it comes to assessing the extent to which functionally irrelevant criteria influence the status attainments of scientists, the "supply-side" research designs that still dominate research on sex, productivity, and career accomplishments in science are simply incapable of determining why science is more fair to one sex than to the other. Models of scientists' careers that are abstracted from the actual settings in which the work is done cannot possibly explain how the structural and interactional features of those settings affect career prospects.

Over the past decade, the "supply-side" approach to the study of occupational status attainment has been supplanted by a research agenda that considers how the organization of work and its structural context shape careers. But the structuralist approach has yet to gain any widespread acceptance among those who study the careers of scientists. Perhaps we are comfortable with the "supply-side" approach because it allows us to measure discrimination as "deviance" from an otherwise meritocratic system based on universalistic principles. As scientists ourselves we subscribe to the ideology of achievement and the notion of science as a special case.

There is much to be learned about sex differences in the careers of scientists by relinquishing the notion of science as a "special case." We certainly have nothing to lose by attempting to apply insights gained from recent social science research into the ways structural arrangements and social-psychological dynamics shape the careers of men and women. Existing studies that do examine the impact of structural arrangements on the careers of men and women scientists are limited to a few case studies of university faculty that are not easily generalizable and large scale comparative studies using gross measures of organizational characteristics.

Moreover, nearly all are based on data collected before universities became subject to equal employment opportunity laws and regulations. Over the past fifteen years there has been considerable variation in the labour market for new PhDs, in the vigor with which equal employment opportunity policies have been enforced, and in organizational policies regarding the hiring and advancement of scientists, yet we have hardly any systematic knowledge of the ways in which these factors have affected the career prospects of men and women scientists.

Nor is there any existing systematic research on social-psychological barriers faced by women scientists. For example, while research studies continue to document the existence of social-psychological barriers with carefully designed randomized experiments using student subjects, I am unaware of any study which attempts to isolate the same processes using college faculty as subjects.

At the 1985 Macy Foundation symposium on gender discrimination in science, it was suggested that the nature of the scientist's work is undergoing a transformation. Increasingly, scientists are involved in the tasks of securing resources, managing teams of people, engaging in public relations, and other aspects of the management of science. If so, this could have important implications for both the structural and social-psychological barriers facing female scientists.

More women scientists may confront the kind of structural barriers that have been documented in research on business settings, in addition to the arrangements that have traditionally contributed to segregation in scientific settings. In addition to stereotypes about women as scientists, prospects for career advancement may also be affected by stereotypes about women as managers. At present, we can only speculate on the possibility of such trends. Until sociologists of science undertake a systematic research agenda to examine directly the structural and social-psychological dynamics of the scientist's workplace, our understanding of the origins of sex differences in the careers of scientists will be limited to the realm of speculation.

5

The History of the Science of Woman

These reflections are part of a quest for a subject, the science of woman. Within the context of the long eighteenth century, they consider a very simple set of questions, namely, whether there was such a science and whether what may or may not pass for one admits of a history. Also queried is whether these questions merit being raised. To be perfectly candid, there are ready answers to these questions, but as they gain in significance from being seen within a wider perspective, what follows is a somewhat roundabout way to them. Men and women have written about women since antiquity. One would think them a perennial subject, were it not for the fact that the topicality of women was so enhanced in some periods as to make them seem almost entirely occluded in others.

In the early modern age, a good deal was said by and about them in the sixteenth century and a great deal again, possibly more, during the seventeenth and eighteenth centuries. Work upon work was composed about their bodies, their minds, their education or lack of it, their rights, their promiscuity, their dress and other artifices. Were they capable of friendship among themselves? Did they love more or less than men? Had they more intense pleasures? Greater pains? Were they witty? Truthful? Faithful? Fickle? Were foreign and ancient languages beyond their grasp? Should they be allowed to own property? To read what they wished? Even novels? To have skills other than domestic ones? Were they able to rule? And if so, could they head despotic as well as more moderate regimes? What of their fertility? Their longevity? What were women like, and what ought they to be?

Women were considered as a unified whole, the female sex, indeed the sex. But they were also differentiated, according to race, culture, nationality, and class. Some were even created as individuals with personalities and talents such as to eclipse their gender; they were sometimes used as any great authority would be: thus was Catherine Macaulay cited by Helvetius and Diderot. Women were studied in different parts of the world and under different climates. Much of what was written about women is to be found under various and sometimes unexpected headings: within travel literature, medical treatises, anatomical descriptions, or essays on topical subjects, such as love, marriage, happiness, population decline, luxury, and old age.

Much of course was said about them in novels. There were also works specifically devoted to women, often, though by no means always, addressing them in their capacity as daughters, wives, and mothers. Some were authored by what were then or have since become famous names: Lady Mary Wortley Montagu, the Baron de Montesquieu, Jean-Jacques Rousseau, Denis Diderot, Madame de Staël, Choderlos de Laclos, Lord Kames, William Robertson, and many more. Others were written by rather less familiar, if not wholly obscure, names: Madame de Genlis, Madame de Monbart, Antoine-Leonard Thomas, Bernardin de Saint Pierre, William Alexander, Elizabeth Hamilton, Madame Dupin, and countless more.

Can any order be brought into all this? Can some shape be given to this body of works that will afford us an understanding of the nature of the knowledge of women contained in them? The history of women, what might be called the social history of women, is well underway. One need but mention early twentiethcentury examples, such as Alice Clark's Working Life of Women in the Seventeenth Century and Ivy Pinchbeck's Women Workers and the

Industrial Revolution, as well as more recent ones, such as Wendy Gibson's Women in Seventeenth-century France, to be convinced of this. Examinations of representations of women throughout the ages are similarly well advanced.

What has as yet attracted less attention is the history of the study of women, the history of women once removed. How is such a history to be written? What should it be considering? To be sure, it is misleading to speak of this area as if it were a terra nova. Work on the representation of women is at the very least a contribution toward a study of what knowledge there was about women, or what was presented as knowledge about them, at any given time.

There are, moreover, already established ways to classify writings about women. They have, for instance, been organized according to genre. This is one of the schemes Vivien Jones resorted to in her recently published collection Women in the Eighteenth Century: Constructions of Femininity. Faced with the daunting task of compiling an anthology under this title, her first batch of texts is grouped under the heading "conduct," bringing together excerpts from various manuals telling women how to conduct themselves.

Bridget Hill's earlier Eighteenth-century Women: An Antbology began in the same way. Treatises on education constitute another such category; both Hill and Jones have used it. Novels and other literary genres, including poetry, satire, medical treatises, and travel reports, are other examples of headings under which writings about women can be gathered so that they may yield a fair account of how women were described and what was prescribed to them. One of the attractions of such a method, apart from the fact that it is relatively uncontroversial, is that a simple chronological reading of texts within a given genre will deliver its history or a good deal of it.

The next obvious way of arranging the written legacy on women is to focus on its content rather than its form, to determine what the predominant perception of women was in the period by, for instance, assessing what register was used to speak of them. Showing how women were aligned with nature has been one of the most common, and perhaps also most effective, ways of giving shape to the vast body of writings on women, not only in the seventeenth and eighteenth centuries but also before and since then. An arguably no less attractive alignment of this kind is that of women and the private. There are considerable advantages to this approach; not least among them is the most evident, namely, its potential scope. It has all the strength and weakness of a well-tried procedure in the history of ideas: following the trajectory of an equation such as women and nature or women and redemption is no different from tracing the history of the idea of happiness, progress, or perfectibility. More important, it can give a sense of historical context more difficult to gain from the analysis of literature by genre. Everything hangs, of course, on getting the right concept or organizing principle to begin with.

Choosing a subject matter such as "sexuality" (whether one calls it such, as Jones does to make for the second rubric of her anthology, or less anachronistically "And the Greatest of these was Chastity," as Hill does to the same end in her collection), affords, on the other hand, the possibility of bringing together various kinds of writings while lessening the risk of presenting a one-sided view of representations of women in a given period. For the danger of writing the history of a particular thesis-say, that women were deemed lower than men on the chain of beings, closer to animals, to matter, and so on-is that it almost invariably invites histories of its anti-thesis: in this example, that they were seen as nearer the angels, the sublime, and the spiritual. Histories that show women as identified with nature will be answered by histories that show them as linked to culture, and so on.

The solution to this is, of course, never to introduce the Madonna without also presenting the whore. This is precisely what umbrella headings such as "sexuality" or "chastity" are designed to achieve. As with any study in the history of ideas, the difficulty is in the selection of the category, the conceptual spindle, if you wish, around which we can twist and wind our thoughts about what was thought of women. The choice will not only depend on the nature of the past; it will be made with a view to present concerns. Conduct, demeanor, virtue, piety, charity, loyalty, courage, and valor were all notions of great import to eighteenth-century women.

Whether women submitted to what was expected of them or not, these were some of the key terms of the debates they engaged in. While there obviously is some overlap between us and our ur-mothers, and much continuity prevails between debates raging then and now, the current conversations about women in the West seem to be dominated by the issues of sexuality and language and by the discipline and practice reflecting on either or both, namely, psychoanalysis.

A cursory glance at any bookshop's women's studies shelves will reveal rape to be one of the central categories of late twentieth-century writing about women. Much that is interesting can be written about rape in the eighteenth century, yet to use this subject as a point of entry into eighteenth-century material on women is rather misguided. Rape was not on any of the very lengthy intellectual, or for those matter social, agendas of the period. Seduction was, but that concept is in want of so much explanation now as to make it an unlikely choice for anyone seeking a helpful analytical device.

Much the same can be said of sexuality or many another of our key conceptual categories. Indeed, though ideas about women might have changed remarkably little over the course of the centuries, the ways in which such thoughts are organized, the discourses in which they occur, often have. Determining whether men and women in times and places other than our own did or not think along lines similar to ours already presupposes not only what is at issue here, namely, what sieve one is to choose to sift writings about women, but a considerable acquaintance with the material. In other words, rather than constituting the most reliable points of entry into history, concepts of the kind under discussion are more likely to be what historical study yields.

One stepping-stone toward women as a subject matter is that provided by the perspective of a particular science or practice, medical sciences being the best case in point. It is tied to the history of representation and examines how women were described, how, to pursue the example of the medical sciences; they were seen as patients, how they were drawn in textbooks of anatomy, and how these perceptions of them affected and were affected by their treatment beyond the medical sphere. Such a history often has recourse to the dichotomies (private/public, nature/culture, reason/passion, and so on) mentioned above. In the case of the medical sciences the view that women are chained to their biology has provided an Ariadne's thread that more than one historian has elected to follow.

This method can take one quite a long way toward an answer to the question "What kind of objects of knowledge are (or were) women?" and is to be valued as a result. What is more, if the science or practice in question is well established, then the history of that science of women is relatively straightforward, especially if, say, it is the subject of university lectures. Admittedly this is of little assistance to those interested in what was said about women in fields of knowledge before these became established disciplines. A concerted effort must also be made in this context to remember that a discipline - no matter how powerful - does not make a culture and that throughout Western history entirely opposite views about women seem to have coexisted.

Moreover, much of what is thought, said, or published about women never makes the grade in any discipline, because of the gender of its authorship or readership, or because the status of women as an independent subject matter is never entirely free of controversy. Not unrelated to this last approach is the biographical one. We can try to remember women we, and arguably others, have forgotten. This is coming to the subject of women through that of famous ones. It constitutes a shift from considering women as the object of knowledge to viewing them as its makers. Though it could never in itself suffice as a way of tidying writings, let alone anything else, on and by women, there remains much to be learned about the ways in which women shaped the world as we know it.

Women's self-perception through the ages also ties in with the preceding approach and can never legitimately be left out of any of the others. The relative paucity of this type of record makes this line of inquiry similarly insufficient on its own. In any case, it would, by definition, be a way of mapping out no more than half of the terrain under discussion. We are left with what might come under the general rubric "feminism." Once again this is a chapter heading in both Bridget Hill's and Vivien Jones's anthologies. The first calls it "Women Protest," while the second owns up to the anachronism of her usage of the term. Right though Vivien Jones is about the term feminism, it is the best and perhaps the only approach to this much coveted object of knowledge called "women."

This is not to say that none of the approaches just mentioned is worth exploring. Though some might be more attractive than others, each has made an appreciable contribution to what we know about the topic today. Moreover, they would be valuable if only because they themselves point to, or help to pinpoint, what wants about them. For something is going amiss in our present endeavors to recover eighteenth-century woman. Compared to similar investigations about man, they seem to face us with not only a quantitative difference for which time and scholarship are the only cure, but a qualitative one as well. Most noticeable is the lack of an overall perspective on the subject at hand.

That the work cannot but be piecemeal in view of the very size of the enterprise is unquestionable. What is less obvious is whether, if we continue to proceed as we are, we will ever venture beyond providing a chapter, the chapter on women, however needed, however absent, however silenced, to whatever kind of history of man happens to be the history of the moment. But to argue this point further, let us change tack again. Looking back over the centuries it seems that any discourse, language, terminology, approach, technique, and so on devised to understand man has sooner or later been applied to women. Marxism, social history, psychoanalysis, to name but the more obvious, have all had their turn.

Something of this process was captured in a remark made in a more general context by an eighteenth-century writer on women when he said that the sexes always follow each other by imitating one another from afar. If this be true, and assuming that it has always been so, then, given that the first half of the long eighteenth century witnessed the rise of the science of man, the second, let us say, must have seen the development of the science of woman. From the 1770s onward there are a number of works about women that are self-consciously different from those revolving around the issue of the equality between the sexes that, in the sixteenth and again in the seventeenth century, had generated the last two major flurries about the sex.

That they are self-consciously different is not in itself telling of their status, for it is a feature of a good deal of writing about women, then as now, that it is justified by its novelty. Interestingly, what is claimed as new is rarely the approach or the methodology; rather it is the subject itself, that is, women, that seems forever new and forever rediscovered, as writers on women tend to think of themselves as so many knights-errant rescuing their subject from neglect. Women artists, women scientists, women in the Church, medical women, women in the guilds, women in the Middle Ages, women always lost and found until we forget them again.

The eighteenth-century texts I am referring to, however, did not claim to have saved women from historical oblivion. Well, not quite. Their authors were well acquainted with writings about women over the past centuries. They wanted to distance themselves from such works for two related reasons. The first was that they believed that writings about women fell within either of two categories: they either praised or denigrated women. These eighteenth-century authors were not interested in evaluating women in this manner. They did not wish to engage in any form of comparison between the sexes. The second reason they gave for breaking with what might have been seen as their predecessors was that the latter were either poets or collectors of women.

Antoine-Leonard Thomas, William Alexander, Mme Dupin, the Vicomte de Segur, and so on were neither. They sought to understand, to know, women. Their interest lay not with particular women but with the sex as a whole. The question is, why? There are many levels at which this question can be taken. On one of them, the answer must point back to the copycat effect just mentioned. A science of man was being attempted; why not also attempt a science of woman? On another is the explanation the Vicomte de Segur gave in the foreword to his two-volume Les Femmes, leur condition et leur influence dans l'ordre social, chez les differens peuples anciens et modernes (1808).

The proper study of man, he argued, consisted in the study of both the sexes. Neither should receive more attention than the other. Favouring either could only ever be justified on the assumption that, their passions, inclinations, and habits being strictly identical, both were depicted in the portrait of the one. Segur doubted this to have been the view underlying the single-mindedness with which nearly all ancient and modern writers exalted men and ignored women.

"On the contrary," he argued, "they have presented man as the being par excellence and have not deigned to preoccupy themselves with the sex they seek to subordinate to him." Poets had, of course, favoured women above all other themes, but their efforts had contributed little toward knowing them. "Il ne suffit pas de les peindre," Segur argued, "il faut en ecrire l'histoire" (It is not enough to paint them; one must write their history). Only the writing of their history could furnish a true understanding of them. This task Segur set himself, promising to run the course of his story between the Scylla of misogyny and the Charybdis of adulation.

Popular as his work proved, Segur was not the first to conceive of such a project, nor to think of it in those very terms. Other eighteenth-century writers had commented on the bias of existing histories. Likewise they had noted that those men who had turned to the subject of women divided themselves between their detractors and their adorers. In equally vehement introductory words, they addressed their fellow men and deplored the absence of a fair history of the sex. Like Segur, each author presented himself as embarked on a mission never yet attempted.

As Thomas, the best-known and most plagiarized writer of this kind, explained, his work was the history of that part of the human species which the other flatters and slanders in turn. This work will be neither a panegyric, nor a satire, but a collection of observations and facts. Women will be shown as they were, as they are and as they could be. What these historians aspired to do for woman was what Rousseau, among others in the century, had done for man. Responding to the call of the Enlightenment, Rousseau had declared that "the most useful and the least advanced part of human knowledge seem to me to concern man."

This study he had undertaken through a theoretical history of man. Historians of woman wanted to tell her story as he had told his. They wanted to come to grips with her nature as he had unraveled his. As it was, history stood half-written, human nature half-examined; half the species was shrouded in darkness. No one questioned whether that history was theirs to tell. Nor did the project become a contentious matter for any other reason. Whatever criticisms a work like Thomas's Essai sur les femmes met with, the need for a history of women was never questioned. That such a history did by no means prove to be the history of man by a different name is perhaps best illustrated by the case of Rousseau himself.

In writing De L'Inegalite parmi les hommes, Rousseau had written about man and for men: "What I am about to say concerns man, and the question that I am examining tells me that I will be addressing men." There is little reason not to take him literally. This is not because women were left out of his critique of civilization, much less because they were painted as passive witnesses to the historical process that took man from the state of nature to commercial society, from innocence to depravity. It was rather because they were represented as being so much at one with this process as to be almost indistinguishable from it. For to the Rousseauian question as to what had happened to man that he now found himself in a corrupt society marked by gross inequality between men, part of the answer was simply woman.

His could only be her history in a limited and rather perverse sense of the notion. Moreover, what little is extant of his history of women, undertaken at the instigation of his onetime employer Mme Dupin, tells an altogether different story, namely that of men's tyranny over women. Again, if one juxtaposes Diderot's history of man and his history of woman one cannot but be struck by the radically different outlook each gives on the merit of the development of civilization. To comprehend why this is so and why Rousseau's history of man, and indeed his fragment toward a history of women, and for that matter any other Enlightenment theories belonging to either of these kinds, were so firmly grounded in the viewpoint of the sex with which they were concerned, two of the period's assumptions must be kept in mind.

Segur has already given us the first: a single history of the species would have made sense only had the sexes been identical. As they were not, two distinct histories were needed. Second, what rendered the idea of a unique history more absurd still was that the Enlightenment perceived the relationship between men and women as one of power. They conceived its dynamic to be that of a struggle for domination. The beginning of this chapter listed, in the form of a series of questions, some of the many issues raised within writings about women.

Now, it is a shortcoming of much written about women in the eighteenth century that it fails to give a sense of the spirit of investigation that attended the efforts of those who undertook to write the history of women. Questions were asked about men. Histories of the period do tend to acknowledge the genuineness of the inquiries about man's nature, mind, and body. Not so when it comes to writing about what was thought and said about women. At the most, what we are presented with are accounts of those who were for or against the legal, social, and political emancipation of women.

Yet a good number of men and women wanted more than just to repeat the prejudices of their day; they wanted to do something other than defend or attack the sex: they wanted to comprehend how the condition of women had come to be what it was. Travelers' reports and the history of their own Western culture told them that the relation between the sexes admitted of a considerable degree of diversity. Lady Mary Wortley Montagu's writings, for one, showed that even within Europe the lot of aristocratic women varied considerably. She was intrigued, sometimes surprised, astonished even, by the difference between woman and woman. Her preconceptions, especially about the confinement of women in the Middle East, were challenged by the evidence of her experience there. It contributed to her readers revising theirs.

What wants in our conception of what was thought about women is that it does justice to neither the sophistication nor the intellectual ambition of what was being attempted, if not achieved. In particular, past attempts to understand the history of the relation of power between the sexes and to come to terms with the nature of its determining factors are lost. When thinking about women, Enlightenment figures did so in the languages that they deployed to think about men. They used Montesquieu and his typology of governments to classify the data brought back by travelers. They used natural law to fill in the stages of their theoretical history and to assess rights and entitlements. They followed the outline of Rousseau's conjectural history of man.

They were trying to get a true knowledge of woman off the ground. There was an Enlightenment project about woman just as there was one about man. Of course not everything that was written about women in the period fell neatly within its scope. But then again, the same holds for eighteenth-century writings about men. Nor it is true that everything that was said of men and women in the period took the difference between the sexes-whether as grounded in biology or as the product of artifice-as its starting point. As Richard Olson has recently argued, many eighteenth-century feminist writers followed through the egalitarian implications of the psychological theories articulated in the seventeenth century.

Such theories of the mind and of the acquisition of knowledge showed men and women, and indeed the whole of the species, to share in a common human nature. Yet while it is undeniable that not every text about women, nor every theory that had implications for them, took difference as its subject matter, it would be mistaken to think the historical approach incompatible with what might be called the psychological one. Indeed, it would be just as absurd as thinking that investigating the origin and history of the inequality between men conflicts with believing them to be equal. What is more, many of the writers engaged in one approach were also engaged in the other. A good, though by no means unique, example is that of the Marquis de Condorcet. The answer to the question of whether there was a science of woman in the eighteenth century obviously depends on what one means by science. If by science of woman one means whatever was meant then, or has since been meant, by science of man, then the answer is yes. Yes, there was a science of woman that traced her history from the state of nature to that of modernity. It traced the different moments in the changes in her condition, isolated the factors responsible, and explained her distinct contribution to the progress of civilization.

It showed her as the subject as well as the agent of this process. It told the history of her becoming what she was, that is, not one single creature and universal entity but the opposite, with different needs and desires depending on whether she found herself in the seraglios of the East or in the relative freedom of Europe, in ancient Greece or in the last days of the Roman Empire. It even sought to take class differences on board: the question of how the emancipation of some women had increased, or was dependent on, the continued burden of others was never far off the page.

If by science of woman one means a body of knowledge conceived in the shadow of the natural sciences, then the answer is also yes. This is so not only because the science of man was partly conceived in that same shadow, but because predictability, for instance, was one of the features of their enterprise most persistently highlighted by historians of women. William Alexander argued:

> As strength and courage are in savage life the only means of attaining to power and distinction, so weakness and timidity are the certain paths to slavery and oppression: on this account, we shall almost constantly find women among savages condemned to every species of servile, or rather, of slavish drudgery; and shall as constantly find them emerging from this state, in the same proportion as we find the men emerging from ignorance and brutality, and approaching to knowledge and refinement; the rank, therefore, and condition, in which we find women in any country, mark out to us with the greatest precision, the exact point in the scale of civil society, to which the people of such a country have arrived; and were their history entirely silent on every other subject, and only mentioned the manner in which they treated their women, we would, from thence, be enabled to form a tolerable judgment of the barbarity, or culture of their manners.

The Enlightenment envisaged a total history or science that would demonstrate the causal relation among all aspects of a given society. The science of man was that project. From its onset it sought to treat men and women as distinct subjects rather than to make man stand for both the sexes. It attempted to explore the differences between them. Given its historical sensitivity, this meant trying to discover the origin and development of the differences.

A difficult task by any standard, it led to some awkwardness and imbalances, not to mention outright tensions, which might explain why, by the time Segur came to write his history of woman, he thought the project had to be undertaken separately from any consideration of man. Indeed, he seemed to think that previous attempts had essentially failed. Consider Buffon's, for instance. In her introduction to his Histoire naturelle de l'homme (1749), Michèle Duchet explains that for Buffon anthropology was the science that enabled one to think about two concepts at the same time: the unity of the species and its diversity. This he undertook in two parts. First he gave a history of the individual, which traced his generation, his development and growth at different stages of life, his senses, and his anatomy.

Next came the history of the species, that is, his compilation and summary of various travellers' reports, which provided a description of the various peoples of the world, with particular emphasis on their physical appearance. Woman's physiology, development, and anatomy find their places alongside a similar examination of man in the history of the individual. Women also feature as prominently, if not more so, than men in the second part of De L'Homme.

What does one learn about women from Buffon? That they tend to be physically weaker than men; that their bones are softer; that, after attaining a certain age, they tend to live longer; that they are shorter; that their breasts are more developed; that in different parts of the world women are shaped in this or that way; that in some nations they are more or less beautiful than women elsewhere or than their own menfolk. Most of what is written about them is comparative.

Even when one would expect clear-cut differences, an element of comparison remains. Moreover, being a woman (depending on the individual) is being more or less a man and, which is important, being a man is being more or less a woman. This is not a view peculiar to Buffon. It is true of much, if not all, of Enlightenment physiology. Femininity and masculinity are matters of degree. Gender is by and large not a matter of clear-cut categories in the eighteenth century, but it is seen on a continuum. Diderot, for one, liked to emphasize how little difference there was, physically speaking, between man and woman.

All this notwithstanding, woman does not meet with the same treatment as man in Buffon's De L'Homme. What is striking in this work is not a matter of absence or silences. It is, on the contrary, an unexpected presence. The woman Buffon wrote about was not just that of the dissecting table nor even only that reflected in the voyeuristic European gaze. She was also the woman with a past, the woman with a history of oppression by men. Not only was Buffon alert to the issue of men's treatment of women throughout the text, but in the section entitled "De L'Age viril" he went so far as to provide an account, albeit very brief, of this history of hers. He explained that whereas bodily strength had once been the guarantor of power, it had become irrelevant with the advent of polished society. Now only mind mattered. And he went on to say:

> Women are not, by a long way, as strong as men; and the greatest use or the greatest abuse that man has made of his strength is to have subjugated and often treated in a tyrannical manner that half of the human species that was made to share the pleasures and the pains of life with him. Savages force their women to work continually: it is they who cultivate the land, who perform the most onerous tasks, while the husband remains nonchalantly lying in his hammock... Among civilized people, men, being the stronger, have dictated laws that always wrong women in a manner proportional to the crassness of mores; it is only in nations civilized to the point of politeness that women have obtained this equality of rank, which is nevertheless so natural and so necessary to the sweetness of society: hence it is that this politeness of manners is owed to them.

Looking for the unity as well as the diversity of the species led Buffon sometimes along an anthropological path, sometimes along considerations of gender. Beyond what relative physical differences existed between them, beyond the abuse men made of their physical superiority over women, was the lack of true reciprocity, which by right ought to have prevailed between them. This initial, though unnatural and unjust, imbalance remained a fact about them, however much it became modified, even reversed. It was a story of the Fall, if you wish, but one in which man was cast as the undeniable sinner. Any study that peeled off woman from the idea of man and tried to do justice to their difference could not, in the eighteenth century, avoid what would over the course of the century assume the status of a commonplace.

The history of the tyranny men had exercised over women and its gradual reversal by women with the advancement of polished society became constitutive of the knowledge about her or of her as an object of knowledge. Whether the oppression of man by man ever became constitutive of the study of man is a matter of controversy. Not so with woman. Hence my earlier comment that feminism cannot be sidestepped; it is unavoidable, for it was integral to the study of woman from its very onset.

That the history of woman, beginning with her subjection by man and progressing through the various stages of her self-emancipation, was constitutive of knowledge about her rendered her study unwieldy within the framework of the study of man. We already touched on this point when mention was made of Rousseau's endeavors in this field. The story of woman could not but run counter to the general drift of that of man, if and when the object of the study of man was to deliver a verdict on the merit or demerit of the civilizing process and that verdict proved negative, as was the case when men such as Rousseau and Diderot stood in judgment on modernity.

Given the general agreement about the dismal condition of women in the state of nature, even the critics of her status in modern European societies owned that women were among the clearest beneficiaries of the forward march of history. Indeed, from their point of view, they may well have been its only beneficiaries. The history of woman was easier to accommodate within the kind of enterprise Buffon was engaged in. His study of man did not overtly stand in judgment on polished society. His was a tableau in which he sought to draw the whole of the species, standing as it were side by side, nuance by nuance, shade by shade, from black to white, from short to tall, male and female. Giving woman a historical perspective and depth within such a tableau was obviously not impossible, since Buffon actually did it.

Doing so did, however, bring to the surface the extent to which Buffon's anthropology was normative, the extent to which he was committed to the view that human excellence was realized in polished European society. In other words, while his work was not conceived as an evaluation of civilization, it was quite transparently critical of its negation, savagery. To have said any more than he did about the historical process that removed woman from that condition would have required, however, more than an appraisal of non-European mores. Buffon's anthropology would have had to be deployed on European culture itself. It would have entailed extending his thesis to encompass, among other things, a comparison between ancient and modern societies. Again, this was by no means theoretically impossible for Buffon. Indeed, following immediately after the passage quoted above is a comparison between their idea of beauty and ours:

The ancients had notions of beauty that differ from ours. Small foreheads, joint or hardly separated eyebrows, were pleasing in a woman's face; a great preference is still shown in Persia for thick and joining eyebrows. Though all but inconceivable, the pursuit of this line of inquiry would have led Buffon along a rather different path. It would have led him to produce a full-fledged history of woman of the kind Mme Dupin and men like Thomas or Segur found wanting.

There was a science of woman in the eighteenth century. It was a French (e.g., Mme Dupin, Thomas, and Diderot), Scottish (e.g., William Alexander), and German (e.g., C. Meiners) affair. It was a female as well as a male affair. For even if few women besides Mme Dupin and Mme de Staël actually attempted to write such a history from beginning to end, many more either worked explicitly within its overall framework, like Catherine Macaulay, or deployed parts of it, like Mrs. Hamilton in her Popular Essays. Others cannot be fully understood except by placing their works within its context, as is true, for instance, of Mme de Graffigny's Lettres d'une peruvienne.

It does have a history, which begins most probably with Montesquieu, goes through the early works of Rousseau and those of Buffon and is taken up by a number of relatively unknown writers such as Thomas and Alexander in the 1770s, gathers momentum around the turn of the century with, among others, Segur, Meiners, and later in the century the Goncourt brothers, and continues into the present day. It may at times have dissipated into analyses of the nature of love and taken on all kinds of forms, including the history of manners, luxury, liberty, or capitalism, but its roots can be found in the eighteenth century, if not earlier.

It was never, as has already been acknowledged, the only study, or approach to the study, of women any more than the science of man proved to be the only study, or approach to the study, of men. The specific nature of the relationship between the science of woman discussed here and, say, Enlightenment theories of human nature and faculty psychology, biology, or even nineteenth-century gynecology is but one of the many interesting and puzzling issues this subject raises. What is clear, however, is that it would be a mistake to ignore the particular character of the intellectual enterprise that the science of woman was or attempted to be.

It will not come as a surprise that on this view of things the third question, namely, whether it is worth one's while to ponder a science of woman and its history, is also to be answered with an affirmative. Without thinking of writings about women as partaking in an enterprise larger than them, larger than anything any of them could possibly achieve independently, we are left with a fragmentary history of women in the eighteenth century and no means by which to follow it into the present. We need every inch of the grand canvas on which the Enlightenment conceived of the subject for us to make sense of its nature then and now.

Think of what would happen to our conception of the history of man in that period if we were to cease to consider the many texts about him as part of that large and formidable project, the science of man! Think of how impoverished our view would be if we did not try to study the nature of this project and gave up trying to write its history! Whatever our reservations about the methods deployed to conceive of the nature of that modern enterprise, we must own its heuristic benefits. Drawing the science of woman out of a shadow it was never intended to inhabit might just also cast a new light on man.

6

Women and Newtonianism

For Eliza Haywood, "Philosophy" is a kind of cure for femininity. This femininity seems to be both a masculine prejudice ("we are accused of...") and a universal reality ("we often feel..."). The woman who takes to Philosophy will conquer equally the preconceptions of men and her own worst inclinations. She will vindicate her sex-and she will escape it. Haywood is referring to the benefits of natural philosophy (what we might call "science"), benefits that are presumed to be available to educated women in general. The study of science is recommended to Haywood's readers as if it were some new womanly duty, and not a challenging or unlikely activity.

In one way, the recommendation is another small piece of a social history of science: "Caught up by the excitement of the 'new science,' educated women, along with men, became an eager audience for the new ideas." Haywood's advocacy fits into a story of women and science that recounts the (often frustrated) attempts of women to gain access to these new ideas. But her recipe for rationality tells us something else: that the new Philosophy could be regarded as inherently suitable for women.

A social history of women's "scientific interests," such as that by Patricia Phillips, must emphasize the role of public lectures and popularizing scientific texts: "the attempt by bourgeois entrepreneurs to capture a wider female audience." It must examine the struggle of particular women to educate them in and to study science. But there is also a rather different history, such as that initiated by Carolyn Merchant: a history of the symbolic use of women in scientific argument, and of the struggle of science-the self-vaunting "experimental philosophy"-to establish and justify itself.

By the 1740s a special, "Newtonian" Philosophy had a secure status as the most powerful form of theoretical knowledge, and its availability had to be demonstrated. Women were symbolically its awed witnesses, its dutiful devotees, and - more surprisingly - its best test. In *The Spectator*, Haywood's own model of polite prose, Addison declared, "I shall be ambitious to have it said of me, that I have brought Philosophy out of Closets and Libraries, Schools and Colleges, to dwell in Clubs and Assemblies, at Tea-Tables, and in Coffee-Houses." He was not thinking of natural philosophy in particular; he was, however, indicating not only that worthwhile knowledge should be made available to his genteel readers, but that such availability was the measure of its worth. Newtonianism, too, is validated by being brought out of closets, and the explanation of it to women confirms its triumph. This chapter will be concerned with the imagining of women as the symbolic agents of its popularization. By Philosophy Haywood means knowledge accessible to those without specialist training or experimental resources. Philosophy is what extends "our Speculations . . . to the greatest and most tremendous Objects," or makes it possible "to pry into the smallest Works of the Creation." Certainly it relies on those fashionable implements, telescopes and microscopes; but it is the name not so much of a body of theoretical knowledge as of an activity at once sublime and ordinary. "Philosophy is . . . the Toil which can never tire the Person engag'd in it." In Haywood's formulation, indeed, it sounds something like a moral duty. The Female Spectator is replying to a supposed letter from Cleora, which has thanked her for "endeavouring to improve the Minds and Manners of our unthinking Sex."

This work of improvement-described as an "Act of Charity"-is all the more important for this (no doubt imaginary) correspondent because women are so frequently barred from "those Sciences which the Men engross to themselves." It is a plea for "the Education of . . . Females." The Female Spectator concurs, unsurprisingly, and remarks that, without "Learning," women become "loitering, lolloping, idle Creatures." But she makes this a special case of what, by the 1740s, is a conventional argument for that female learning.

> Knowledge is a light Burthen. . . . But of all Kinds of Learning the Study of Philosophy is certainly the most pleasant and profitable:-It corrects all the vicious Humours of the Mind, and inspires the noblest Virtues. . . . [T]he more we arrive at Proficiency in it, the happier and the more worthy we are.

Those who have "the Female Part of their Family at Heart" would be wise "to instruct them early in some of the most necessary Rudiments of Philosophy:-All those little Follies now ascrib'd to us, and which, indeed, we but too much incur the Censure of, would then vanish, and the Dignity of Human Nature shine forth in us." The polite reader is told that acquaintance with natural philosophy will make her morally better and raise her from the condition of femininity.

In the earlier Essays of Lady Mary Chudleigh, the same ideal is articulated in a breathier rhetoric of self-exhortation (the imagined female readers addressed with sentences that frequently begin "Let us . . ."). Physicks . . . will show us Nature, as she variously displays her self, as she manifests her self in material Objects . . . from the glorious Orbs which roll over our Heads, to the minutest Insect that crawls under our Feet; discover to us Beauties which Art can never imitate, and which common Spectators do not observe.

This comes from an essay, entitled "Of Knowledge," that shares Haywood's ambivalence about the capacities of women. It encourages its female readers to believe that "all useful Knowledge" is accessible, but it is also always on the point of admonishing them for the feminine follies that will exclude them from knowledge. Readers must be deaf to "such as can talk of nothing but what is not worth the Knowing, of the little mean concerns of the Animal Life, their Domestick Affairs, the various Efforts of their Passions, the Triumphs of their Vanity, and the numerous Instances of their Folly." Distracting and distracted, women of this type are everywhere. Perhaps only a minority can turn away from "Romances and Trifles of that Nature" for a better contemplation: "to survey all those solid Globes, which swim in the fluid Aether, see vast Masses of fiery Matter whirl'd round their Axis with an amazing, an inconceivable Rapidity."

Evidently, the seeing and surveying talked of here are peculiarly metaphorical. They are in the mind's eye of those with an understanding beyond that of "common Spectators." If only the exceptional woman seeks some understanding of natural philosophy, and in particular of celestial mechanics, that is but evidence of the special value, and the uplifting character, of that knowledge. In Benjamin Martin's The Young Gentleman and Lady's Philosophy, one of the texts dedicated to popularizing Newtonian physics that I will discuss later, the female character in the dialogue, Euphrosyne, tells her brother (who is also her instructor) that she has been ridiculed for her interest in natural philosophy.

"It is a Pity that any, even of our Sex, should so far betray their Want of Prudence as to ridicule a philosophical Disposition in others, only, for Want of a Taste for the Science themselves," he observes. It is as if it is necessary to regret what he calls "the inconsiderate Part of Mankind" in order to establish the privilege of Philosophical knowledge. (And here a female character is particularly useful to Martin, for if a woman can apply herself to grasping Philosophy, surely any gentleman should be able to do so.) "Till very lately, Philosophy has not been the Subject of Conversation, and it is but rarely so now." But making some appreciation of Philosophy into a social qualification to rank with the other arts of conversation is just the ambition of these writers. In a culture that so valued taste, a "Want of a Taste for the Science" is to be seen as a major failing.

So, when Richard Steele's The Ladies Library, an anthology of didactic passages for female readers arranged by topic, discusses the benefits of scientific knowledge to women, it is in the section on modesty. For modesty is "directly opposite to whatever is bold and indecent, and in an especial manner to

Curiosity" and any feminine tendency to curiosity is best turned to the "Wonders" of "Nature." Inquiries into nature are "useful and entertaining to all those whose curious Minds are always in Action, and for want of nobler Objects descend to Scandel and Impertinence." Again, natural philosophy will save women from themselves.

Its power to do so is registered by the text's exclamations on the scale and organization of a universe comprehended by Newtonian mechanics: "Oh Miracle! Oh Prodigy!" And there can be no doubt as to the consequence of this comprehension: "The Searches of curious and humble Minds into Nature will more and more confirm him in holy Admiration of the Greatness and Goodness of God. There are no Minds so weak as to be Incapable of these Meditations."

Here is an occasion when the slip to the masculine pronoun is telling. For it is a point at which the text forgets that it is written for women, and instead finds itself using a woman's (imagined) understanding as a test of the potency and clarity of a new kind of knowledge? Throughout texts written in the early eighteenth century to make Philosophy available to women, this very availability is treated as a validation of the new science. The art of explaining Philosophy to a woman is a demonstration of its truth. This is one of the reasons why the dialogue form is popular.

The best-known example is probably Elizabeth Carter's translation of Algarotti's Sir Isaac Newton's Philosophy Explain'd for the Use of the Ladies (1739), which, like Benjamin Martin's work, uses a female character to catch the lucidity and the awesomeness of "Newton's Philosophy." Algarotti has produced "a complete Treatise of the Newtonian philosophy" designed to be "lively" and engage his readers as would "a Composition for the Theatre." The Marchioness of E listens to the narrator's account of the new knowledge, asking appropriate questions, and the limited drama is in her compliant delight and amazement at the answers that she receives. A knowledge intended to displace other theories needs to show the pleasure of complete conviction.

So the Marchioness begins "extremely desirous of becoming a Newtonian," and she is told at the end of her exhaustive course of instruction, "The Light of Newtonianism has dissipated the Cartesian Phantoms which deluded your Sight. You are now really a Newtonian. In between, she has been brought to admire and celebrate the "Spirit of Observation" and "the Study of Experiments," dispelling "ill-grounded Fears," "Ignes fatui," "Superstition," and "the Marvellous."

In particular, she has been given an "Exposition of the Newtonian universal Principle of Attraction" and shown its effects. "Light and Truth itself address you in the Language of Sir Isaac Newton," she is told. She replies, "Let it dissipate any Remains of Darkness that may still obscure my Mind, and conduct me into this new World of Philosophy." Her delighted conviction is the new truth in operation. Because, as a woman, she is intellectually ingenuous, she is the best witness of this truth. The dialogue form allows her to put it archly: "I perceive . . . that there is nothing secret to Philosophy; we may hide ourselves from Men, but not from Philosophers." There is no resisting the knowledge that she now has.

In his conclusion, the narrator refers to her as his "fine Conquest" and almost makes explicit the buried rhetoric of seduction: "If I could give a just Description of my fair Disciple, my Book would never want Readers, nor true Philosophy a numerous Train of Proselytes." It should, in the end, be impossible to say no. In Martin's Young Gentleman and Lady's Philosophy, too, a woman's ignorance is useful in the celebration of Newtonian science. The male character, Cleonicus, tells his sister that her inquisitiveness is virtuous.

Philosophy is the darling Science of every Man of Sense, and is a peculiar Grace in the Fair Sex; and depend on it, Sister, it is now growing into a Fashion for the Ladies to study Philosophy; and I am very glad to see a Sister of mine so well inclined to promote a Thing so laudable and honourable to her Sex. Her anxieties about the obscurity of "that Science," stated in the book's first dialogue, are met by his assurance that "Abstrusities" either are irrelevant or "may be explained in a more easy and familiar Manner by Experiments. Fear not,

Euphrosyne, the greatest and most delightful Part of this Science is within the Ladies Comprehension."

This is, in effect, a reassurance to all his readers. The attentive woman allows the text to show that Philosophy rests on universally intelligible principles. It is less, indeed, that Euphrosyne depends on Cleonicus for knowledge, and more that he depends on her for the appropriate questions. If she is ignorant and modest she can hardly ask the wrong question, which only the misinstructed could supply. Natural-philosophical explanation is thus at its most comfortable when confronted by naive ignorance (fearing only skepticism and atheism). In Martin's text, it is precisely because "useful Science is of neither Sex, nor any Party" that women can be converted to it.

Cleonicus tells his sister, "I expect to see you proselyted to this, not more modish than true Philosophy, before we leave the Subject. I can tell you, Sir Isaac has no small Party among the Principal of the Fair Sex." Dialogue allows the doctrine to be liberal and condescending at the same time; Cleonicus can even stoop to correct his sister's feminine desire to gain only "such a Competency of Knowledge as is fit for a Woman." A woman's "Senses," says Martin in his introduction, are "formed as accurately" as a man's, and "therefore these philosophical Subjects must be, in this Way, equally intellikible to both; consequently the ladies may be admitted to the Pleasure and Advantage of these Speculations as well as Gentlemen." A woman who can rise above what Cleonicus calls "this Woman-hood of yours" can reach to the modest, awesome facts of the new Philosophy.

Martin himself made a living encouraging this ambition. He has Cleonicus complain that Philosophy is not taught in schools but must be got either from books or from those "who sometimes read Lectures on that Subject." Martin was one of those lecturers-one of the several apostles of Newtonianism whose audiences routinely included women. "Knowledge," as he wrote in 1743, "is now become a fashionable thing, and philosophy is the science a la mode."

One of the pioneers of this fashion was John Harris, who published his Astronomical Dialogues between a Gentleman and a Lady in 1719. His female character, Lady M, has all the readiness for instruction that these lecturers symbolized in the person of an inquiring "lady" (perfectly cultured, as well as unknowing). She also has that inclination to conquer femininity that runs through most of the texts that I am discussing, wryly telling her "gentleman" instructor, "You have Philosophised me out of many a fair Pleasure already; Censure, Satyr and Gossiping are almost gone." "Philosophical" explanation, she tells him, can "get rid of many Fears and Terrors, too incident to our Sex" (she is particularly reassured to find that "The Affair of Comets" is accountable by Mathematical Calculation"). Yet, as in Martin's and Algarotti's texts, the woman validates Newtonianism even while it ennobles her. Harris's dedication indicates how this works:

> I don't perplex my Fair Astronomer with any thing but the true System of the World: I mislead her by no Notions of Chrystalline Heavens, or Solid Orbs: I embarrass her with no clumsy Epicycles, or imaginary and indeed impossible Vortices: But I shew her at first the Celestial World just as it is; and teach her no Hypotheses, which, like some other things taught at Places of great Names, must be unlearned again, before we can gain True Science.

Having less to unlearn, a woman is a better auditor than many men. Her immediate and grateful understanding of what even natural philosophers have only recently comprehended sanctions Modern knowledge:

> I can't help reflecting upon the Arrogance, as well as Ignorance, of the Ancients, in supposing their Knowledge to be the Bounds of all things; and glad I am that we know something which they did not. . . . I will . . . thank God that I am a Modern, and alive now.

Harris may think this, but it is his female character who says it for him. By her comprehension, the ancients and the Cartesians are routed. It is because "Newtonian Physicks, or Natural Philosophy," is radically distinct from older forms of learning that it might be made "intelligible to any common Capacity and inquisitive Genius." Such intelligibility is not just an ideal; it is test and proof of Philosophy.

"We must render the various Arts and Sciences as easy of Access, or the Pathways to knowledge as direct and plain, as possible," writes Martin. Sometimes, addressing an explanation to a woman seems but a way of signifying the accessibility of that explanation. Jasper Charl ton 's The Ladies Astronomy (1735), for example, explicitly states that this address signifies an avoidance of "Mystery" and that his work is actually written for "the Publick in general."

When Martin's Euphrosyne is shown "Experiments on the Air-Pump" in the final dialogue of The Young Gentleman and Lady's Philosophy, she becomes a representative observer. Her observations are ingenuous and therefore trustworthy, guaranteeing the integrity of experiment. She can confirm the experimental philosopher's performance because of her lack of knowledge or prejudice, and she does so on behalf of readers of either sex. Some who popularize or recommend natural philosophy do, however, presume that the understanding of women is inherently different from (and inferior to) the understanding of men.

It now seems, indeed, ironical that Algarotti's Il Newtonianismo per le dame should have been translated by a woman of such formidable learning as Elizabeth Carter when it begins by declaring, "I have endeavoured to set Truth, accompanied with all that is necessary to demonstrate it, in a pleasing Light, and to render it agreeable to that Sex, which had rather perceive than understand." In a manner both cordial and patronizing, the author makes clear his belief, common enough at the time, that women are not usually capable of abstraction from particulars: "Lines and mathematical Figures are entirely excluded, as they would have given these Disccurses too Scientific an Air, and appeared formidable to those, who to be instructed must be pleased." Even this text finds certain combinations of "ladies" and Philosophy incongruous.

It is predictable, then, that incongruity is the proferred amusement of eighteenth-century satires on female learning in general, and women's interest in science in particular.

Some Nymphs prefer Astronomy to Love; Elope from mortal men, and range above.

This preference was apparently sufficiently topical to command a section of that part of Edward Young's Love of Fame (1727) "On Women." His female enthusiast substitutes well-known Newtonian lecturers for other consorts:

Of Desaguliers she bespeaks fresh air,
And Whiston has engagements with the fair.

The Newtonian woman is a contradiction in terms, and everywhere the traditional satirist can find incongruities:

What vain experiments Sophronia tries!
'Tis not in air-pumps the gay Colonel dies.
But though today this rage of science reigns,
(O fickle sex!) soon end her learned pains.
Lo! Pug from Jupiter her heart has got,
Turns out the stars, and Newton is a sot.

As in Pope's later Epistle to a Lady, the poet's couplets work at turning a woman's activity into an oxymoron. (And as also with Pope, the couplets are then used to represent the poem's "good woman" as a miraculous reconciler of normally warring opposites.)

Evidently, the very word Philosophy could seem ludicrous to some, when put in the minds or mouths of women-just as The Spectator asked for any easy laugh merely by listing Newton's Works among the contents of the library belonging to the affected Leonora. In Thomas Wright's play The Female Vertuoso's, the sense of Philosophy as what one character defines as "a Stoical and Undaunted Mind" is invoked to show how peculiarly unphilosophical women are likely to be.

Lady Meanwell is an enthusiast for scientific projects, but, as her "honest" husband puts it, she "makes indeed a High Boast of her Philosophy, but she is not a bit the less Cholerick for it. She is still Woman all over." In this play, women aspire to Philosophy but remain slaves to their passions: indeed, any female interest in science is construed as but a strange and helpless passion. As the "gentleman" who is the author of Man Superior to Woman puts it, "A severer Imprecation cou'd scarce be utter'd against the lovely Sex, than to wish those Science-mad." Women are most of all excluded from Philosophy: "Every Branch of that is built upon Reason, and Reason they have nothing to do with."

Man Superior to Woman was produced in response to Woman Not Inferior to Man: or, A Short and Modest Vindication of the Natural Right of the Fair-Sex to a Perfect Equality of Power, Dignity, and Esteem, with the Men. By Sophia, a Person of Quality, and was in its turn answered by Woman's Superior Excellence over Man. The three texts were published together in a single volume in 1743, as if they represented entertaining debating positions, rather than the deeply held beliefs of particular authors. Yet, even if we cannot quite trust the tone of these texts, they do give an idea of what arguments about women's relations to the new Philosophy were available.

Woman's Superior Excellence over Man finds at the root of natural philosophy an empiricism available to all: "There is nothing more wanting than sensation, reflection and attention in observing the different appearances of nature, to discourse on their effects." Only "mannish learning . . . takes the disposition of different persons to different sciences for an effect of natural temperament, when in reality it is more often the casual effect of necessity, chance, or education." In this argument, Newtonian astronomy offers a paradigm of universal and accessible knowledge: "Any one will be capable of remarking that the luminous bodies in the heavens are of an igneous nature . . . and to judge of their motion and courses, there needs no more than comparatively to consider their different and successive appearances by the help of telescopes."

Such science is open to women in a way that older kinds of learning have not been: "The mind is always in action, and she who has once observed the main springs of nature, and knows how it proceeds in one thing, may without much drudgery, discover its manner of operating in another."

However, those works that purport to open a Newtonian universe to women do not imagine such an unflustered and systematic scrutiny of nature. Women are invited to gaze on nature, but they must do so with rapture as well as with understanding. They are most likely to feel (and to be morally improved by) what Lady M in Harris's Astronomical Dialogues calls "the Rapturous Pleasures of Science." Amazement is an important component of Newtonianism (and perhaps most familiar in the exclamations of James Thomson's poem "To the Memory of Sir Isaac Newton"-the celebration of what it calls an "amazing mind").

Benjamin Martin's Panegyrick on the Newtonian Philosophy, published ten years before his Young Gentleman and Lady's Philosophy, catches nicely, if confusingly, the sense of an understanding at once satisfied and overwhelmed by a new kind of knowledge: "Philosophy . . . fills our Minds with sublime and august Ideas; Ideas strange and incredible to the uninstructed unphilosophic Mind." It is as if the true Newtonian feels amazement on behalf of all those who remain uncomprehending. The experience is given as an ideological necessity, for the Philosopher must, on his observation of the heavenly "System," acquire "a most sublime and august Idea of the Works of creating Power and Wisdom, highly worthy of the divine Author." In Thomson's poem, such "Power and Wisdom" seem entirely Newton's; in the "official" Newtonian version, of course, Philosophy reveals the true scale of God's activity.

"The Friends of Philosophy are the Friends of Mankind," writes Martin in the preface to his Panegyrick. This explicitly addresses the "Gentlemen and Ladies" who have subscribed to his lectures, and who are treated as if they are exceptional individuals who recognize the truth of his motto: "Felix qui potuit Rerum cognoscere Causas" (happy the person who can know the [mechanical] causes of things). "While others trifle away their time in low, sensual and unworthy Amusements, you have the Happiness of a rational Curiosity, and are capable of the noblest Methods of improving it."

On the frontispiece of his Young Gentleman and Lady's Philosophy, a man points a woman to the starry heavens, which is where those possessed of "rational Curiosity" gaze for validation of the new Philosophy? He also gestures at what is guaranteed to overwhelm his favored "lady." When Cleonicus has given his sister an account of comets, he asks, "What think you of that?" as a woman, she is suitably amazed: "Think! What should a Woman pretend to think of such Matters, as I believe I may venture to say, surpasses the most philosophical Heads." Feminine exclamation records the power of Newtonian explanation.

Harris's dialogues make use of the same enraptured female character. Having had the nature of the sun and the stars explained to her, Lady M exclaims that the notion of stars as "Suns to some other Systems of Planets" excites "a glorious Idea . . . of the Almighty Power!" She claims to be stunned by God's creation but appears just as impressed by the scope of the explanation that she is hearing. Such dialogue allows popularized natural philosophy a double claim to truth: through the male character, it confidently reduces all that can be observed to Philosophical principles; through the female character, it pauses in awe before the immense patterns that those principles reveal. This dialogue is how Philosophy justifies itself.

"They who contemplate Nature, my Euphrosyne, always find their Admiration and Pleasure encreasing with their Knowledge": such is Cleonicus's assurance in Martin's Young Gentleman and Lady's Philosophy. His "lady" is a source of ideologically necessary "Admiration and Pleasure," as well as a ready receptacle for knowledge. No doubt a man performing public lectures "in which the Properties, Affections, and Phaenomena of Natural Bodies, hitherto discover'd, are exhibited and explain'd on the Principles of the Newtonian Philosophy" needed to persuade readers of the delights they might purchase from him. But the promise of delight is not just merchandising; it is integral to Newtonianism.

This is why Newtonians need, and they dabble in, poetry. John Theophilus Desaguliers and Benjamin Martin, lecturers in natural philosophy with no other pretensions to poetic achievement, both take to verse to celebrate Newtonianism-as if what Desaguliers's poem calls "The Newtonian System of the World" is enough to tug even a Philosopher away from prose. Henry Pemberton's A View of Isaac Newton's Philosophy is prefaced by "A Poem on Sir Isaac Newton".

The various explanatory dialogues of Harris, Martin, and Algarotti are punctuated by mottoes and descriptions taken from poetry. For poetry, like women can exclaim in wonderment, under the pressure of all that the new Philosophy reveals. So Martin's dialogue is prefaced by "On the Usefulness of Natural Philosophy. A Poem," describing how "Man . . . Thro' Nature takes a philosophic View, / While Wonders, rais'd on Wonders, strike his Eyes!" Martin includes his own panegyric to "Gravity," with regulation exclamation marks, and treats science as a feminine deity under whose kind influence all will prosper:

All hail philosophy! Celestial Fair! Sent from above, replete with ev'ry Good, T'improve each striving Faculty within to mend our Morals and refine the Heart.

In The Seasons, James Thomson-above all a poet of exclamation-had called on "serene Philosophy" as "Effusive source of evidence and truth!" Effusiveness is just the rhetoric of the poetry deployed in justification of that Philosophy and is proof of its comprehensiveness, its clarity - and its compatibility with proper religion.

John Millburn writes that, in his dialogue, Martin "did his utmost . . . to lighten the scientific text with liberal doses of poetry, no doubt hoping that the market for the Magazine [of which this text was but a part] would thereby be increased." Perhaps these doses (which included, indeed, many passages from Thomson's Seasons) did render his text more palatable to female readers, in the same way that they are shown to translate celestial mechanics for the benefit of Euphrosyne.

Perhaps Martin does imagine curious "ladies" reacting as Euphrosyne does to an account of the seasonal variations: "Their Nature explained by the Orrery, and their Properties and Qualities as finely described by the Poets, give me perfect Ideas thereof." But the marriage of poetry to natural philosophy is common enough (and strained enough) to suggest something more than a sugaring of the pill of scientific knowledge. For Newtonian texts frequently propose a natural affinity of poetry and Philosophy.

One explanation is offerered by Cleonicus in The Young Gentleman and Lady's Philosophy: "The great Works and Scenes of Nature, you'll find, are the most agreeable Themes of the Muses." He echoes Lady M in John Harris's Astronomical Dialogues, who claims to find in all the information about planetary bodies that she is given "a rich Fund of Images . . . to embellish our Poetry." This new knowledge demands the muse not merely to turn it into lyrical awe, but also to show that it is directly comparable with what poets have always thought and observed.

So, while Martin's dialogue is full of passages from avowedly Newtonian eighteenth-century poems like Henry Baker's The Universe and Moses Browne's Essay on the Universe, it relies equally on Ovid and Dryden. And Algarotti's Sir Isaac Newton's Philosophy Explaind, which frequently works from the poetry that its "lady" already knows to the explanatory Philosophy that she must attain, has no reservations about using Pope-arguably an anti-Newtonian poet. As her instructor takes her from poetry to Philosophy, he remarks that Pope himself "cannot be offended at my leaving him for a Philosopher, and such a Philosopher as Sir Isaac Newton." The poet who envisioned a triumph of dullness in which Philosophy, that lean'd on Heav'n before, Shrinks to her second cause, and is no more might not have agreed.

Poetry, in these texts, is what women know. It provides the data of awed yet accurate observation which is to be turned into knowledge by Newtonian Philosophy and its agents, the lecturers. The poetry of proper wonderment records the aspiration to comprehend nature, the first requirement for a Newtonian convert. Consistently, as in my opening example from Haywood's Female Spectator, this aspiration is best spoken for by a woman-untrammeled by older kinds of learning, and yet eager to transcend her femininity.

This is why Elizabeth Tollet, one of the many commemorators in verse of Isaac Newton ("Immortal and secure thy Name remains,/ Which scarce the habitable World contains"), provides her Georgian readers with a translation of "The Praise of Astronomy, from the first Book of OVID's Fusti." The early astronomers were the first "to leave behind/ The Crimes and Pleasures that debase Mankind"; they transcended law, war, and ambition-but also "mean Desire" and any interest in merely cosmetic beauty: "'Tis thus that Science can the Heav'ns obtain." A (much worse) male poet of the period, Henry Jones, celebrates the superiority of those drawn by public lectures to Newtonian mechanics more condescendingly and (inadvertently) more ludicrously:

Thrice happy few who wisely here attend The Voice of Science, and her Cause befriend, Let others, heedless of their youthful Prime, Squander on empty Toys their fleeting Time; 'Tis yours with Reason's searching Eye to view Great Nature's Laws, and trace her winding Clue. Such ambition can, of course, be challenging as well as compliant. Perhaps following the lead of The Female Spectator, Toilet takes the ancient Egytian astronomer Hypatia as the symbol of a woman's ambition "the Mind to raise,/ To follow Nature in her winding Ways." Haywood had referred to this fabled "Philosopher" as a precedent for the "great Perfection" in "this Science" (i.e., natural philosophy) that women could reach. Tollet's "Hypatia" depicts knowledge of nature as unmysterious enough to be available to women, and therefore as energetically guarded by men. Women remain untutored.

That haughty Man, unrival'd and alone, May boast the World of Science all his own: As barb'rous Tyrants, to secure their Sway, Conclude that Ignorance will best obey. The poem goes through the kinds of knowledge that are denied to women, with all their variously desirable effects, beginning with moral and political wisdom, and proceeding via mathematics to scientific knowledge. It is to this that the poem most aspires-although it also manages to comprehend most of what is officially beyond it: from geology to microscopy to the Newtonian universe. The female astronomer escapes all limitations in her observations of the heavenly bodies: "Yet, as she may, her Forces she explores,/ And far above the Orb sublunar soars."

Perhaps in order to transcend any topical controversy, Tollet's poem is put into the mouth of an ancient Egytian. However, this produces an embarrassment that returns us to the very meaning of Newtonianism, and of its need to recruit women (even if only in fiction) to its cause. Whether that Spirit which o'er all presides Infus'd through all its equal Motions guides, Or from the whole distinct, himself unseen, Conducts and regulates the vast Machine, Let Heav'n decide.

Such lines apparently require Toilet to add an endnote, explaining awkwardly that such "Doubts," which might "be thought exceptionable," belong only with "the Character of an Heathen and a Platonist." For, in the age in which Toilet writes, the new mechanical Philosophy is sanctioned exactly by the sense and certainty that it gives to Christianity. Indeed, she herself includes in her collection a poem, "On the Thunder-Storm, June 1726. In Allusion to Horace," specifically directed against any who would believe that an explanation of thunder from "Causes natural" can be complete to itself. "Mistaken Fools! It was He assign'd to all/ That universal Law we Nature call." God is "the great Geometer," and all properly sustained Philosophy leads-without "Doubts"-to him.

Women are therefore employed by writers or appealed to by lecturers as ingenuous witnesses to the religious probity of Newtonian Philosophy. Popularizations of science in the eighteenth century are full of assurances that the new mechanical Philosophy improves its devotees, in the words of the periodical The Ladies Diary, "by giving us a clear and extensive Knowledge of the System of the World, which . . . creates in us the most profound Reverence of the wise Creator." If women are taught about science, it is that they might know it to be no friend to skepticism, materialism, or infidelity. But all the assurances and pronouncements to this effect seem to tell us of anxiety.

We might take for a definition of Newtonianism the subtitle of Benjamin Martin's A Panegyrick on the Newtonian Philosophy: "Shewing the Nature and Dignity of the Science, and Its Absolute Necessity to the Perfection of Human Nature; the Improvement of Arts and Sciences, the Promotion of true Religion, the Increase of Wealth and Honour, and the Completion of Human Felicity." Newtonianism was the impulse to "shew" all this. Yet, in the matter of "true Religion," Newtonians did not necessarily hold to the same beliefs: Martin himself, like James Thomson, was what we might call a deist; the Newtonians who determined religious orthodoxy and whose arguments have been so brilliantly charted by Margaret Jacob were Anglicans; William Whiston, one of the best-known Newtonian lecturers, was publicly what Newton himself was privately-an Arian, opposed to the doctrine of the trinity.

So when Martin's Panegyrick concludes with a poem "On the Anti-Newtonians; or, Pseudo-Philosophers of the Age," he can be read as externalizing dissent and heterodoxy that would otherwise be internal to Newtonianism. The religious as well as practical "Usefulness of Natural Philosophy" is what licenses the new knowledge. Attacking supposed atheism and skepticism is a necessary antidote to doubt. Elizabeth Carter, translator of Sir Isaac Newton's Philosophy Explain'd for the Use of the Ladies, is representative in directing against "stupid atheists" her description of how only God can have "taught the newborn planets where to roll:/ With wise direction curv'd their steady course,/ Impress the central and projectile force." It is not clear who or where these "stupid atheists" might have been. They are the useful other for those who would be reassured by Cleonicus's instruction of his sister in Martin's dialogue:

> Our Principles and Notions of Religion are much more correct and rational than they were formerly; and to what is this owing, my Euphrosyne? To our having a more correct and rational Philosophy: you will find it a never-failing Maxim, that the better you understand Philosophy, the better you will understand Religion.

Women listen to doubts dispelled and skeptics fended off. Newtonianism seeks, or shows itself seeking, "the ladies" because they are the untutored auditors who could endorse the new Philosophy by being enabled to comprehend it.

7

Corporate Relations in Science and Technology

Our universities are among the more remarkable institutions of modern society. Through their faculty and students, they pursue complex roles of scholarship, education, and community service, often with internal tensions among these roles. Depending upon the vantage point and the times, they seem both resilient and fragile, both proud and beggardly, both aloof from and involved in public issues. They vary tremendously in size, revenue sources, academic traditions, and public involvement. Universities stand for important values in our society. These include free and open communication, respect for individual views, and insistence on excellence, disinterested objectivity, fastidiousness and honesty in the reporting of research results, and dedication through education and research to enhancing the state of basic and useful knowledge about ourselves and about the worlds around us. On a more practical plane, universities are very complicated organizations that must find the means to support their commitments to faculty, staff, students, physical plant, and various external communities. These responsibilities require collective, as well as individual, endeavor to adjust to changing times and new opportunities, while still maintaining essential values.

The present may prove to be a watershed period in university relationships, as well as in our economy. For a host of reasons and with a nearly bewildering array of financing mechanisms universities and companies are seeking common ground. This very conference reflects the ferment and the sense of opportunity, since several of the host institutions have had only limited organized relationships with industry in the past. In many states, including my own state of Washington, there are concerted efforts to recruit and to build a high technology industrial future with considerable emphasis on the potential contributions of the research universities. Many of our most prominent scientists have become identified with these efforts.

In the broadest terms, university relationships with industry are intended to serve the public interest by facilitating technology transfer, improving productivity, and enhancing the competitiveness of the nation in world markets. While there is respect for knowledge itself, the predominant theme of public investment in basic research in this country has been the potential application of such knowledge in industry, agriculture, and medicine. One need only recall President Lyndon Johnson's dramatic call - upon swooping down in his helicopter in front of the Clinical Center at the National Institutes of Health - that we scientists "unlock the secrets of the laboratory."

The spectrum of university- industry arrangements ranges from individual and collective consulting to research contracts to cooperative research programs and formal research partnerships. For the university and for the faculty members, however, summarized the potential advantages of these arrangements: increased income, resources for program expansion, broadened opportunities for students, access to special equipment or research tools, and longer-term support for high-risk projects, presumably with fewer strings attached than from government funding; and the potential risks: creating imbalances of faculty, students, and space; using up the "seed corn" of basic knowledge, while seducing or otherwise exploiting students and faculty into more targeted, narrower training and research; inhibiting communication, publication, and peer review; raising numerous potential conflicts of interest for the individual and the university; and losing public confidence and jeopardizing government funding.

To be realistic and not too romantic about the often-troubled past, we should note that universities have found themselves negotiating over or adjusting to requests and requirements of the funding source, whether wealthy individuals, foundations, industry, or government. In the Daedalus volume Limits to Scientific Inquiry, Don K. Price reminded us, "It has been easy to forget the atmosphere of the time, less than a half-century ago, when the Federal Government considered research grants to private universities improper if not unconstitutional, and when the leaders of the National Academy of Sciences objected on principle to letting private universities accept government funds."

The tensions of university-government relations are beyond the scope of this chapter, but are the subject of a major National Academy of Sciences review at this time. We should keep in mind, as we eagerly seek productive relationships with industry that the several highly publicized, multi-million-dollar, multi-year contracts between individual companies and specific research groups at universities represent only a few tens of millions of dollars annually, compared with the $3.5 billion per year provided by the National Institutes of Health alone. It would be folly for both industry and academia if the government comes to view industrial investment in university research as a substitute rather than as a supplement.

In the *New England Journal of Medicine* specific examples of three coherent institutional mechanisms for enhancing technology transfer: active patenting and licensing efforts, especially through university research foundations; not-for-profit contract research laboratories; and faculty practice plans in medical schools. These three mechanisms offer instructive historical context for our discussions of the participation of academic scientists in research contracts and venture companies in the biotechnology arena and other promising areas.

In most discussions about the uncertain boundaries of the interests of companies, universities, faculty members, students, government agencies, and the public at large, the emphasis has been placed on the relationships between individuals and companies or between universities and companies. I wish to emphasize certain aspects of the sensitive and crucial relationships between faculty members and their own universities as I review specific models of university-industry relationships.

MODEL 1: INCOME FLOWS FROM CONSULTING

Consulting arrangements are a critical element of university-industry relationships. Often, many years of consulting by one or a few specific faculty members, working closely with counterparts in the company, lie at the core of a major research contract or partnership arrangement. A good example is the longstanding relationship between Bert Vallee of Harvard and Monte Throdahl of Monsanto. Another is the consulting relationship of Howard Goodman with the Hoechst Company.

Generally, consulting is permitted - or even encouraged - by universities as a means for faculty members to supplement their incomes. Other goals - including two-way technology transfer, opportunities for students, and development of company-university partnerships - are usually implicit. Information about the existence of a consulting arrangement itself, let alone the financial terms and the technical domain, is generally considered private and confidential. Most universities, including my own, simply set limits on the amount of time that the full-time faculty member may take away from academic duties or away from the campus.

A common figure is one day per week, or fifty-two week days per year. When weekends, evenings, vacation and holiday time are added, considerable latitude is apparent. At the University of Washington, any outside consulting must be reported in advance and approved by the departmental chairman, or the dean, with a note that the activity is considered appropriate. Even so, there seems to be little attention to the income flows or to overall time commitments.

Some universities have sought to develop consulting ties on a program or departmental basis so that more faculties can benefit, the time commitments can be shared, and more expertise can be brought to the parties served. In some situations an informal clearinghouse function is mounted, with openness about the opportunities and stimulation of additional faculty to participate, if they choose. A more formal arrangement is the associates program, whereby numerous corporations pay annual fees for the right to participate in visits to university laboratories, briefings by faculty, and generally generic consulting exchanges. The associates programs, long a feature at MIT, are being adopted in many areas of the country to facilitate the interchange judged crucial to high-tech regional development.

Both consulting on an individual basis and consulting through associates programs can be enhanced if the university faculty generates patentable discoveries. The origins of patenting useful scientific discoveries in this country lie in Benjamin Franklin's founding charge to the American Philosophical Society in 1744 and in Article 1, Section 8, of the U.S. Constitution. There have been some notable financial successes from university patents. These include the irradiation of milk to activate vitamin D and the discovery of anticoagulants at the University of Wisconsin; the development of stannous fluoride as a dentrifrice at Indiana University; and the development of Gatorade at the University of Florida.

Whether through university research foundations at arm's length, or through active licensing programs within the university administration, many universities are trying to utilize the liberalized provisions of federal grants and contracts with regard to university patenting. As one can see, the University of California system, MIT, Stanford, Wisconsin, and Cornell stand out among these universities in terms of activity and yield. Some of the others have barely begun. Johns Hopkins, the University of Pennsylvania, and Yale also rank in the top ten for life sciences R&D.

In terms of the division of net income between the faculty members and the university, the standard protocol at the Wisconsin Alumni Research Foundation is 15 percent to the inventor and 85 percent to the university foundation. In this case, faculty participation is strictly voluntary. At the Indiana University Foundation, the inventor receives 20 to 50 percent, depending upon the amount of university resources utilized, and the university share is divided evenly between the inventor's department and the rest of the university. In the celebrated case, now under review, of the CohenBoyer patents for the basic gene splicing and cloning techniques, the proceeds would go one-third to Cohen and two-thirds to Stanford, and one-half to Boyer and one-half to the University of California. Both Cohen and Boyer voluntarily assigned their shares to their respective universities.

Patenting and licensing can be effective and, in extraordinary cases, lucrative. However, a major "winner" is necessary in order to make a patenting program successful and even then it takes years to realize substantial revenues. There is no comparison to the sensational financial returns for those who have benefited from the speculative fever of venture capital investments and equity holdings during the past couple of years. Nevertheless, it is increasingly apparent that that speculative fever has abated.

MODEL 2: INDUSTRIAL RESEARCH CONTRACTS TO UNIVERSITIES

Academic appointments and university facilities are generally too confining for major technological or commercial work. Multidisciplinary centers or laboratories have become a favored mechanism for organizing "big science" with government and sometimes private sector contracts. Preeminent in the use of this mechanism is MIT, to which the federal government turned during World War II to mobilize academic talent for the defense effort, but many major universities have large contract research units. Faculty are enabled to undertake projects simply not feasible within the academic departments, recruiting large numbers of technical staff, building special facilities, gaining access to government and other sources of information and spinning-off companies.

Generally, faculty do not stand to gain increased personal income from these contract research laboratory arrangements. Extraordinary funding for research institutes of laboratories in the biotechnology area has arisen lately with the establishment of the Whitehead Institute at MIT, the Hoechst Department of Molecular Biology at the Massachusetts General Hospital, the Du Pont - supported Department of Genetics at the Harvard Medical School, and Monsanto support for the Department of Medicine at Washington University.

The source of funds in these examples is the private sector, but the results are similar to those with federal funds: resources to expand faculty, staff, and facilities, accompanied by needs to clarify roles, accountability, and access by others to the research results. We might as well acknowledge that to many faculty in arts and humanities departments, medical schools as a whole, with their growth and reliance on a combination of NIH funding and hospital revenues, appear much like giant contract research laboratories!

One of the most interesting examples of the not-for-profit research unit is the Wharton Econometric Forecasting Association (WEFA) at the University of Pennsylvania. The growth and commercialization of econometrics bears some curious parallels to the pattern in genetic engineering. During the 1950s and 1960s, the National Science Foundation (through the Social Science Research Council) supported economists who developed complex mathematical models of the economy, involving hundreds of simultaneous nonlinear equations to express the relationships among a host of economic activities. Such models of the U.S. economy were devised at Wisconsin, Michigan, and the Brookings Institution.

There was general skepticism about their practicality. Few guessed that over the next decade such models would yield economic forecasts that would become basic economic planning tools for most of the leading corporations of the world and for many governments, or that one company founded by a Harvard faculty member, Otto Eckstein, would be worth $100 million on the stock market a decade later. In order to overcome limitations in resources, personnel, and pay scale, Lawrence Klein, one of the pioneers in this field, and his colleagues at the University of Pennsylvania set up a private, not-for-profit corporation with Klein as chairman of the board and still full-time professor of economics.

The university extended a $250,000 line of credit, treating 40 percent as equity in the venture and the remainder as debt in exchange for the data, software, and use of the Wharton name. WEFA agreed to carry all subscribers to the pre-existing forecasting service and to donate the proceeds to Penn. The annual payment to the university grew to $150,000 by the mid-1970s. WEFA's revenues from new clients were plowed back into the operation. Klein accepted modest consulting fees from WEFA and continued his research, extending his models to other countries and initiating Project LINK to create a model for the worldwide economy. He received the Nobel Prize in Economics in 1980.

Also in 1980 the university decided to sell 80 percent of its equity in WEFA, gaining an estimated $7 million. This decision represented a mutuality of interests. It generated essential capital for the expansion of data banks, software, personnel, and field marketing to keep WEFA viable and competitive. It brought the university endowment for an Economic Research Institute, repayment of certain guaranteed loans, a 20 percent residual interest in WEFA until 1985, and access to WEFA's models and data base for use by students and faculty.

Klein and his colleagues continue as consultants. Despite the highly beneficial past and future arrangements, news of the sale triggered quite a stir on the Penn campus over the agreement between the purchasing company and the proposed Economic Research Institute, over the continued use of the Wharton name, and especially over the confidentiality of the negotiations leading up to the sale. Just as this conference provides an opportunity to share experiences, awareness of these events of 1980-81 at Penn might have been helpful to the Harvard administration in advance of its abortive proposal to help set up a company with a leading faculty member, Mark Ptashne.

A new twist in the model of industrial research contracts is the use of tax-sheltered R&D financing through limited partnerships. Genetic Systems, Inc., is a small company in Seattle with rapidly growing links to private laboratories, drug companies, and university-based researchers. Highly focused, specific research contracts - including contracts in the School of Public Health at the University of Washington - have been funded through the limited partnership mechanism. The researchers are not - or at least need not be - investors!

The most important development of the contract mechanism is the evolution of research partnerships, with significant research and technical support roles, carefully defined, for both the university and the company scientists. The Monsanto-Harvard Medical School contract was the forerunner of these partnerships. More than a transfer of funds is involved. The complementary research roles must be defined and the development of techniques and materials must be coordinated. Those involved gain a far better appreciation of the values, imperatives, capabilities, and constraints of the other partner.

MODEL 3: NEGOTIATED SHARES OF EARNED INCOME OR EQUITY POSITIONS

Among the diverse arrangements of faculty and institutions to expand research, service, educational, and income-generating activities, an especially welldeveloped and at least partially relevant model for basic science faculty can be found in the negotiated arrangements of faculty in the clinical departments of most medical schools.

Medical practice plans were stimulated by a desire to enhance clinical service as an essential counterpart to teaching and research, by a need to tap additional sources of funds in the face of increasing costs and decreasing real faculty salaries, and by an opportunity to take advantage of altered external circumstances, namely the availability of Medicare and Medicaid financing for previously unbillable clinical care in teaching hospitals. Especially for medical schools associated with state universities, the option to step free of restrictive personnel, salary, and benefit policies was an additional attractive factor.

The response has been quite diverse in institutions around the country, reflecting different traditions and circumstances and reflecting different power relationships within individual schools of medicine and teaching hospitals. Negotiations in most schools have led to formal written financial agreements that succeed in keeping key faculty and in giving incentives to emphasize - but presumably not overemphasize - clinical service.

The plans provide supplementary income to the individual faculty member, negotiated balance among practice, teaching, and research for the department, and unrestricted funds for the school and for individual departments. In many schools, the dean is able to use some of the funds to assist basic science departments. These plans represent a significant source of revenue for medical schools, increasing from $90 million in 1970 to $727 million in 1979, according to compilations from the Association of American Medical Colleges. The negotiation is the essence of the process - requiring faculty to be explicit about institutional goals and objectives and the different contributions of participating faculty. A. S. Relman has highlighted some of the serious difficulties in establishing and updating these practices plans and their income distribution formulas. The most pervasive is the wide variation in incomegenerating capacity and in academic orientation of the participants and their departments, exacerbated by the fact that high-earning capability may bear little relation or even an inverse relation to academic contributions. The same is true in the commercialization of genetic engineering, or other basic fields. Just as there are haves and have-nots among clinical departments, there are striking differences within and among basic science departments in the potential for revenues from outside sources, assuming that a desirable balance of outside and academic pursuits can be negotiated. Ironically, surgeons are now envious of the biochemists!

Teaching hospitals have some surprising analogies with off-campus research ventures, both nonprofit and for-profit. Hospitals are sites of considerable income flows, whether for the individuals involved or for the institution or for both. The hospitals are often physically separated from the medical school itself, and from the rest of the university. They generally have separate boards of trustees and administrators, yet they are essential to the mixed academic-service roles of the medical schools in educating students and advancing medical knowledge.

The excitement of clinical or applied work tends to "seduce" students away from basic sciences. Conversely, clinical challenges, like corporate challenges and advances in techniques and instruments, may greatly stimulate basic research, a factor in these relationships that the historian DeSolla Price has emphasized. The negotiated practice plan approach may be useful for basic science faculty, as a mechanism for making explicit and concrete some of the heated and often symbolic debates over values, activities, commitments, disclosures, and potential conflicts of interest in their industry relationships.

Requirements for disclosure of outside activities, whether for income or not, vary tremendously across institutions, depending upon local political factors and sources of funding. Faculty must agree on what activities are subject to disclosure, in what detail, and to whom. Faculty will bring different values, different preferences, and different current ties to such discussions. In these negotiations, students' interests and intellectual property need special protection. Very sensitive analyses are required to define which activities are truly related to responsibilities of the faculty member to the department and to the university, and then to define any kinds of income-generating activities that might warrant inclusion in a faculty income-sharing plan.

Precedents are the departmental consulting groups via associates programs and the assignment by Cohen and Boyer of their patent shares to their universities. Another instructive example is the assignment of a certain percentage of the equity in a new firm called Zymos (Greek for "yeast") to the Washington Research Foundation. Hopefully, other well-established faculty will be similarly generous toward their own universities. Dealing with equity shares will be a particularly awkward problem for the faculty negotiations, since they represent potentially lucrative and distinctive aspects of the commercialization phenomenon in biotechnology.

The value of equity shares is often difficult to establish, subject to great fluctuation and to manipulation and promotion. Equity shares are not the only sensitive matters, however. The individual faculty member who consults or initiates outside research ventures or writes a book is benefiting from the institutional resources and reputation, as well as from his or her own record, ideas, and energy. The lesson from the clinical practice plans is not that negotiation of faculty roles is easy, but that it is feasible. Faculty plans in the basic sciences could capitalize upon the growing sense that intensive relationships with companies can, indeed, be a legitimate and desirable adjunct to traditional academic roles - both for the individual and for the institution. As partners in the research enterprise, we must learn and respect the values and driving forces of universities and of companies, as well as of the government agencies. In this process, those of us in universities should be especially sensitive to the interests and anxieties of our faculty members and our students. We should draw them into open discussions about the mechanisms to foster appropriate university-industry relationships.

THE NEW INVESTMENT IN SCIENCE AND TECHNOLOGY IN FRANCE

It is difficult to speak specifically about the French program in science without first considering the context of the present French government's policy. This government has undertaken major economic, political, and social reforms. In particular, from its very beginning it recognized the relative decline and vulnerability of the French industry over the past few years and introduced a policy for industrial and economic development,in which the key word was "reindustrialization."

This policy included several elements. The first element was to convince the French people of the paramount importance of industry, especially necessary in a country that has not yet fully integrated the industrial activity among its values and its culture and which was hoping, too quickly perhaps, for the "post-industrial" era. The second element of this government's policy was to create the conditions for people to accept more readily radical changes in their work environment and the social structure, basically through a renewed social participation; such an acceptance is a necessity for the continuous thrust of technology to introduce new products, new sources of energy, and new ways of life.

The third element was to increase investment and to modernize industrial equipment. In most of the Western countries, but particularly in France, there has been a stop in the increase of productive investment in the last ten years. Therefore, the government had to introduce many different mechanisms for attracting money toward industry; furthermore, the urgent need for massive investments in many major firms has been a key element for nationalizations. The fourth element of this general policy is a strong belief in high technology and the research to support this technology. From the very beginning, a major objective was to bring universities, government laboratories, and industry together to enhance the effort in technology. This would apply to both high-technology industries as well as to basic industries.

The subject of the new investment in science and technology in France is one of the prime ingredients for a stronger, more competitive industry as well as a show of faith in the future. It requires the government to begin long-term planning and decision-making, an unusual task for governments that would rather solve short-term problems and ignore long-term issues. The first step taken by the government was to establish a ministerial department for research and technology. Jean-Pierre Chevènement, a prominent political figure of the Socialist party, was appointed to be its head.

One year later, a second significant change occurred. The three departments of research and technology, industry, and energy were combined to create one very large department called the Ministry of Research and Industry. This ministry has become a good forum for interactions and exchange of ideas between research and industry. In France research is shared between three groups: universities and the National Center for Scientific Research, also classified as a university group; government laboratories, such as INRA (agronomic research),

INSERM (medical research), CEA (atomic energy research), and industry. Industry is now the largest contributor to the French effort in research.

Just twenty-five years ago, industrial research and development in France was at a low level with very few companies conducting research. This changed under the administration of President Charles De Gaulle when a large industrial research effort was promoted. Most significant to the strategy for the development of science and technology was the enactment of legislation called the "Law for Programming and Orientation for Research," in which both the quantitative and qualitative objectives for the next five years were stated. The passing of this exceptional law was a difficult but necessary undertaking because it insured funding for a long-term scientific effort.

The law states clearly that scientific research and development and technological development are to be national priorities. Between 1981 and 1985 the percentage of the Gross National Product devoted to research will increase from 1.8 to 2.5 percent, thereby increasing by 40 percent the spending for technological development in five years. This process began in 1980 and there have been 12 percent annual increases in each of the three successive budgets. Changes can already be seen and the stage is set for more improvements in the next decade. However, one must be reminded that this action came after ten years of decreasing spending for scientific equipment and, therefore, the need was very acute.

Part of the new funding went to renovate equipment in universities. A large part of it was to reinforce the cooperation between university and industrial research. The government's contribution to the increased funding for research will be matched by industry. This means that industry also must increase its expenditure for research and development by 40 percent in five years. Another step taken by the government was to create tax incentives and devise a new system of indirect aids to industry. Equally important was the establishment of a mechanism for developing the financial and legal structures of university-industry cooperation: it is now possible to establish institutional linkages between public laboratories and industry in order to promote joint ventures including research, development, and preindustrialization phases.

An exchange of people between university and industry was also encouraged and a system of sabbatical years in industry established. At present, more than two hundred people participate in this exchange program each year. Last, the administration of public universities and public laboratories was made more flexible. In addition to meeting the scientific and development needs broadly, we also are setting priorities among those needs: through the "mobilizing programs," efforts by university, government laboratories, and industry are focused on aspects of industrial development that are considered to be the most important.

Three of the main programs lie in the field of biotechnology, new sources of energy, and the major one, electronics, which includes computer information systems, robotics, and other areas. In these programs, funds can be allotted to universities and industries through various cooperative arrangements. In conclusion, I should like to emphasize three important aspects of the French program. First, France has demonstrated a deep commitment to scientific development by increasing its budget. It should be noted that this budget increase for science came at the expense of other programs because the overall national budget did not increase in real terms. Second, the emphasis on science and technology is being made within the overall context of reindustrialization. Third, the proposed changes concerning the scientific community at large are now possible since a renewed sense of commitment has emerged among researchers along with the reassessment of this national responsibility.

Of paramount importance in this change of attitude was the "Colloque National de la Recherche" held in January 1982. Prepared during the fall of 1981 by numerous meetings throughout France, this large conference was opened by President François Mitterrand, closed by Prime Minister Mauroy, and attended by over three thousand scientists. It is now generally recognized that this national conference marked a turning point for the French research policy, which shows that only a strong political will can transform the attitudes of the scientific community and the perception industry has of this community.

REACTORS

Beginning about fifteen years ago there was an intense discussion in West Germany on what was called the growing technology gap between the United States and Europe. Government, industry, and the scientific community in my country then, had concerns very similar to the ones that are being expressed here. Although you may be rightly concerned about the future, I feel the United States is doing very well.

For a long time the German research system has been characterized by complexity and multiformity. As you know, in the forty years since World War II, the Federal Republic of Germany has grown greatly. We have a population of sixty-two million people, and last year the gross national product was 1,500 Deutsche marks or about $650 billion. The total national research and development budget was 36 billion D marks or about 2.3 percent of the gross national product.

Of this money approximately 50 percent came from public funds. Universities spent more than 6 billion, industry 22 billion, and other institutions 8 billion D marks for research and development. The number of research personnel in universities is approximately 73,000 men and women. There are 248,000 scientists and engineers in industrial laboratories and about 53,000 people in governmental laboratories. The constitution contains four basic principles that apply to research and research promotion. First, freedom to do research and to teach is guaranteed. Second is the importance of the division of powers between the federal government and state governments. Third, the budgeting rights of the federal and the state governments are assured; and fourth, a private enterprise system is guaranteed.

Characteristically universities are engaged in pure science, and the constitution provides for cooperation between federal and state governments in the support of universities. We also have technical universities which were established to promote applied education and research, and very tight relationships exist between the technical universities and industry. Both scientists and managers in industry often have lecture contracts with universities or may be active members of university faculties.

The main institutions that interrelate government, universities, and industry are the Commission of the Federal and State Authorities; a science council; a West German University Rectors' Conference; and the German Research Society, which was founded in 1920. The Research Society has a budget of 800 million D marks, and is funded 75 percent by the federal government and 25 percent by state governments.

We also have an old tradition of academies of science. There are five in number. The first one was established in Gottingen in 1751 by King George II of England, the Elector of Hanover. Perhaps the best known is the Max Planck Society founded in 1911. There are now forty-eight Max Planck institutes with an overall budget of 860 million D marks. They are jointly funded by the federal government and the states with a contribution of about 10 percent from other institutions. The "Big Science" Establishment consists of thirteen institutes with a 1,700 million D marks budget and 16,000 employees.

The Fraunhofer Society is a special institution that might be of particular interest here. It is dedicated to applied research and contains twenty-seven institutes with a budget of 250 million D marks. Of that total 165 million D marks comes from contracts with third parties, mainly industry. The system contains a bonus arrangement wherein the greater the sales of the product of an institute the more basic support for research that institute receive from the federal and state governments.

West Germany also has a Confederation of Industrial Research Associations. It has ninety members, and 240 million D marks are spent by the federal government and 80 billion D marks by industry in a joint venture. About two-thirds of the research supported by the Associations is carried out in universities. In industry, research and development is mainly done in three areas: chemicals, steel and mechanical engineering, and electrical engineering. Direct federal government research and development support is mainly for basic research and secondarily for research and development in those fields where industry cannot assume the major responsibility such as nuclear, space, and environmental research.

The total direct governmental budget for research in 1983 will be 6.9 billion D marks, and of that amount 4.6 billion will be spent in industry. Indirect governmental support for research and development can be obtained by such means as claiming special allowances or tax deduction, and so forth. Cooperation is mainly based on personal relations, on mutual confidence, and on excellence. We should not expect too much in too short a time from these contracts. Therefore, continuity of support should be guaranteed.

The German federal government recognized this need. Because we have budgeting for five years ahead, contracts can be made for five years and even longer. In special fields permission can be obtained to contract for as long as twenty years if that time is needed to start a new reactor development plant, for example. The new government of West Germany is also dedicated to research and development, and the first priority will be given to basic research.

Just a word of reaction about the Hoechst-Massachusetts General Hospital contract. Obviously both sides had matching interests, and they were able to agree on a contract that promoted and protected those interests. It is very important to maintain freedom of scientific communication and cooperation between the countries of the free Western world and the different institutions within our countries. Recently two large chemical and pharmaceutical German companies placed similar contracts with the universities in Heidelberg and Cologne and activities such as these will continue in my country.

8

Science, Engineering and Mathematics

Group Work

Group work has become popular in disciplines ranging from the humanities through the social sciences to the sciences. For some professors, the group work represents an unusual or isolated experience, which they attempt during one class period or for one project or assignment outside of class. For others, group work has become the focal point of the course and has caused them to rethink entirely their curricular content, syllabus problems, laboratory exercises, and methods of teaching.

Although few professors may be as inexperienced as Peter Adams, and few would create the complicated mess likely to result from the scenario depicted above, most faculty members have not explored the research on group work. Even fewer have delved into the literature on the significance of gender and race dynamics within groups.

In contrast, a recent study revealed that students, particularly minority women students, understand the significance of group work. Their highest priority advice to other women minority students seeking graduate degrees in science, engineering, and mathematics was to become a member of a study group. Moreover, many of these minority women revealed that they had been excluded from study groups, which they felt had hindered their success in graduate school.

If the dynamics of race and gender are understood and used effectively, group work may enhance the learning for all students, especially women and men of colour. Even more important, if these dynamics are ignored or misunderstood, group work may actually inhibit or detract from learning. This chapter will explore parameters such as group size and selection, roles and leadership, assignments and grading, student resistance, and the particular interaction of gender and race with each one.

SETTING UP GROUPS

Like our professor Peter, faculty inexperienced with group work may assume that dividing the class into groups requires brief forethought and little explanation to the students. Particularly at the college level, where considerable student autonomy and maturity are assumed and where we may have no information about our students' prior achievement, faculty may assume that self-selection or random assignment are reasonable ways to divide the class into groups. But simply asking the class to form itself into groups with four members each or to count off often results in situations actually inhibit-or fail to enhance-learning for the more vulnerable students.

Studies have documented that when students choose their own teams, they tend to choose others that they know and who are like themselves. And study groups formed outside of class informally or without faculty supervision often lead to exclusion of women and minority students. A graduate student in engineering recounted her difficulties in completing group projects by her because she found she was excluded from groups formed by white women, as well as those by men of colour or white men.

In addition to group size, the research suggests that other parameters such as abilities, race, gender, and previous experiences can be critical to successful groups. Ideal group size varies according to the nature of the task or project and class size. Most research documents that teams should include between three and six members, and one tested cooperative learning method for mathematics is called "Groups of Four". Although much faculty report that groups larger than four may encounter problems with meeting times and poor participation by one or more group members, for some tasks larger groups may be useful. Given the current trends for large cooperative teams for scientific research, some experience with relatively large groups may be appropriate in upper division undergraduate or graduate level courses.

As with all parameters surrounding group work, the size of the group should be related to its objectives or tasks. For example, for a laboratory experiment in an introductory course that depends upon each member having access to the same equipment during a short time, more than three people on the team could be prohibitive. In contrast, a team of five or six may be best for a senior design project lasting several weeks in which each person completes a large part of the project alone, and then the team synthesizes the results of all members for a final product or theoretical conclusion (the so-called "jigsaw puzzle" approach). Thus, before selecting their groups, teachers should reflect on what should be learned from the task and the ideal way to accomplish it.

Faculty selection of groups, as opposed to random or self-selection, permits the teacher to take race, gender, abilities, and experience into account. A useful alternative in upper division undergraduate and graduate courses is to explain the important characteristics needed for viable groups and then ask the students to use those characteristics in forming their own groups. Thus, after being informed about group dynamics, the students are allowed to take some responsibility for forming groups. Even if the professor does the selecting, however, the students need to learn about the importance of group dynamics.

What are the significant characteristics faculty or students should consider in selecting groups? The cooperative learning literature for the K-12 classroom emphasizes forming groups composed of individuals with mixed abilities. In the public schools, where mainstreaming can result in wide variance in student ability within one class, and standardized testing requires that all students reach a certain level of proficiency, mixed-ability grouping helps to minimize discrepancies in group progress. But at the college level, the need for mixed-ability grouping is less. Because most science, engineering, and mathematics courses are lock-step, passing the prerequisite courses lessens some of the variance in students' abilities. Most faculty are forced to assume that students in a given class have roughly the same abilities. For the initial group assignment, most professors prefer not to make ability a major consideration. After the first examination, project, or other major assessment, performance ability might become one of the bases for reassignment of groups (along with other factors such as dysfunctional personality combinations)-if it appears that the performance among groups is widely disparate.

INTERSECTION OF GENDER AND RACE

In contrast to abilities, race and gender should be considered in initial groupings, much of the K-12 literature advocates having each group statistically reflect the overall racial/gender mix of the class as a whole. This literature supports the notion that having minority perspectives represented in each group will help the majority to understand other approaches and ideas of people from diverse backgrounds. For example, a class of twenty-five students, five African American and twenty white, and approximately equal numbers of males and females, might be divided into five groups, each containing four white students and one African American student.

Although this apparently "equitable" distribution may be helpful in exposing the majority to minority perspectives, it may, in fact, be harmful to the minority students. Particularly when the subject is a nontraditional major or career choice for the minority, distributing-or, often, isolating - one minority student within each majority group may lead to the minority student dropping out of the group, the course, or the major. The work of Treisman demonstrated that effect for African American students at UC-Berkeley in mathematics and for Hispanic students at UT-Austin.

A similar phenomenon may haunt women pursuing nontraditional majors such as science, engineering, and mathematics. Four females and sixteen males would not be an uncommon gender distribution in an introductory calculus-based physics class. Four groups of five students, with one female in each group, appear to be an equitable (or at least representative) division along gender lines. But the research on study groups at Harvard and other work suggest that women are more likely to drop out of the group if they are the only female, particularly if the subject is a nontraditional one such as science, engineering, or mathematics.

In the college science classroom, where, in contrast to K-12, dropping out or switching majors is a viable option, the research does not support having each group reflect the overall statistical profile of the class for gender and race. Developing individual groups that contain a critical mass or at least more than one person of the minority gender or race leads to less isolation or "spotlighting" of women or men of colour. The calculus-based physics class used in the example above might still be divided into four groups, with two groups containing two women.

Although such groupings result in some groups with only males, the few women in the class are less likely to experience isolation and drop out. The intersection of race and gender further complicates group selection. For instance, assigning an African American woman to a group consisting only of white men clearly constitutes isolation. But questions arise about whether the African American woman is still isolated when another woman, not African American, or an African American male, is assigned to the group, along with the white males.

Somewhat different, but overlapping, issues surface over definitions of racial minorities for scientific purposes. The National Science Foundation has defined Asian Americans, because of their relative overrepresentation in science compared to their percentages in the overall population, as not a minority or protected class in science, engineering, and mathematics. Although Asian American men are not a minority, Asian American women are underrepresented, in a status similar to that of white women. Even so, the differential treatment of Asian American women compared with white women in our society means that they will bring varied experiences and expectations to the group work.

By not defining Asian Americans as a racially underrepresented group, we also overlook diversity among them. Although some groups of Asian Americans such as Chinese Americans and Japanese Americans may be relatively overrepresented in the workforce of the sciences, engineering, and mathematics, other groups such as the Hmong are clearly underrepresented. A growing body of literature has begun to air the misconceptions about the designation of Asians as a "model minority" and their prowess in science, engineering, and mathematics.

These misconceptions particularly affect some Asian American women, Asian Americans from certain ethnic backgrounds (such as the Hmong), and some Asian American men. Lumping all Asian Americans as a monolithic group obscures not only differences in country of origin and language, but also in status and class, such as immigrant or nonimmigrant, which may have more impact on their numbers and performance in science, engineering, and mathematics than race or gender.

For some groups, race may be a more significant factor than gender for underrepresentation. For example, repeated studies have documented that minority women find both racism and sexism to be significant barriers, with many women ranking racism as more problematic, particularly at the undergraduate level. One study suggested that sexism may cause more difficulties than racism at the graduate level.

A complicating factor for minority women, which may shed some light on differential responses, was uncovered in the Brown (1995) study. Her study revealed that women graduate students in science, engineering, and mathematics who were easily identifiable as nonwhite reported more difficulties with racism. In contrast, those, such as some Cuban and American Indian women, who stated that others appeared to perceive them as white reported more problems with sexism.

LEADERSHIP AND GROUP ROLES

Viewing women or all members of a designated racial group as similar can obscure diversity within groups. Individual differences become especially prominent in the choice of group leaders and assignment of roles. Assigning a Hispanic woman the role of group leader, assuming that the other group members include a Hispanic male and a white male and female, places her in a role counter to the stereotypes of male dominance for her race and gender. Although many Hispanic women do not fit the stereotype and feel comfortable with assuming leadership positions, in an introductory course, when students do not know each other or the teacher, this initial leadership task may be difficult for some Hispanic women.

For the first group task or project, encouraging students to select their own leader and assign their own roles typically results in group members who feel secure. That works well when the professor has chosen a project in which each member has a clearly defined task and responsibilities. The self-selection of roles within a group facilitates both group comfort and functioning.

ROTATION AND STEREOTYPES

Even though students may prefer to select their roles initially in group work, roles must be rotated throughout the course, with monitoring to assure that each student fills each role for a variety of tasks. Reports from the engineering industry reveal problems when such rotations fail to occur. If students are permitted to stay with the same group all semester, filling essentially the same role to complete several projects or smaller tasks associated with a semester-long project (not an uncommon phenomenon in a senior engineering course), the overall group project may be excellent. All group members may receive an A, because each did her or his part well and the group functioned well as a whole. But failure to rotate roles can become especially problematic when skills learned in the classroom need to be translated to the work setting. Because they were not forced to assume new roles, members may have missed some skills and perspectives developed by other project members in varied roles. In the industrial setting, if the role available in the work group for the new employee is not the one which she or he assumed in the senior group project, the new employee is at a severe disadvantage.

Gender may be a factor in preference for, or comfort with, certain roles. Sometimes a woman prefers or may be assigned the role of group manager. Growing up as a female in our society may have provided her with better skills in social organization than most males. She may be better at working with other members of the group to ensure that the group functions smoothly to complete the task on time; her overview of the process as a manager and her writing skills enhance her abilities to produce the final report on behalf of the entire group. In contrast, a man may have more experience with computers and seem to prefer to work more with the hardware than with the group. He may develop superior computer programs to solve design problems encountered by the group and enhance the written portion of the final report with outstanding computer graphics.

As new employees in the industrial setting, both the woman and the man above may lose their jobs. It is unlikely that the role each assumed repeatedly in the class group will be the only role needed on the job. The man has not learned the social skills and management strategies useful for handling group dynamics, and the woman has insufficient experience with the hardware and software. We professors must do more than delineate clearly the group roles required for a particular task in order for the group to function smoothly. Monitoring each student's role during each project permits rotation and ensures against students' avoiding roles that require new skills or that run counter to their expected gender role.

DESIGNING PROJECTS

Changing a course to incorporate group work takes much thought and effort. An error made by some faculty in the science, engineering, and mathematics classroom is to make no change in the assignments traditionally used in the course.

Some simply expect the students to do the usual assignments in groups. Assuming that the traditional problems, experiments, or projects were designed for individual work, they are unlikely to be effective for groups. Moreover, students rapidly perceive that this is a task they could complete on their own, perhaps even more quickly, and they resent the group work as unnecessary-especially if it is to be done outside of class.

OVERCOMING RESISTANCE

In the work world, teams or groups are used to solve problems where the perspective, skills, or knowledge of one person are inadequate or where the complexity and/or amount of time required are excessive for one. Each person actively depends upon the other members of the group because they understand that they cannot complete the project alone. They cooperate with the group because their self-interest depends on successful completion of the team project.

Problems or projects assigned to groups also need to incorporate complexity, time pressures, and a variety of skills, so that teamwork is critical to their solution. For the faculty member who has taught the course using traditional, individual assignments, the transition to groups involves substantial rethinking and work. Contrary to an expectation of some teachers that group work will lighten their class preparation, it involves considerably more time and preparation, especially for the first few times.

Development of guided design problems, complex projects, and multifaceted experiments with appropriate roles usually requires much planning and up-front time for faculty. It may take more time than conceptualizing a new course or redesigning the content of a previously taught course retaining the traditional teaching methods. For a faculty member who has never worked in a setting in which teams are used or taken a course with extensive group work, it will be challenging to rethink ingrained patterns of teaching and problem solving.

Class problems and projects need to draw on experiences and issues significant for males and females and people of all races. Overall course objectives and tailoring the problems for teams serve as the primary principles guiding this development. However, gender or race may influence the decision if the professor has undertaken group work because of the research suggesting that women and men of colour may respond well to cooperative learning and practical applications. When that becomes a major motivation, the teacher may wonder whether it is worth the work to redesign the course-especially if the students' initial response is indifferent.

One source of student resistance may be assignments that are inappropriate. Because until recently most students have been taught content mainly by lectures in science, engineering and mathematics courses, they do not expect to actively participate, and they may oppose groups because they require more work. And some of the most resistant students are often high-ability, high-achieving minority women. When many faculties using group work reported this to me, I explored some of the reasons. Although no statistical data were collected about this, the belief of the faculty, based upon conversations with students, was that the resistance stemmed from the fact that the students had worked long and hard to develop skills that had helped them to do well in science, engineering, and mathematics.

Many of them also had significant outside responsibilities such as families and full-time employment. They viewed group work as another situation in which they would have to be responsible for someone else (i.e., they would have to teach the other students and bring them along) and/or as an additional complication to an already difficult schedule. After the initial opposition, however, almost all students, including these high-achieving minority females, reported great satisfaction with group work as an experience that aided their learning, if assignments were appropriate for team efforts.

FAIR ASSESSMENT

Students may also resist because of concerns over how group work will be assessed and reflected in the final individual course grade. Many faculty also express discomfort with assessment of group work. Studies reveal a range of approaches from not assessing or counting group work at all to making the common group grade count as the individual final grade for each student. Faculty also vary in the extent to which they take complete responsibility for grade assignment to each individual or consider student assessments of individual contributions to the group effort. In some cases, the teacher assigns an overall project grade and adjusts the individual student grades based on all students' assessment of their own work and that of each other team member. This assessment conveys to students that the group work is important (i.e., it counts as part of the course grade), that the group product as a whole will be assessed (i.e., the professor will grade the product, possibly in relationship to other group products or against a standard of what is a correct answer or good outcome), and that the teammates' perceptions of individual contributions also count.

In cases where students undertake group work, but the grade assigned is based upon a laboratory write-up done individually by each student, a different message is conveyed. Students will recognize the significance of individual performance. Group work and cooperative learning count only as they enhance the individual laboratory report. In contrast, making the group work count for 100 percent of the course grade and making the groups grade the same for all its members relay a very different message. Such an assessment implies that group work counts for everything and that individual's will do well only when the group functions to produce an excellent product, which will in turn benefit the grade of each individual group member.

Although this last example may seem to give extreme emphasis to group work and penalize individuals in groups with one or more nonfunctioning members, in certain cases it may be an appropriate assessment. In a senior-level engineering course, after which most students will take jobs in industry, a major course objective may be to teach students to function well in teams. In industry, all members of a team may experience low salary increases or lose their jobs if they fail repeatedly to function well and produce. Perhaps the best method to prepare students to grasp the importance of group functioning in the work world is to have all members of a team receive the same individual grade.

This last example stresses the important principles that should underpin all assessments of group work: the assessment should be appropriate to the significance accorded group work and consonant with the course objectives for the use of group work. Students receive conflicting messages when a major course objective is teaching students to work in teams but group work does not count toward the final grade. It appears equally inappropriate to base the entire final grade of each student on the group project grade, while not including group work as a primary objective of the course. In general, a combination of individual and group assessment works well for most courses; however, in some cases, course objectives (a senior engineering course) dictate that all group members receive the same grade.

Issues of race and gender may enter into assessment of group work, particularly during the evaluation of the contributions of individuals. Research on gender roles in group dynamics documents differences in the ways individuals are perceived and treated, based on their gender. Studies in formal groups of both men and women have demonstrated that men talk more than women and exert more control over the topic of conversation.

White men also interrupt women much more frequently than women interrupt men, and their interruptions more often introduce trivial comments or statements that end or change the focus of the women's statements. Further, the more frequent use by women of "tag" questions ("This is true, don't you think?"), overuse of qualifiers, and polite and deferential speech forms may make women's comments more easily ignored or ineffective. A more insidious form of ignoring women's contributions occurs when a point made by a woman is later attributed to a male in the group, who then receives credit by having his name attached to the idea.

In peer evaluations of individual members by themselves and others in the group, the contributions of women may be undervalued because of gender bias. In science, engineering, and mathematics groups, the women's ideas and skills may be further underrated if they have played the role of group manager or facilitator. Ironically, if they have done an excellent job of making all members feel included and facilitating smooth group functioning, much of their work may have been barely perceptible to others.

In the sciences, where experimental data, ability to work with hardware or equipment, and theorizing may be highly valued, people in those roles may be perceived as particularly valuable or hardworking, which may be reflected in their peer evaluations. In contrast, the role of group manager or facilitator may be devalued and receive lower peer evaluations, particularly when that role is compatible with the gender expectations for women. Most faculties who undertake group work in the science classroom assume that it represents a positive force for retaining women and men of colour - if they even consider the impact of group work on gender and race in making their decision.

Aware that cooperative learning and reduction of competition may attract women and men from some ethnic/cultural backgrounds, faculty may assume that use of a group format will facilitate learning for individuals traditionally underrepresented in science, engineering, and mathematics. But if professors do not know about the powerful effect that gender and race dynamics may have in groups, they may set up groups in ways that deter men of colour and women, as Professor Adams did.

After receiving disastrous midterm evaluations, Peter Adams read the research on group work, paying particular attention to race and gender. This led him to set up the groups in his classroom quite differently for the second half of the semester. Even though it meant that some groups were all male and two were all-white and also had male leaders, he did not isolate individuals as the sole representatives of their race or gender in the study groups. Peter paired women as laboratory partners and replaced the blackboard competition with an exercise to encourage cooperation between the partners. He monitored the groups carefully and stepped in where necessary to ensure smooth functioning, which removed some of the responsibility from the group leader.

Because the course was at the introductory level, Peter chose to make the group project worth only 20 percent of the final grade. Half of the project grade was based on individual contributions; all group members received the same grade for the other half of the project grade. By the end of the semester, Peter received glowing evaluations. Several praised him for really paying attention to the students' criticism of the course and making mid-course corrections to improve their learning experience. Every student but one commented on how much she or he had learned and how the group work had facilitated their learning. Thus, when faculty members consider gender and race in determining group size, leaders and roles, and assignments and grading, they may enhance the learning for all students-especially women and men of colour.

9

Women in Science and Engineering

At the outset we should emphasize that this chapter is organized in a somewhat atypical fashion; that is, we have merged the existing literature on this topic with our own original results, rather than having composed separate literature review and findings sections. This unusual organization reflects the explicit purposes of our study: (1) to synthesize what others have learned about this important topic and then (2) to test those themes by analyzing two national data sets. Further, we illustrate rather than report all the data that served as the bases of our empiricism, in keeping with the study emphases: We do not want to overstate the importance of our own results, compared to the much more extensive work of others, in reaching our conclusions. In sum, the conclusions that we report represent an integration of the work of previous researchers and of our own original efforts.

Underutilization of women and minorities in science and engineering is a problem of national priority; social equity and the quality of U.S. labour are involved. Although the numbers for minorities remain discouraging, women have nearly reached or even exceeded parity with men as entrants into numerous scientific fields; nevertheless, their representation in many specialties remains substantially below their distribution in the population.

Not only does the lack of parity raise obvious social concerns, the quality of the science and engineering labour force is at issue, for even though the supply of scientists and engineers appears, at least for the present, to be adequate to national needs, larger labour supply pools translate into higher quality scientific workers, thereby increasing marginal labour productivity and, in turn, the productivity of the overall economy. Put another way, all else being equal, we would expect that the more women and minorities enter these fields, which are known to be powerful contributors to national productivity, the larger will be the nation's stock of scientists and engineers, the greater will be the quality of that stock, and the greater will be the productivity of the nations's labour force.

Underrepresentation of women and minorities in science and engineering is not a new topic in science policy research. A recent review of the literature identified no less than 120 empirical and theoretical undertakings related directly to the issue. During 1995 and 1996 alone, many new articles on the subject were published or presented at national conferences. In addition to the ubiquitous commentary-type articles, this substantial literature ranges from studies that consider specific questions by examining small samples in single institutions to major national investigations of virtually all the conceivable, related issues.

Although our efforts were targeted on the postsecondary education years, we quickly learned that most postadolescent behaviours in regard to science and engineering can be understood clearly only by reference to earlier life experiences, probably most notably to very early socialization and to behaviours that become manifest in the adolescent years. What emerged from the literature synthesis was a robust early-years-to-employment explanation of why women, and to a lesser extent minorities, are underrepresented in particular areas of science, mathematics, and engineering.

This "life-sequence" approach identifies three major concepts that seem to capture most of what distinguishes majority females and minorities from majority males in regard to science and engineering study and employment. After briefly describing our methods, for each of the three concepts we begin our treatment with the early years of life, progress on through the school and college years, and finish long after college matriculation, at a time when some individuals are employed and still others are in graduate school. We conclude the article with some policy implications.

TESTING THE THREE CONCEPTS

The majority of our effort in this study was directed toward understanding and synthesizing the results of the extensive research completed by others. For this we employed standard integrative review strategies. Once we had discerned the lessons of previous work, we were ready to test those explanations ourselves. It is important for the reader to understand that the data presentation below is illustrative only. The tables necessary to present all or even most of the data that yield the findings far exceed the space available. This is important to know, because the reader may otherwise spend considerable time searching futilely for the data that demonstrate the finding being reported.

Our data sets included the 1971 and 1980 Cooperative Institutional Research Program (CIRP) files, which contained substantial information from the precollege years, taken at the time of college entrance and extended through undergraduate and graduate education and employment, and the National Longitudinal Survey of Youth (NLSY), which annually (through 1993) interviewed persons between the ages of 14 and 22 in 1979. The CIRP data, and to a considerable extent the NLSY data, were almost entirely categorical as opposed to continuous.

This necessitated an exclusively limited dependent variable approach to the empirical analysis. We estimated binomial logit, multinomial logit, and ordered logit models by maximum likelihood methods. Because the estimated parameters of these models are not always easily interpreted, we focus our discussion on the estimated marginal effects of the explanatory variables (evaluated at the sample means) on the outcome (education and employment) probabilities.

Because the outcome probabilities must sum to one, the marginal effects must sum to zero. Since the explanatory variables are typically dummy (indicator) variables, the notion of a marginal effect requires some elaboration. We calculate the marginal effect of each variable as the incremental effect of a change in the variable from its sample mean, holding constant all other variables at their sample means. The interpretation is that the sample means represent the probabilities of selecting someone with the given characteristics. We then estimate the effects on the outcome probabilities of marginal changes in the probabilities of drawing individuals with the given characteristics.

Although a particular marginal effect may appear to be small, this does not imply that the estimated coefficients on the given variable are statistically insignificant in the underlying logit model; indeed, many are significant. Further, it must be remembered that these are marginal effects; that is, the contributions of other variables are held constant. For example, it will be noted that having a parent who has a science or engineering occupation adds to the likelihood that one will major in science or engineering, quite aside from other aspects of that occupation, such as income level, and quite aside from one's personal traits, such as high-school rank and high-school preparation in science and math.

Where number of cases permits (CIRP), we estimate separate models for white males, white females, black males, black females, Hispanic males, and Hispanic females. Most often our analysis (CIRP) is limited to white males versus white females or males versus females (NLSY). Full information from the CIRP analysis is contained in our report to the National Science Foundation (1996); full information from the NLSY is in McClure, 1997. Because all of the explanatory variables are dummy (indicator) variables, each set of dummy variables must have a left out reference group in order to avoid a perfect correlation among the explanatory variables.

Where only a single dummy variable is included, the left out reference category is obvious. For the high-school rank variable, those in the bottom 50 percentile served as the left out reference group. For the parental income variable, PARINC7 served as the left out reference group and represented parental income in the middle of the income range (where PARINC1 is the lowest income category and PARINC12 is the highest income category). We utilize the CIRP data for the illustration of our analysis; the NLSY analysis is virtually identical. For purposes of analyzing factors that determine the probabilities of selecting a first choice from among competing college majors in the "freshman" year, we aggregate CIRP choices into five broad categories of college major: physical sciences/engineering, biological sciences, liberal arts, business, and all others.

The underlying choice framework is represented by a multinomial logit model. (For analyses of persistence to the degree, graduate study and employment in physical sciences, mathematics and engineering [PSME], ordered logits are used.) The final multinomial model includes seven sets of explanatory variables, each set consisting of one or more dummy variables. These variable sets are high school rank, self-rating of math and natural science preparation for college, the presence of a college prep program in high school, parental occupation in the science and engineering area, parental income, expectations regarding sources of college financing, and marital plans. The sample size is 9,628. We estimate a pooled model and control for gender and ethnicity with dummy variables. We also estimate separate models for each of the six gender/ethnic categories.

First we discuss findings from the pooled samples. The estimated multinomial logit model correctly predicts 46.7% of the first choices of college major. The estimated marginal effects for the pooled sample are reported. The magnitude of the effects may be evaluated by recalling that theoretically the marginal effects must lie between -1.0 and +1.0; but also note that the variables may not be statistically significant. As reflected by the negative signs (-), holding constant other factors, white females (WFEMALE) and Hispanic females (HFEMALE) are less likely (than white males) to select science and engineering or business as their first choice major and are more likely to select a major in liberal arts.

For example, if the probability that a student is a Hispanic female increases by 10 percentage points at the mean, the probability of selecting a major in physical science or engineering falls by 1.5 percentage points. Black females (BFEMALE) also are less likely (than white males) to select their first choice from physical science/engineering or business; however, black females are more likely to select a major in the biological sciences and in the liberal arts. Black males (BMALE) are less likely (than white males) to select their first choice from science and engineering and are more likely to select business. Finally, Hispanic males (HMALE) are less likely to select biological science or business but are more likely to select physical sciences/engineering.

Turning to the separately estimated multinomial logit models, we find the following predictive accuracy rates for first choice of college major: white males - 37.5%, white females - 55.0%, black males - 40.4%, black females - 51.7%, Hispanic males - 51.9% and Hispanic females - 56.7%. We report the separately estimated marginal effects. Our illustrations of the data are of the major differences, among groups, in the marginal effects of the determinants of first choice of college major as they pertain to selection of majors in science and engineering. Among the six gender and racial/ethnic groups, being in the top 25% of one's high-school class has the largest positive effects on the selection of science and engineering for white males.

The effect of better than average preparation in math and natural science is the highest among Hispanic males. A 10 percentage point increase in the probability of reporting better than average preparation increase the probability of selecting a major in science and engineering by 2.2 percentage points for Hispanic males and 1.7 percentage points for white males. Among males, having a parent in a science and engineering occupation has the largest effect on the probability of selecting physical science and engineering for Hispanics. For example, increasing the probability of having a parent in a science and engineering occupation by 10 percentage points increases the probability of selecting a major in physical science and engineering by 8.0 percentage points for Hispanic males; next is a 1.1 percentage points effect for white males.

In the case of the biological sciences, blacks exhibit the largest positive effects of having a parent in science and engineering. A 10 percentage point increase in the probability of this variable increases the probability of choosing a major in biological sciences by 1.5 percentage points for black females and 1.4 percentage points for black males. For Hispanic males the effect is to lower the probability of selecting biological sciences by 7.7 percentage points; for Hispanic females the effect is a 1.0 percentage point gain. Anticipation of reliance upon work, savings, or GI benefits (WORKSAV) has the largest effect on selection of a major in physical science and engineering for Hispanic males. This effect is negative and indicates that a 10 percentage point increase in the probability of relying upon work, savings, or GI benefits reduces the probability of selecting a major in physical science and engineering by 2.0 percentage points.

Group differences in estimated marginal effects result from differences in parameter estimates as well as differences in the mean values of the explanatory variables. One way to separate out these effects is to construct Duncan dissimilarity indexes. These indexes measure the distance between any two distributions across mutually exclusive categories. The index is bounded between 0 and 1. A value of zero indicates that the two groups are identically distributed across the categories, whereas a value of 1 indicates no overlap in the distribution, i.e. perfect segregation.

The index can be interpreted as an estimate of what proportion of one group or the other would have to shift categories in order to render the two distributions identical. If we predict a distribution for a given group based on the estimated model for white males and then calculate the dissimilarity between white males and the predicted distribution for the given group, the value of the index is a measure of how much dissimilarity remains after controlling for different parameter estimates between white males and the given group. In other words, the index measures the contribution of group differences in the values of the explanatory variables to overall dissimilarity.

Similarly, we can calculate the dissimilarity between a group's actual distribution and its distribution as predicted from the white male model. In this case the value of the index is a measure of the dissimilarity arising from group differences in the models generating the outcomes, i.e., dissimilarity stemming from group differences in the parameter values or structure. The Duncan Dissimilarity Index (DDI) analysis indicates that the disparity between white males and others almost always has more to do with differences in the effects of explanatory variables (i.e., their coefficients) than with differences in the values of the variables themselves. (For example, it is not so much differences in the number or set of math courses taken, that explain differences between male and female persistence, as it is differences in the utility gained from the particular courses that are taken.) This is true for all females in the first choice of college major. For example the DDI between white males and white females is 20.4, which means that 20.4% of the white female freshmen would have to change their first choice of college major in order to have the same college major distribution as white males. If the effects of the explanatory variables on choice of college major for white females were the same as those of white males, only 3.4% of white females would have had to change majors in order to produce identical distributions.

By comparison the DDI between the actual college major distribution of white females and their distribution predicted on the basis of the estimated model for white males is 19.0. In other words the gender differences in the effects of the explanatory variables require that 19.0% of white females change their first choice of college major in order to produce identical distributions for college major.

This is much larger than the change required solely on the basis of gender differences in the values of the explanatory variables. This illustrates the nature of the analysis, the form of the findings, and the bases for the results reported below. The following section integrates the extant literature with our own findings; the specific data reflecting our own finding are not presented, as is consistent with the purpose and emphases of our study, not to mention space limitations.

In preface we should note that centering our discussion on the most powerful concepts explaining the underrepresentation of women and minorities in science and engineering (a conclusion based upon a synthesis of the literature and our findings) results in a somewhat artificial grouping of particular variables and in omission (in the discussion) of others, which often are noteworthy by themselves. In a few cases the variables omitted may be of greater explanatory power than included variables, which were selected for discussion only if they contributed to an understanding of the most powerful concepts.

The three concepts, self-concept/self-efficacy, peer influence, and goal commitment, are all closely connected. We begin with self-concept and self-efficacy, two closely related abstractions that constitute an important body of research in psychology and social psychology. An individual's development of the first of these, self-concept, is fundamental to development of the latter, self-efficacy. The early development of self-concept bears importantly on the achievement of science outcomes for women and minorities later in life, that is, through science and engineering self-efficacy. In turn one's self-concept/self-efficacy is impacted importantly by peers, all of which affect one's relative commitment to science and engineering. In each of the three sections below, we begin with definitions and a discussion of the relevant literature and then progress to a discussion of our own results.

SELF-CONCEPT AND SELF-EFFICACY

Self-concept is perception of self; self-efficacy is belief in one's ability to perform a given behaviour. The evidentiary literature is quite compelling that self-concept and self-efficacy strongly affects the achievement of science and engineering outcomes for women and probably for minorities, too, although the evidence regarding minorities is much more limited.

Self-concept is both hierarchical and temporal in nature. General self-concept is at the top of the self-concept hierarchy; positive, subordinate self-concepts generally contribute to positive general self-concepts, although the former may be complementary rather than complimentary. General or overall self-concept is observable in very young children and is quite stable, but with age becomes situation-specific as the hierarchy is descended. (Subordinate) verbal and Mathematical self-concepts and self-concept hierarchies begin to develop by about ages 5-8; they are distinct and separate by late adolescence. Self-concept has been linked empirically to achievement. These statements pertain to the overall population. What of differences for identifiable student groups?

Generally, in elementary school boys and girls do not vary significantly in math/science ability, confidence, or interest; however, many math/science gender differences are evident by the end of high school, with the junior high-school years probably being transition years for most youth, but particularly for girls. It is instructive to note that these patterns are consistent with self-concept theory and with empirical evidence: the absence of self-concept differentiation in the early years and the distinctiveness and separateness of math and verbal self-concept in later years.

Generally, self-efficacy, rather than self-concept, is employed by social scientists to explain behaviour related to science and engineering outcomes. This choice is supported by the definitional differences. Self-efficacy has a more specific contextual meaning than self-concept. As typically used, self-concept might be seen as the general conception of self one brings to personal decision making. It is the basis for forming one's sense of self-efficacy, which relates to specific personal decisions, such as career choices in science and engineering.

Self-efficacy theory, which usually is credited to Bandura, begins with the notion that human behaviour is devised through cognitive processes, with performance-based experiences being most important. Learning about ourselves involves evaluating "differential consequences"; it involves acquiring and evaluating personal information. The elements of the learning process are four in number: We learn through "performance accomplishment," which is very important and is based upon mastery; "vicarious experience," which involves making social comparisons and is less powerful; "verbal persuasion," which is widely utilized but is of limited utility; and "emotional arousal."

An appreciation of these four factors is important to understanding the issues addressed herein: As specific obstacles arise, one's self-efficacy will be instrumental in determining whether one decides to cope with adversity, to what degree, and how persistently. Bandura observes significantly that the "strength of conviction" in one's self-efficacy will affect one's willingness to see a task or goal to completion and even whether one will make an effort: "Weak expectations are easily extinguishable by disconfirming experiences, whereas individuals who possess strong expectations of mastery will persevere in their coping efforts despite disconfirming experiences".

Strong self-efficacy can turn threatening obstacles into events perceived as safe. Self-efficacy has been shown to predict performance accurately in 85% of tasks confronted. With these ideas in mind, let us return to gender differences as they may pertain to science and engineering. On essentially all characteristics hypothesized to affect science and engineering-related educational and career choices, girls do not differ from boys in the early years of life, years before the development of the distinctively different subordinate self-concepts; however, numerous, important self-concept/self-efficacy differences related to science and math are evident thereafter.

As a point of departure in examining gender differences related to science and engineering, ability differences between boys and girls in math and science are almost universally agreed to be minimal over all age ranges. Although some differences usually are noted in empirical work, analytical models almost uniformly find no significance for ability measures when other factors, such as number of science and mathematics courses taken, are controlled. Even so, certain exceptions are instructive. Mathematical abilities do decline earlier and more steeply for girls, and at the high end of the ability continuum, differences clearly are noted; for example, males outnumber females 4:1 in the number of individuals earning more than 600 on the SAT-Math test.

Nevertheless, girls tend to earn somewhat higher grades in science and mathematics. Overall, the conclusion is that ability differences fail to account for important gender disparities in science and engineering and that we must look to other explanations. Such differences are noted on a number of other measures. The number of mathematics courses taken almost invariably is a primary predictor of majoring and persistence in science and engineering. By the end of high school, boys substantially exceed girls by this measure. One's expectations of the probability of success in a given endeavor are known to be an important factor in formulating behavioral choices. Levels of expectations in science and math are lower for females than for males. There are several reasons for this.

Males rate the usefulness of science and math higher than do females, who even rate science and math as more useful for males than for themselves. Female ratings of science and mathematics usefulness decline for girls as they mature a phenomenon that does not characterize the maturation of boys. No doubt female "other directedness" plays some part in this that is the desire to please others. Linn and Hyde conclude that of all variables examined, only usefulness of math and science appears to affect persistence, and that this difference by gender has existed for many years.

Usefulness of science and math has been connected empirically to valuing science and math, males valuing these subjects more than females. The importance of "usefulness" to science-and-mathematics-linked academic and career choices is illustrated by analogy to the gender differences in the valuing of athletics: Because traditionally girls have valued athletics less than boys, it is hardly surprising that historically more boys than girls have engaged in athletics, although, of course, this is changing.

It is similarly no surprise that boys voice a greater interest in and more positive attitudes toward science and mathematics than do girls, although, again, the differences emerge only after the elementary school years. Before adolescence, interest levels are essentially the same. In one study interest even surpassed ability in predicting self-efficacy in engineering, and self-efficacy was found to intervene to mediate effects of such factors as stress, coping, and gender and ethnicity on achievement.

The same is true for confidence in science and math. Relatively and on average, women are more likely to lack such confidence. The disparity in favor of boys emerges by high school, and this relative confidence may not be supported by ability differences. In turn, confidence in science and mathematics has been connected to test-taking skills in math/ science; for example, boys are more willing or able to attempt time-saving shortcuts in solving problems.

A caveat should be inserted here. Gender-linked variables do not necessarily translate into gender-linked effects on the critical outcomes. For example, the only causal relationship Sherman and Fennema could find among math usefulness, performance, and course plans was a moderate one between math being perceived as a male domain and math achievement, and the relationship was only for girls in the high school-years. This caveat notwithstanding, by the end of high school, these perceptual differences are associated with gender disparities in science and engineering-related decisions.

Perceptions of math usefulness generally predict intentions to take math courses and math achievement, although the greater course-taking propensity of males is not clearly detectable until grade 12 and is not strong in predicting enrollment in mathematics courses even at the collegiate undergraduate level. That female self-efficacy is involved in these disparate changes, is of little doubt. Girls' self-esteem drops precipitously after adolescence, with the drop for Latinas being the greatest; whereas African-American girls do not decline in self-esteem (they do dislike schools and teachers). (There may be an important clue here to understanding gender differences if it can be shown that the socialization of African-American girls differs from that of other girls and that African-American female socialization is similar to that of majority males.)

The manifestations of gender difference take several forms. Older boys rate their ability as the "secret" of their success in science and engineering, whereas similarly situated girls cite their personal diligence, skill, and effort. If girls experience problems in math, they perceive this as personal failure. Especially boys, but girls as well, believe that male understanding of science and math is superior, even when it is not. Boys overestimate their abilities; girls underestimate theirs.

The connection between self-concept or self-esteem and ability in science and mathematics is important. Students are more likely to enroll in optional math courses when they perceive themselves to possess high math ability or feel confident in math, although relatively few studies attempt to determine whether the links are causal, and when they do, the results are far from clear.

Math comes to be viewed as a male achievement domain; the same is true for science. Boys consider math to be a masculine subject; however, girls are less likely to gender-type math than are boys, and although girls may perceive math-related careers as masculine, they do not necessarily view math as inappropriate for them. They do believe that studying science is more important for boys and that it will be of greater utility for boys. But again, these differences rarely are detected until the self-concept differentiation years, and they are not clearly evident until late adolescence. For example, gender-linked mathematics enrollment patterns do not materialize until grade 12 and are still weak among college undergraduates.

Clearly, self-efficacy in science and math, on average, is less evident for females than for males. The explanations would appear to involve important gender-linked perceptual differences that take many forms but that usually involve perceived male-female role disparities. The important policy question is, what changes between preadolescence and adolescence? Of course, differences in socialization experience are thought to explain many if not most of the gender differences, but what are the specific mechanisms leading to gender differentiation in science and engineering?

Identification of specific causal agents is not far advanced. Attitudes of parents and other family members, teachers, counselors, and peers are variously known or believed to play some part but most evidence is more impressionistic than hard. In regard to race, it appears that self-efficacy and self-confidence are primary factors in African-American male consideration of math/science careers whereas for females personal interests are paramount; nevertheless, African-American male/female interest levels are approximately equal. African-American males give broad consideration to career possibilities, relative to females. Disturbingly, African Americans do not appear to reflect on their personal abilities in these considerations.

SELF-CONCEPT AND SELF-EFFICACY

What do our results say about these issues? First, our conclusion from the literature that self-concept/self-efficacy is important to understanding underrepresentation of women and minorities is supported strongly. The associated variables in our data sets are second only to measures of commitment (which we connect to self-concept/self-efficacy below) as predictors of science and engineering study and employment.

The best measure of science, math, and engineering self-efficacy available in the CIRP files is at the point of college matriculation, when, as our findings show, the perception that one's preparation in math and natural science is "better than most"' is associated about equally with the greater likelihood of selecting physical science/engineering and biological sciences, rather than "other" fields, as the first choice of college major. The marginal effect, that is, the effect holding all other variables in the analysis constant, is a substantial 1.6 percentage point increase in the probability of choosing science/engineering majors for each 10 percentage point increase in the probability of perceiving oneself to have a relatively good science/math background.

The most closely related outcome measure available in the NLSY is "major field of study in last college attended." Here, there are four presumably good measures of self-concept (as opposed to self-efficacy), and all are related to majoring in the physical sciences, mathematics, and engineering; for example, a personal sense of pride is strongly associated with majoring in these fields and is strongly and negatively associated with majoring in nonscience fields. The reverse is true in regard to the relative feeling of personal failure. These findings are for all matriculants. What about selected subgroups? First, the fact that white men are most likely to perceive their math and natural science preparation to be better than most is noteworthy. The comparative mean values (from CIRP) are white men, 43%; white women, 31%; black men, 26%; black women, 16%; Hispanic men 23%, Hispanic women, 17%. These are substantial differences. It is little wonder that the numbers of women and minorities entering science and engineering are relatively small.

How do the effects of self perception vary by race and gender? Results from CIRP, such, yield answers to this question. The positive marginal effect of the science and math preparation variable on the probability of choosing a major in physical sciences/engineering is larger for white males than for white females, African Americans, and Hispanic females. Only Hispanic males show a greater positive effect of relatively strong math and science preparation on the probability of selecting physical sciences or engineering as the first choice major.

In short, one of the important reasons white men are more likely than women and minorities (save Hispanic men) to select math/science majors is that they perceive themselves as being relatively well prepared in math/science; i.e., their self-efficacy in science and math is stronger. In the NLSY files, mathematics knowledge scores are available, whereas an independent measure of science and math self-efficacy is not; therefore, one cannot know to what extent math knowledge, which is a very powerful predictor of majoring in PSME for males but is insignificant for women, acts through self-efficacy, independently, or in tandem.

The other pertinent findings from NLSY are more extensive and are somewhat different, in that they largely reflect general feelings of self-concept rather than specific science/math self-efficacy. (Of course, unless both science and math self-efficacy and knowledge are contained in the data set, it may not be possible to separate the effects of the two.)

Two NLSY measures of self-perception are strong predictors of majoring in PSME for both men and women, as are the feeling that one is in control of one's direction in life and that "luck" is not an important factor in achieving one's ends; however, the predictive power of each of these variables is modestly stronger for women majoring in PSME than for men: generally, positive self-perceptions and a feeling that one controls one's own destiny has a greater utility for women in PSME than for men. Put another way, the women whose self-concepts and sense of control are less strong are more likely to major in non-PSME fields. Yet, as the CIRP results show, self-efficacy in science and math is most clearly demonstrated by white men in science and engineering.

Turning to the biological sciences, first our stated expectations in regard to math and science preparation are met: For the CIRP sample, self-perception of above average math and science preparation has a larger impact on the probability of selecting a major in PSME than in selecting a major in biological sciences. Further, we can see that a reported "stronger than most" math and science preparation has a larger positive effect on the probability of selecting biological sciences for white women than for white men. The same is true for black females versus black males. Hispanic males and Hispanic females are about equal in this regard.

For the NLSY sample, too, the self-concept and sense of control variables are far less important for the biological sciences than is the case for PSME, both for men and women, although generally they are a bit more important for women in the biological sciences than for men. Math knowledge is essentially inconsequential for the biological sciences outcomes. The gender and (for the most part) racial/ethnic differences that exist in these regards are almost completely limited to PSME.

Consistently, for the self-efficacy/self-concept variables, easily the largest differences between groups are found between Hispanic males and females. These results are instructive, because gender roles tend to be most sharply distinguished among Hispanics; that is, traits held to be more masculine tend to be quite clearly associated with male behaviour, and those held to be more feminine tend to be quite clearly associated with female behaviour. In other words, if in fact socialization experiences do vary by gender and racial/ethnic group, if in fact these differences do manifest themselves in self-concept/self-efficacy variations by gender and racial/ethnic group, and if in fact those differences do lead to female and minority underrepresentation in science and engineering, then we would expect those differences to be most clearly shown among Hispanics, especially Hispanic males, whose roles are most closely linked to being family providers. This is precisely what occurs. Not only is this math and science perception variable most strongly associated with physical sciences and engineering matriculation for Hispanic males, the absence of such perception is most strongly associated with their matriculation in the liberal arts.

There is one other variable in the CIRP data set that should impact directly on self-concept, if not self-efficacy. That variable is one's grades earned in college, and the outcome measure is degree attainment. We would expect that earning good college grades would be more important for white women than for white men, because self-concept/self-efficacy is supposed to be more critical for the former group than the latter in the pursuit of science and engineering majors.

Indeed, that is what the results show. For the physical sciences and engineering, the effect of having earned undergraduate grades of B or higher has almost twice the effect on achieving an undergraduate degree and almost a 50% greater effect on earning a masters degree for white women compared with white men. The patterns are of the same general order in the biological sciences; however, here, the effects of higher grades are more beneficial for white males in earning doctoral and professional degrees.

Parental influences. One other set of variables in our data sets would appear to be important to the formation of science and math self-efficacy and, in turn, to science and engineering outcomes. Those variables relate to how parental occupations and educational backgrounds impact whether individuals come realistically to "see themselves" as scientists or engineers.

Others have concluded that parental backgrounds are germane to science and engineering achievement of their offspring, although most of this research is of a relational rather than causal nature. Jackson, Gardner, and Sullivan (1993) report that women who enter male-dominated fields such as science and engineering tend to come from intact families, have mothers who work, and have parents who are well educated and consider success to be important. Worthley (1992), too, reports that science persistence is associated with having highly educated parents.

The Jackson et al. work finds that women who become engineers are likely to have fathers who are engineers and that they are likely to marry engineers. The AAUW study (1991) reports that families (and schools) are the greatest effectors of science and engineering aspirations, and Astin (1993), from more recent CIRP data, finds a positive relationship between majoring in engineering and having a father who is an engineer. The engineering students in Astin's sample are clear that their parents want them to become engineers. Our view is that parental backgrounds work their effects on their children primarily through demonstrating the feasibility of science and engineering careers, that becoming a scientist or an engineer is a reasonable expectation, in a word, that it is efficacious.

We, too, find that having a parent engaged in physical science and engineering occupations increases the probability of majoring in the physical sciences and engineering. The NLSY files show a greater effect for males than females. The differences among the six CIRP groups in these regards are particularly instructive, being uniformly greater for males than females and by far the greatest for Hispanic males (followed by African-American males).

The connection to self-efficacy, and in turn to science and engineering career commitment, is suggested by our earlier discussion regarding Hispanic culture. We hypothesize that for minority men, especially Hispanics, having a parent who is employed in physical sciences or engineering is very instrumental in creating a perception that such an occupation is a realistic goal, and that this perception reinforces science self-efficacy and supports the student becoming committed to that goal, i.e., to science and engineering study.

Our reasoning is that minority males encounter many inhibitors to majoring in science and engineering and that parental role models serve as powerful counterforces. The reason that the marginal effects are less for white men is probably because they are less likely than minority men to encounter obstacles to majoring in science and engineering; therefore, parental role models are less vital. The quite different effects for women, minority and majority, may well reflect their more "eclectic" decision structure; that is, in deciding whether to major in science or engineering, women may be less prone to the influences of parental occupations because of the attractiveness of family-oriented goals. For the biological sciences the patterns are far more mixed for women, although the magnitude of the effects often is strong.

The CIRP data reveal that the marginal effects of fathers' occupations in science and engineering on the science and engineering outcomes for their children are even larger later, in shaping employment patterns, than they are in selection of first majors (a pattern not found in the NLSY data). Clearly, individuals working in science and engineering occupations in 1980 were substantially more likely to have had fathers whose occupations were in science and engineering than in some other field (CIRP data).

Further, the effects for the entire sample of white men and white women were almost totally a function of the effects on the males: increasing by 10 percentage points the probability of having such fathers increased the probability of white males being employed in science and engineering occupations by almost 5 percentage points, but for white females the effects were essentially zero. In a pattern that became clear when we examined all the "family influence" variables, white men appeared more responsive to such variables than did white women. Again, we hypothesize that female goal conflict is a major cause for the smaller effects for women.

An important exception to the pattern for family influence variables was the effect of mother's education level upon the physical science/engineering higher degree attainment of their daughters (CIRP). Mothers' college degrees affected female degree attainment positively and male attainment negatively. Because white women, on average, have weaker math/science self-efficacies than men, it may be that maternal role models are more essential for women in science and engineering than for men.

Further, for those in the physical sciences or engineering, the effects of parental degrees persist at least through the master's degree; in fact, they grow modestly stronger for both men and women, before declining at the doctoral and professional level. For the biological sciences, the patterns for women are very weak, providing still more evidence that women (as well as men) who pursue degrees and work in the biological sciences are substantially different from those in the physical sciences and engineering.

Interacting with physiological change, peer influence, we believe, is the "missing link" that explains much of the great transformation of girls, during and after adolescence, from being full and equal participants in science and math to much smaller representation. We largely credit Holland and Eisenhart's, Educated in Romance (1990), for this insight. Holland and Eisenhart explain how female self-concept, self-efficacy, classroom experiences, and external goal orientation come together to deny women their representative places in the science and engineering professions: It is the influence of peers that is critical to how these forces play out.

Although their focus is on the college years, they observe that the origins of the phenomena are in the onset of adolescence, which marks not only a clear demarcation between boys and girls in regard to science- and math-related behaviours, it signals the beginning of distinctly different paths of gender-linked general personality development.

From its nationwide survey, the American Association of University Women (AAUW, 1991) concludes that adolescence is a critical time for female self-identity development. It is a time of both dramatic biological and psychological changes; it is a "critical moment" in the development of one's lifetime choices and decisions. The AAUW survey shows that prior to adolescence, girls are "confident, assertive and feel authoritative about themselves". In subsequent years their self-esteem declines dramatically. Notably, adolescent girls rank "being popular" as the most important personal concern, whereas boys list competence and independence. Girls report not being happy "with the way I am", growing more timid and tentative, and becoming more conflicted. Their physical appearance is of great importance to them.

The similarity of these observations about the female self to female self-efficacy changes in science and mathematics is striking. Lack of self-confidence, low self-esteem, timidity and tentativeness, are all descriptions that fit many postadolescent girls in regard to science and mathematics, as is the perception on the part of girls that boys are more able in math and science than they are.

Logically, the dramatic decline in female self-esteem that occurs during adolescence would be expected to cause girls to become more other- rather than self-directed. Their primary concern with popularity suggests strongly that girls are likely to be particularly mindful of what their peers think of them: how they behave, their values and orientations, what they like and do not like.

This other-directedness might be expected to result in openness to the suggestions of parents and teachers, provided that those suggestions do not run counter to the values of the peer culture, in which case the outcomes might be far less certain. Nevertheless, generally, one might assume that this other-directedness influences girls to develop superior academic habits, for example to complete homework assignments, study dutifully, and generally be more diligent in academic matters than are boys. Clearly, the AAUW data suggest that girls may lack the self-confidence to set their goals independently, that they may pursue life goals reflective not of what they want, but of what others want them to do. Again, the importance of commitment to goals accomplishments is clearly noted.

If adolescent girls are so susceptible to the influences of others, especially peers, what is it that others cause girls to do? Teachers, and to some degree parents, of course, want girls to be good students, often even to study science and math. Female peers, on the other hand, according to the AAUW findings, primarily value popularity. Because this and related values emerge dramatically during adolescence, popularity almost certainly is in part a reflection of personal appearance and by implication, involves appeal or attractiveness to boys. Holland and Eisenhart demonstrate that females gain much of their self-esteem through their relationships with males. The effects are circular: Validation of girl's and later women's behaviours by males leads to greater acceptance by peers, all tending to reinforce female perceptions that their sense of self-worth is connected importantly to the perceptions of males. This means conforming to what both female and male peers conceive of as appropriate female behaviours and values.

On average, this suggests a lessening, not a strengthening, of girls' commitment to science and math; why, to a considerable degree, girls begin to lose interest in science and mathematics beginning in the junior high years; and why girls come to view science and mathematics as the domain of boys. In discussions of our findings our academic colleagues and our students often expressed initial skepticism about this conclusion. They questioned the implicit assumption that girls were more concerned about and affected by boys than vice versa.

Certainly, adolescent as well as postadolescent boys are vitally interested in girls. What differs, we believe, is how this interest plays out in relative commitment to science and engineering occupations, how males come to view work as an obligation because they see themselves as family providers, whereas girls often come to view work and family as equally attractive alternatives.

At the time of college entrance (CIRP data), individuals were asked whether there was "some chance or a very good chance that he or she will marry while in college or within a year after college." At first glance this variable may appear to be a very indirect measure of peer influence; however, the variable directly reflects the precise effect peers are held to have on young women: the promotion of the importance of relations with men over academic values. Indeed, plans for marriage may be viewed as a very potent test of goal conflict/commitment (the third and final concept, which is discussed in the next section) for women versus men. Our reading of the literature is that it is indeed peers who are most fundamental to greater goal conflict for women than for men, specifically as that conflict reflects science and engineering versus family goals.

Generally, students who were relatively less interested in marriage and thus more committed to careers were more likely to plan to major in biological sciences than in other fields. Among white females, having plans for marriage in college had the largest positive effect on the probability of selecting liberal arts, with much smaller positive effects on the probabilities of selecting physical sciences and engineering. Among white males, the only positive marginal effect of having plans for marriage in college was on the probability of selecting business; the marriage variable had a negative effect on the probability of selecting each of the other majors, including science and engineering.

Black women with expectations of marrying while in college were especially less likely to declare biological sciences as their first choice of major. Among Hispanic men marriage had a positive effect on the probability of selecting science and engineering, whereas for Hispanic women marriage plans exhibited the largest negative effect on the probability of selecting biological sciences and the largest positive effect on the probability of choosing "Other," which includes the "undecided major" category and might have indicated a relative lack of commitment to earning a degree. Our question here is how college peers might have impacted those plans.

In the 1980 CIRP follow-up survey, respondents were

asked whether they had ever married. The results for the total sample were strongly in support of the peer influence (and goal commitment) hypothesis: Across the board, marriage impacted the probability of obtaining a college degree far more for women than for men. Among whites the impact was ten times as large for women; among black women it was twice as large; and, consistent with observations made elsewhere herein, Hispanic women were far less likely to have graduated if married, whereas Hispanic men were the only group to show a negative effect from never having married. In other words, having married increased substantially the likelihood that Hispanic men had achieved a degree.

These results may suggest strong support for the importance of socialization and indirectly the role of peers in that process, but also for the role of culture - if indeed these influences can be separated at all. The results from the NLSY are supportive, although the form of the data is somewhat different. Asked at the time of college entrance what they would "like to be doing at age 35," 20% of females, compared to less than 2% of males, selected "married, family." This difference directly demonstrated goals differences by gender, but indirectly may have reflected how those goals came to differ, that is, to some extent at least, through differences in socialization and, specifically, to differences in the influences of peers.

What about the science and engineering students? If we read the literature correctly, peer influence should have a strong effect on the underrepresentation of women, but at what stage of life? Are the effects felt primarily before college, during college, after college, or are they spread evenly across all stages? The answer would appear to be primarily before college, largely because the behavioral changes that begin for women at adolescence are cumulative; deficiencies such as fewer math courses taken often preclude later progress in these fields. The evidence from our empiricism is in two parts. First, female attrition in PSME is roughly the same as for males (NLSY). Indeed, although female attrition is 73% for women in the PSME, overall, compared to 72% for males, attrition in the physical sciences and engineering is actually slightly greater for males than for females, being 75% and 72%, respectively. Only in the biological sciences are the attrition rates uneven, favoring males to a considerable degree. Second, the marginal effect of the marriage variable upon degree attainment in physical sciences and engineering among white women is small, which is perhaps a rather obvious result in light of the fact that female and male attrition rates are about even.

The original CIRP survey in 1971 contained some information that was highly relevant to the peer influence hypothesis, although a direct connection to the importance of peer values is lacking. The primary variables in question reflected incoming students' self-ratings in regard to general popularity and to popularity with the opposite sex. Among five related self-concept variables, popularity with the opposite sex was clearly the most potent predictor of not achieving degrees in the physical sciences and engineering; general popularity also was a negative factor. The literature would suggest that peer influence likely was a primary culprit.

The fact that these patterns did not hold, but rather were very weak for white women in the biological sciences, was consistent with observations made elsewhere herein regarding why these women were less at risk than women in physical sciences and engineering. Finally, the relatively small coefficients for these variables among women in science and engineering almost certainly reflected major self-selection effects; that is, those who place a high value on attractiveness to men are less likely to enter science and engineering in the first place, once again drawing attention to behavioral changes that occur prior to college entrance.

We may also examine labour force status of science and engineering majors. Overall, employment status essentially is unrelated to having been married; however having never been married reduces the probability of full-time employment in science and engineering and increases the probability for the other categories (part-time employment, unemployment, and out of labour force) for white males, while increasing the probability of the former and decreasing the probability of the latter for white females.

Clearly, the effects of peers in socialization take their toll primarily prior to college admission. Perhaps collegiate peers help to prevent women from "catching up" later on. Although the "marriage variable" is at best an indirect measure of possible peer influence, marriage and child-rearing could be viewed as the ultimate tests of the influence of peers in leading women toward what Holland and Eisenhart (1990) call being Educated in Romance and away from science and engineering.

Necessarily, much has already been said about goal commitment. Obviously, self-efficacy and peer influence contribute directly to personal goal commitment. From the literature and from our findings, we infer that science and math self-efficacy largely form in elementary school but are often retarded for women during adolescence by the interaction of physiological changes and peer influences, sometimes resulting in reduced or conflicted commitment to science and engineering study and work.

Commitment is known to be the most potent predictor of persistence in almost all human endeavors. For women, their interactions with parents, K-12 science and math teachers, and peers appear often to lead to formulation of goals that are externally directed; that is, their important life goals frequently are formed largely in response to the desires of others. Women are socialized to seek to please. Thus it is not surprising that most women tend to be interested in careers emphasizing human interaction (as are many men), even if within science and engineering. The evidence is noteworthy.

Both men and women tend to view math and science more as "masculine" fields of study. For men this perception probably reinforces their tendency to persist in these fields; for women the reverse probably is true. Women are attracted to fields seen as more nurturing, fields such as the social sciences and humanities. Men exhibit nurturing behaviours too, but predominantly when that nurturing is in fields perceived to be masculine. For example, men are quite willing to be helpful and supportive of women in math and science classrooms, laboratories, and on math and science homework.

From her study with Hewitt, Seymour (1992) concludes that female self-worth in science and engineering is, in fact, extrinsically based, and that for many females, selection of a college major in science and engineering is externally rather than internally driven. Persistence, too, is connected directly to degree of goal commitment, specifically in engineering. Thus, women, more so than men, require a "genuine interest" in their chosen careers. In short for many women commitment to science and engineering goals may be quite tenuous.

Men are known to be more "single-minded" than women in regard to work and careers, a characteristic suggesting greater science and engineering goal commitment. Women perceive an incompatibility between careers in science and family life, and they see raising a family as an attractive alternative. The effects may be direct. Marion and Coladarci (1993) demonstrate that those women who place a high future value on family are less likely to take science and engineering courses; Seymour (1992) finds that female science and engineering students switch majors due to lack of personal goal commitment; and Lewis (1991) reports that those women who do wind up studying mathematics are "extremely job oriented".

The literature demonstrates that male/female differences regarding career and commitment continue into employment. Employed female scientists and engineers are less involved with their work than are their male counterparts although the gap narrows for those holding master's and doctoral degrees; for both bachelor's and master's degree holders, time for personal lives is rated as more important by women, compared with men. Tobias (1992) raises questions about faculty prejudices against women, in particular bias against women who have strong family commitments.

We would expect that any individual who is marginally committed to any goal, in this case a science and engineering degree, would be less likely to tolerate unsatisfactory or adverse conditions than one who is fully committed. In short, all else equal and on average, men should be more likely than women to persist in science and engineering. Of course, we already know that most female "attrition" in science and math occurs prior to college entrance.

We have already noted that one of the largest family influences on science and engineering outcomes was whether parents were engaged in science and engineering occupations and how the effects were quite different for women and men. We spoke of the more "eclectic" decision structures of women in these regards. Also, we have observed that female commitments to science and engineering goals may be reinforced by having a well-educated mother.

From the CIRP files, commitment was best expressed by one's stated purpose in attending college. For the NLSY sample, identifying the desire to be employed in science or engineering at the age of 35 was easily the strongest predictor of majoring in PSME. The relationships were much stronger for men and for PSME, but also were strong for women and for the biological sciences.

A strong desire to gain a general education and to prepare for graduate or professional school was the measures. Among those who had been enrolled in degree programs in the physical sciences and engineering, white women were less likely than white men to have expressed these goals at the time of admission, and although the stated desire to attend graduate or professional school had positive effects on the probabilities of enrolling in physical sciences or engineering for both white males and white females, these effects were generally higher for white females.

To us, these results emphasize the importance to white females of being committed to science and engineering, if they are to achieve these ends: At the time of admission, white women are less committed to science and engineering, generally, than are white men, but those white women who are committed, as attested to by their graduate or professional school goals, will achieve in science and engineering at relatively high levels.

Arguably, an even stronger indication of commitment is whether one plans science and engineering as a likely career.

In fact, for the CIRP students, specifying science and engineering as one's likely career in 1971 was strongly and positively associated with being employed in a science or engineering occupation in 1980, and for the NLSY subjects, desiring to be "employed as a scientist or engineer at age 35" was the strongest predictor. Further, the effect was noticeably larger for males compared with females and for PSME as opposed to biological sciences. Our conclusion is that, on average, women who select science and engineering majors may be less committed to science and engineering careers, which may be to say that they are more conflicted about career and family.

Probably the greatest realization that has come to us from this work is that studying the phases of science and math education separately is problematic. One cannot understand why women, and to some degree minorities, are underrepresented in science and engineering unless one understands that the related behaviours are formed over at least half a lifetime, but especially in the years prior to college. Although collegiate interventions no doubt can increase female (and minority) participation rates, the critical damage is done much earlier.

The essential proof of this statement is that attrition rates in postsecondary education are very similar for men and women; it is the difference in the numbers of men and women who enter science and engineering curricula, the much-discussed "pipeline effect," that largely explains gender differences in graduation rates, graduate study, and employment in science and engineering. These gender differences also are evident for minorities. Science and engineering matriculation patterns of minority men are far more similar to those of majority men than to minority women.

The gender disparities among minorities are especially large in the PSME, but again it is differences in science and engineering matriculation rates, not persistence rates, that are at odds. The patterns for the biological sciences are more mixed by gender, not only in regard to minority matriculation but also in regard to attrition rates. It is important to note that most of the problems are in the physical sciences and engineering, not in the biological sciences. Students in the biological sciences may be at no greater risk than students in general, or at least causal patterns are not at all clearly evident, even for white females.

The core contributors to participation in science and engineering, particularly PSME, are self-concept/self-efficacy, the influence of peers, and commitment. General self-concept forms at an early age and differentiates into mathematics and verbal self-concepts before adolescence; prior to this time, socializing forces are relatively evenhanded in the treatment of boys and girls, although the seeds of later disparities clearly have been sown through differential socialization.

Adolescence is the critical period, a time when differentiated self-concepts begin to transform into math and science and other self-efficacies. For girls numerous actions of family members and education personnel, but especially those of adolescent peers, promote values at odds with math and science pursuits. By the beginning of high school, boys possess superior science and math characteristics, compared with girls. As a result, by the end of high school, on average, females have studied less science and math than have males, and the former are behind on many factors that contribute to the pursuit of science and engineering careers.

By this time, on average, female aspirations, expectations, and especially commitments to science and engineering careers are markedly less than for men. Even those women who do enter science and engineering curricula - a group that is already highly "pruned" - are less committed, on average; they are more likely to be conflicted about career versus family. Nevertheless, both men and women respond negatively to many features of science and engineering study, especially in the introductory courses, and most of both genders migrate out of science and engineering, the proportions remaining being about equal. What can be done?

The primary foci must be on early interventions aimed at improving female science and math self-perceptions and counteracting pertinent influences of peers, interventions that will lead to greater science and engineering self-efficacy and commitment. Science and math self-perception is a function of one's knowledge of math and science concepts and one's confidence in math and science. Special efforts to expose female and minority students to elective math and science courses in their pre-college years is important to enhancing both the skill acquisition and the confidence necessary to making science a feasible choice for a college major.

Increasing math and science course requirements should not be precluded. To reap the benefits from skill acquisition, female and minority students must come to believe that they can use math and science tools effectively. We have some ideas about the kind of environments that might contribute to improved science and engineering self-efficacy and commitment, in particular for women.

Families clearly can be highly instrumental to the science and engineering related aspirations and commitment of their children. Special attention should be given to matters of early socialization. Proactive rather than reactive strategies probably will prove most useful. A specific example of the power of early socialization is seen in how the educational levels and science and engineering occupations of parents impact the science and engineering achievements of their children. Why not exploit this relationship (as some programs already are doing), not only for the children of such professionals but also for females and minorities who lack such parents? Why not expose many more female and minority youth to the work environments of female and minority scientists and engineers? And why not target such youth for recruitment to science and engineering careers?

Clearly, we must develop also more and better interventions for the adolescent years, especially in support systems. Strategies might include focus groups that would make girls and minorities aware of how their aspirations are formed, in particular the role of peers, and how powerful can be the detractors from science and engineering careers. Individual counseling sessions probably should follow. One obvious strategy is to make girls aware, early on, of the costs of adherence to peer norms, for example, the costs of avoiding math and science courses in high school and the way they come to gain their perceptions of their own science and math abilities, skills, and attitudes.

At the postsecondary level, it is not uncommon for some colleges and universities to structure student living arrangements according to various "themes." Consideration should be given to structuring housing arrangements so that female and minority science and engineering majors can live in proximity to one another, thus permitting the reinforcement of science and engineering goals and proactively working against detractions. Professional counseling and counseling by science and engineering faculty probably would be productive, too.

Space limitations have caused us to concentrate here on what appear to be the central factors contributing to underrepresentation of women and minorities in science and engineering; however, our primary omissions have been of additional aspects of our three central factors, rather than of some unidentified factors. That is, we believe that other factors, such as education personnel, teaching methods, and structural traits, exert their influences chiefly through our three central concepts. What follows are a few illustrations of these additional aspects.

Evidence exists that in the high-school years, though well-meaning, science and math teachers fail to challenge young women as much as they should. Treating women as "the weaker sex" is no favor to them, at least when science and engineering careers are considered. Science and math teachers should interact with their female students with no more delicacy than they do their male students. They should challenge them, engage them rigorously in discussions, and expect high performance of them. They should insist that females, as well as males, do their own lab work, answer difficult questions, and justify their responses; in short, they should engage their female students much more in the give-and-take of intellectual discourse and provide them much less in the way of deferential, unchallenging treatment.

If these and other such approaches were carried out in precollege years, the problems of the college years would be more manageable; however, there still would remain the need to address many structural issues in college-level science and engineering programs, especially in the introductory courses. In the end the issue for science and engineering education will be how to make necessary changes while maintaining high quality. Science and engineering course work is rigorous, on average requiting more time and effort than course work in most other fields.

Science and engineering programs usually attract more highly able students than do most other fields and on average produce relatively competent graduates; yet, the criticisms of these programs by their students, white men as well as others, cannot be discounted. We wonder, for example, whether in introductory physical sciences courses there are not better alternatives to the almost exclusive reliance upon mathematically based problem solving, whether a greater mix of strategies might not yield superior results? We wonder why cooperative learning strategies could not be encouraged, and why science and engineering faculty might not be persuaded to encourage rather than discourage students to persist in science and engineering programs?

Our sense is that if science and engineering faculty merely became aware of the implications of many of their present practices they would be able to design adaptive strategies that would increase, not decrease, their program quality, overall. Our observations in outstanding science and engineering programs in private liberal arts colleges tell us that the proposed changes are clearly possible, even likely, where faculty sense that course enrollments must be maintained in order to maintain program viability. Perhaps the incentives and disincentives are not yet adequate in larger and public institutions.

We note the promise of one particular technique for environmental enhancement of science and engineering units. We observe from our findings that coming to know a professor or administrator is especially important for women in terms of raising the probabilities of persisting to higher degrees in the physical sciences and engineering. This finding supports considerable personal testimony from science and engineering professionals, especially members of minority groups, who emphasize that it was a particular individual, usually a faculty member, who was instrumental in their science and engineering persistence and success.

Finally, in this work we have set aside value judgments on whether women and minorities ought to pursue educational and career goals identical to those of men, either in general or in science and engineering in particular. Rather, our intent has been to shed light on what factors can improve the prospects of underrepresented groups entering and succeeding in science and engineering fields, should they choose to do so, in other words, the enhancement of free and open choices.

10

Development of Women in Information Technology

Progress in science and technology is critical to the ability of U.S. organizations to stay competitive in a global marketplace, as well to continuous improvements in the standard of living American workers expect. In today's world of e-commerce and instant communication, companies depend on technological and computer expertise at all employment levels. Therefore, jobs in information technology and related fields have increased dramatically in recent years, and this trend is expected to continue well into the future.

THE INFORMATION TECHNOLOGY JOB SECTOR

The Information Technology Association of American (ITAA) estimates the U.S. information technology (IT) workforce in the range of 3.6 million workers, and IT employment is projected to be among the fastest growing, according to Hecker (1999). Database administrators, computer support specialists, and all other computer scientists are projected to increase 118%; computer engineers, 109%; systems analysts, 103%; and computer programmers, 23%. Kurtz (2003) notes that eight of the 10 fastest-growing U.S. occupations from 2000 to 2010 were in information technology. Additionally, employment in industries peripheral to high-tech but generated by purchases of high-technology industries has also increased substantially.

Substantial evidence documents the importance to organizational effectiveness of skilled and motivated IT workers. In a survey of information technology executives, conducted by the ITAA and published by the U.S. Department of Commerce, "50% cited a lack of skilled/trained workers as 'the most significant barrier' to their companies growth during the next year." This was viewed as a greater problem than economic conditions, profitability and lack of capital investment, taxes or regulation.

An additional 20% of the IT executives reported that the shortage was a barrier to their companies' immediate growth. Further, an international survey of approximately 1,500 chief information officers conducted by Deloitte & Touche Consulting Group, cited in the same article, noted that IT managers throughout the world were experiencing a difficult combination of unprecedented demand for IT workers and high turnover rates, reported to be as high as 45%.

In addition, this 1997 U.S. Department of Commerce report discussed the alarming possibility that the nation's ability to develop innovative products would be inhibited due to a shortage of IT workers, resulting in both a reduction of U.S. competitiveness as well as a constraint on economic growth. Just to be able to staff their organizations, IT hiring managers will be required to pay close attention to the career development issues facing their employees.

CAREER ISSUES IN INFORMATION TECHNOLOGY

Defining "information technology" is subjective because it involves different types of industries and firms. The U.S. Congressional Office of Technology Assessment defines "high technology" firms as those engaged in designing, developing, and introducing new products and processes. According to the Department of Labour, the IT industry includes all scientists, engineers, and technicians who create and apply new technologies regardless of their industry.

Other occupations within IT include engineers, scientists, mathematical and computer specialists, technicians, managers of these positions, as well as those involved in delivering products or services within technology. The complexity and variety of skill sets required within IT contributes to career issues that are unique to employees in this industry. For purposes of this study, we use the following broad definition of information technology: "a term that covers all forms of technology used to create, store, transmit, interpret, and manipulate information in its various formats".

Information technology employees require extensive knowledge of the theories and principles within their field, as well as hands-on training in hardware and software applications. Therefore, most IT workers need specialized post-high school education, which may range from an associate degree to a doctorate. During the last 10 years, the number of students receiving university degrees in computer science has actually declined. The U.S. Department of Education reports that the number of bachelor-level computer science degrees awarded by American universities declined more than 40% between 1986 and 1994.

Research has begun to address some of the key career development issues of IT employees. Finegold, Mohrman, and Spreitzer (2002) looked at the age of technical workers (under 30, 31-45, and over 45), their organizational commitment and their willingness to change companies. Tan and Hunter (2003) also explored factors affecting IT personnel turnover, such as project challenges and opportunity for personal growth. Igbaria, Parasuraman, and Badawy (1994) examined measures of work attitudes, such as job involvement and quality of work life, in their study of information systems staff.

Appelbaum, Ayre, and Shapiro (2002) assessed the outcomes of career management and development within three different organizations in the IT sector. According to Lee (2002), IT professionals reported greater career satisfaction under circumstances of professional enhancement related to career planning and strategy. Some studies have looked at the relationship between technology and other work variables (e.g., a special 2003 issue of the Journal of Vocational Behaviour), such as technology-enabled work, on-line/virtual teams, and telecommuting.

GENDER AND CAREER ISSUES IN IT

In this exploratory study, we examine another dimension of the broad arena of IT careers: the link between gender and career and personal outcomes among IT professionals. The gender gap in the U.S. workplace as a whole has been documented for decades by scholars. While statistics show that women have indeed made significant gains in employment and wage parity over the years, research continues to find that the salaries of females do not progress at the same rate as those of comparable males.

In fact, a high-level woman within any industry is still rare. Meyerson and Fletcher (2000) report that women compose 10% of senior managers in Fortune 500 companies, less than 4% of the ranks of CEO, president, executive vice president and COO, and less than 3% of top corporate earners. Even though progress has been made toward equality in the workplace, Rheem notes that women still experienced unfair treatment and negative attitudes on the job.

The gender gap appears to be even wider in the IT arena, at all levels of employment. The ITAA estimate of women workers in the overall IT workforce dropped from 41% to 35% between 1996 and 2002. According to Women at Work (2003), a recent research report published by the American Association of University Women (AAUW) Educational Foundation, a national organization that promotes education and equity for women and girls, women account for only 25% of professional IT workers. A recent survey of IT executives published by eWeek suggested that men outnumber women in IT leadership positions by over six to one, and only about 11% of the top 500 U.S. technology companies have women corporate officers.

Gender issues in IT may begin as early as middle school. According to another AAUW Educational Foundation study, many girls find computer work tedious, sedentary, and anti-social. Through high school, girls are less likely than boys to enroll in computer science classes, and the disparity increases in more advanced classes. ITAA data show that women earned only 22% of all computer science and engineering undergraduate degrees in 2000, a figure that has not changed since 1998 despite the rapid growth in the technology field (and commensurate employment opportunities).

Sherry Turkle, professor of sociology at Massachusetts Institute of Technology and co-chair of the commission overseeing the AAUW research, notes, "The commission makes it clear that girls are critical of the computer culture, not computer phobic. Instead of trying to make girls fit into the existing computer culture, the computer culture must become more inviting for girls." During a panel discussion held during the winter of 2000 at Loyola University Chicago, a discussion of how to involve high school girls in technology supported the AAUW study findings.

For example, both panelists and participants commented that girls may not be encouraged to explore new skills or tinker with objects, at least to the degree that boys are. Further, girls may have more difficulty in taking risks and may set unrealistically high standards for themselves, both potential liabilities in the fluid, ambiguous world of information technology.

The differences between women and men's approaches to the field of information technology may be heightened by societal and cultural differences in the U.S. workplace as a whole. For example, numerous scholars have argued that women may seek to avoid the politics and tokenism of corporate America. Meyerson and Fletcher (2000) suggest that as women approach the top levels of a firm, they may become disillusioned with the corporate ladder and jump off. Yet the U.S. Small Business Administration estimates that 9.1 million women own businesses in the U.S., almost 40% of all businesses. Women may be disillusioned by business practices in industries that are male dominated and thus may be starting their own firms.

Moore and Buttner (1997) linked a woman's leaving an organization to start her own business to career frustration, and the 129 female entrepreneurs in their research pool were able to incorporate previous career frustrations into positive aspects for their new companies. A similar career strategy among IT workers was identified by Lee (2002), who called it "technopreneurship"-IT professionals setting up their own technology-related businesses.

A subtle illustration of gender differences in IT is reflected in the design of high-technology products. Anita Borg, founding director of the worldwide Institute for Women and Technology and founder of Systers, an international electronic community for technical women in computing, is credited with leading a worldwide movement to improve the relationship between women and technology. Borg noted that personal digital assistants and handheld devices were designed to fit in a breast pocket, while pagers and cell phones clip onto a belt. How many women tote their handheld devices in a breast pocket or clip a pager to a belt clip?

In this chapter, we address some key career issues affecting all IT professionals, with a special emphasis on women. Our interviews focused on work preparation for current position, professional goals, work environment, flexibility, balance between work and professional realms, and the perception of gender equality in areas such as job security, promotions, and pay. The results provide some useful insights for companies that depend on retaining and motivating IT staff.

Twenty interviews were conducted with individuals in various areas of IT who held a variety of positions in for-profit and nonprofit organizations, including executives, managers, consultants, and academics. A detailed summary of the respondents, including titles, tenure in IT, and type of employer, is provided. In addition, we were able to follow up with 12 of these 20 respondents in 2004 to determine their current positions. Eight of 12 had stayed within IT, while four left to enter completely different fields, ranging from physical therapy to real estate.

As shown, length of time in the industry ranged from three months to over 21 years; range in their current role was from one week to over 21 years. The average length of time in the IT industry was 4.9 years, while the average length of time in the position was 2.6 years (due to reported job changes, including promotions). Three of the interviewees, 15%, were born outside the U.S. There were 12 females and eight males (60% and 40%, respectively). The age range was 18 through 55, though the distribution was heavily concentrated in the 25-34 group.

During the interview process, the respondents were given the option of completing the interview via e-mail or face-to-face. Twelve of the interviews were completed via e-mail and eight in person. The respondents were all personal or professional contacts of the principal investigator, who conducted all 20 interviews. While this sample was not ideal, as it included people known to the researcher, it did permit probing for personal factors as well as professional gender and career issues. We examined length of interview transcripts as well as the questions addressed, and concluded that the interview format did not appear to affect data collection and results.

Interviewees were asked about various aspects of their professional life, including their background and preparation, their work environment, and their balance of work and personal obligations. Respondents were also asked to share their perceptions on the status of women within the technology industry as well as their position.

The qualitative interview data were organized and content analyzed as follows: The principal investigator typed transcriptions of all 20 interview notes and constructed an Excel table of the results. To maintain consistency, the principal investigator reviewed and unitized every interview text into a series of sentences and brief phrases. The data were then organized into categories, searching for emerging themes, first within an interview and then across the series of interviews. This process is similar to Tan and Hunter's use of narrative inquiry in their study of information systems professionals (2003). Our search of emerging themes, coupled with the Excel table of the respondents' comments, provided the means for searching for patterns in the data.

The data results are grouped into three general categories: individual career issues, elements of the IT work environment, and gender and career issues in IT. While our sample size was limited, our respondents nonetheless provided some intriguing insights into the job of the information technology professional.

Seventy-five percent of our interviewees reported that some form of education had prepared them for their current position. However, the range of education varied widely, from technical to general, and included both degree programs and individual courses in the following areas: economics, computer science, computer applications, business administration, engineering, library sciences, liberal arts, and psychology. One respondent said that his "liberal arts background helped him to be a free thinker," which is necessary to solve problems within the ambiguity of technology business development. Additional educational preparation included courses in areas of programming, e-commerce, and information systems.

Participants reported a wide range of sources for additional preparation, including prior work experience, both within their current organization and external. Only 15% of the respondents reported that their prior work preparation in the same area of their same organization helped them fulfill their present responsibilities. This is understandable since many were new to their current position and had noted elsewhere in the interview that they were self-motivated learners (thinking ahead to the next new challenge versus being content in one role for any length of time).

Other additional preparations included formal and informal "lessons." Formal preparation included computer courses or related technical training, technology conferences/ Internet seminars and certifications, while informal preparation included mentoring and self-motivation. The latter was a common theme throughout this research; many respondents viewed asking questions and being a self-starter as a key to their success. This supports research in other industries about the importance of informal, on-the-job learning.

Other themes in our interviews were being able to "go with the flow" and being comfortable with a rapidly changing environment. Interviewees reported excitement and enthusiasm at learning new things, rather than dismay that there was no "tried and true" path. The areas that had the most impact on people's ability to perform their current job included coursework, work experience, and, most notably, mentoring and being a self-motivator. Specific nontechnical skills considered important included "people skills." As one participant commented, "I learned people skills, not 'teachable' skills. I can't say enough how important that is, no matter what you do."

PROFESSIONAL GOALS

Ninety percent of respondents had not completed all of their career goals (even the highly accomplished said "there is much more to be done"). These individuals viewed life and career as a series of steps, versus one end goal, with the common theme of lifelong learning and challenges. One interviewee viewed "life as a series of professions" and another echoed the view that "when I stop learning, it's time to move on to something else." Despite accomplishments in many areas, many felt that they had "only just begun." Our results support Lee's findings (2002) concerning the importance of career strategy and professional enhancement among IT professionals. Tan and Hunter (2003) also found that the majority of their sample of IT personnel considered themselves "problem solvers."

As shown, 55% of interviewees reported working in an environment that was teamwork-based and relied on questions to learn and be productive as a team.

The IT environment and its reliance on teamwork and asking questions becomes especially important when linked with the interview data about professional goals. Respondents reported that to advance professionally, they needed to learn by asking questions and being self-motivated. Representative comments about teamwork included:

- There is a lot of open exchange of knowledge and help when needed.
- We work together to make sure that the areas where our work will overlap each other goes smoothly.

- I work in an open and flexible environment where you can feel comfortable and ask for help anytime you need to.
- It's a very tight knit group and very supportive.

Participants also reported working with a diverse group of individuals on a daily basis. This is not surprising considering that the interviewees were all from different areas of IT, and IT can affect an entire organization. Representative comments regarding this subject are as follows:

- I work with a large variety of people in different contexts ... they tend to be very gifted in their careers.
- My immediate group ranges from liberal to conservative and are an incredibly diverse group ... they are all very competitive with a common passion for technology.

A common passion for IT was evident regardless of whether the work culture was traditional or nontraditional. One interviewee described her environment as "working in a culture of contrasts, both is equally passionate and committed to technology." Speaking of his employees, another participant said, "Most would consider their work also as their hobby".

Flexibility of hours worked. Three-fourths of the interviewees reported that their required work hours were flexible, while the rest reported they were not. However, many participants said they worked long hours, so that even though their hours were flexible, they worked the traditional hours in addition to evenings and weekends. One interviewee stated with a smile, "I can pick my 18 hours [per day] any time I want them," and another admitted that "like 90% of driven professionals, I work too much."

Work versus personal life balance. Despite the long hours reported, 70% of our respondents believed they had a good balance between work and personal life, while the remainder reported an imbalance. One reason for this pattern of results may be our small sample, which was heavily concentrated in a younger, childless age group. Of those who felt they had a good balance, a few said they had a balance because they had chosen it. One individual shared this about her company's expectations.

I personally have a good balance because I make an effort. The duties here are endless and the pressure to continue education is high. The typical person who succeeds here is one who is not married, has no children and dedicates their life to their job. Although I am dedicated, I do not sacrifice my personal life for a career gain.

Other participants within the 70% reported that they had balance because their organizations valued personal and family time, even sponsoring events for the employee and his or her family and friends. As one person stated, "The Company values family so there is that balance. It's an organizational value."

GENDER AND CAREER ISSUES IN IT

Equal treatment: industry and position. Overall, 60% of our participants reported that within the industry women were not treated equally to their male counterparts, while 80% report that within their position (or comparable positions) there was equality. This difference in perception from industry to specific position may be due to the under-representation of women in the field of technology, specifically upper management. Participants cited the number of women as evidence of inequality yet did not have specific examples. A few reported that there are too few women even to comment or speculate as to equal treatment. While our sample size limited the conclusions we can draw, summarizes some interesting comparisons provided by our respondents.

Interviewees were also asked to share their perception of the treatment of women within their industry and their position along specific dimensions, including: sexual harassment, derogatory language to women, and stereotyping women's skill sets. Overall, participants perceived that there were differences in treatment within the industry, but generally not in their position or current positions. Many also commented that the behaviours they observed or perceived were not industry-specific but occurred in many industries. Interestingly, there was a consistent discrepancy between what participants observed or perceived on a (macro) industry level compared with a (micro) position level.

Participants were also asked if they perceived women within the IT industry to be more vulnerable than men in terms of job security, promotion, equal pay, and balancing work with family. The results for each of the areas differed: the majority of interviewees perceived women as equally vulnerable as men in the realm of job security. One respondent who was undecided reported that it is an issue with both genders, "especially when you get older." Of those who reported an inequality, they attributed it to women being able to bear children and felt that pregnancy can affect job security.

Promotion was the category that was most closely and evenly split and also had the fewest "undecided/depends." Of those who felt that women were more vulnerable, the topic of women as childbearers again surfaced and comments included, "women with kids can be seen as a liability," and "I don't think women are always considered for promotions because they are seen as having to raise their kids ... hopefully this will change as the new generation of management slowly moves in."

Others report the continued existence of an "old boy network," and women sometimes failing to know about promotional opportunities. Others who were undecided reported that promotions may not be equal, but not because of gender, having observed, "Incompetent men and women promoted and competent men and women passed over." These individuals said that it depended on the organizational culture and "who is at the top making decisions." Interestingly, the interviewee's gender was not a determining factor of the perception of equality.

Equal pay was another issue that was closely split, and, as with promotion, interviewee's gender did not determine their perception. Of those reporting that women are not equal in pay to their male counterparts, two of the seven cited statistics on the amount of money women earn compared with men. For example, according to Messmer's (2003) data, salaries of upper-level IT women hires were estimated to be about 9% lower than those of comparable men.

The area of balancing work and family had the fewest responses supporting the equality of men and women as well as the most "undecided/ depends" responses. Again, gender was not a predicting factor. Of those who perceived equality, it was attributed to working in a flexible industry, one where you can work anywhere and anytime. Of those perceiving inequality, it was attributed to societal expectations that women are in charge of the family unit. One interviewee shared an experience where a male boss wrote up a female subordinate for being late due to a childcare crisis, and the same day let his male staff off early to go to the racetrack. In summary, though there were differences reported between the genders, many were undecided or believed that the organization's culture was the determining factor in a family-oriented company, more balance was accepted and encouraged.

Our research revealed similarities and differences across this small sample of IT professionals. Despite its limited nature, our research nonetheless suggests some interesting elements about career development and gender issues in IT. Across a variety of backgrounds, education was cited as most important to job performance, yet that education varied widely and involved both technical and "softer" skills, such as people management and working with others. This is important because many IT professionals deal with a diverse group of individuals that may include people from client companies (and a potentially different culture).

However, technical education was not reported as the most important skill for success, and interviewees had traveled down a number of career paths to their current positions. Transferable skills and flexibility were key success factors in this dynamic industry, as opposed to others, such as finance or accounting that demand a highly specialized skill set. The first impression of IT may be that a highly specialized skill set could work in one's favor, yet the reality is that with an ever-changing industry, it is more important to be flexible and able to learn the technical aspects along the way (versus as a prerequisite).

The need for flexibility may be unique to the early stages of the IT evolution, and once it takes on a more definite form and labour demands subside, a specialized skill set may become the norm. The industry requires diverse skills, especially when projects have various components and affect many areas of an organization. The team effort and collaboration is required. Having all of the information is not as useful as being able to "go with the flow" and being comfortable with ambiguity, since many IT projects break new ground.

The work environment tends to be based on teamwork and the ability to ask questions to do the job well and ensure continuous learning. Coworkers necessarily rely on others for their expertise and to further their own knowledge, if not to solve the problem at hand. Team-based problem solving is integral to tackling the most difficult problems and it was rare to find within the interviewees any position where it was not needed. The structure of the jobs required reliance on others, even within nontechnical areas of IT.

People with various skill sets were forced to work together, resulting in a diverse group working in sometimes opposing business cultures. But they all shared a passion and commitment to the technology field. The work brought them together and kept them together. Nevertheless, there was evidence of a glass ceiling at some level, and the work characteristics beyond that ceiling may prove very different.

Interviewees reported that even though their hours were flexible, they often worked long hours which could be a problem for those with heavy obligations outside of work. Women in charge of their families may find that in technology, even though the work schedule is allegedly flexible, it is still very demanding. Availability is required of technology workers, and many were at the mercy of their client's business hours. Weekends and lengthy workdays were not uncommon among our interviewees, and promotional opportunities may dwindle for those with heavy family responsibilities, regardless of gender.

The participants in our study generally reported a good work/family balance, perhaps because many are single or had fewer family responsibilities than those in other industries. This may, in fact, be a characteristic of an industry that discourages women from entering the field at all, and undermines a possible first impression that technologists can conduct work 'anywhere, anytime'.

Despite the fact that many reported a gender-based equality within their position, many disbelieved that equality existed within the industry. Since women are not equally represented at higher levels of IT, the macro-perception may be that they are not given equal opportunity, while on the micro-level they seem to have the same opportunities. This difference in perception may also be affected by the level of job attainment, and by a glass ceiling that starts above the general level of those interviewed. It is also possible that IT reflects the same issues and behaviours that are present in other male-dominated industries and is not unlike other industries.

Behaviours such as sexual harassment, derogatory language, and stereotyping of women's skill sets may be equally represented across various industries, as opposed to being IT-specific. Interviewees perceived the area of balancing work and family as being most pertinent to women, in terms of unequal treatment. This could be because women continue to be expected to bear the responsibility as head of the household and, therefore, to have more obligations outside of work than their male counterparts. Individuals reported that this situation may be changing and could be attributed to an "older" school of management thought and would change over time as the "new economy" mentality became part of management. Participants pointed out that in organizations where culture includes a "family value," the balance is much more agreeable and is probably promoted by the employee.

This study was exploratory and included individuals within various areas of IT. Open-ended questions were used to reveal otherwise inaccessible areas that the researcher would then have the freedom to explore. However, this approach limits the ability to generalize the findings within IT. These data do provide interesting preliminary findings about career development issues among IT professionals. One of the challenges is that as the industry evolves, the defining segments and sub-segments may change dramatically, and career progressions will also change.

Continued trend analysis is also useful in tracking changes within this field. Specific areas for future research include expanding participant demographics such as the age range, and interviewing or surveying boys and girls to determine their use and perception of technology. An in-depth analysis of work culture and the status of women within various segments of IT would be useful for determining differences in career attainment and whether there are glass ceilings.

The perception of equality in a position and inequality within the field should be explored. Focusing on the attrition of women in IT and of those seeking a mathematics, engineering, or computer degree may help identify underlying issues. A shift in accepted male oriented business practices and societal perceptions of women's skills may be needed to create true gender equality.

THE GLASS CEILING FOR WOMEN IN TECHNOLOGY

The Information Technology Association of America (ITAA) released a study indicating there are 346,000 vacant IT positions in the United States. Certainly this growing area of computers and technology has lured females in its direction, away from traditional roles and career paths. However, once in the field of IT, the environment may not be as attractive to some women, who find themselves amid the male culture of technology. In 1971, the female portion of computer systems analysts and other specialists was only 9%. By 1990, this proportion had jumped to 35%. In 1996, the Department of Commerce noted a decline in the proportion of females to 30%. A similar trend existed in the women's share of computer and information science bachelor degrees.

Several explanations emerge for why women enter the IT field, exit it, and encounter obstacles to managerial positions within it. For example, glass ceilings for women in IT may result from educational aspects and family characteristics, corporate cultures, or sociological factors. This chapter is the qualitative portion of a large empirical study that asked respondents to complete an on-line questionnaire regarding the glass ceiling for women in technology.

During the initial stage of our work, we contacted members of Systers, an informal on-line organization for women working in the field of information technology. Systers was developed in 1987 as a small mailing list for women in "systems." There are now over 2,500 systems in 25 countries belonging to this organization. We asked Systers members for opinions and comments on both the subject matter and the design and wording of our empirical questionnaire. Sixty respondents indicated willingness to cooperate by completing the survey and commenting on the instrument.

Due to the vast amount of time required to participate, we were not surprised that only 60 of the approximately 2,262 domestic and international members responded. First, the questionnaire was not applicable to individuals not in an intermediate-to-large organization. Several members indicated in e-mail that they are consultants or work in small organizations where promotions are infrequent. Second, some members are in academia where the hierarchy is flat or in positions with no career ladder. Finally, the international dimension suggests that there may be a language barrier for some members, which may explain why all responses were from domestic members.

The number of persons falling into these categories was unattainable. While each member may place a profile of themselves in the Systers database, it is not required, so an exact percentage of respondents was impossible to calculate. However, the women who did respond were eager to express their views, and their intriguing and insightful comments inspired this chapter. Although we received 60 responses, to avoid redundancy we categorized them into three specific areas: educational aspects and family characteristics, corporate cultures, and sociological factors. The comments quoted herein are an attempt to represent everyone who responded to our study.

EDUCATIONAL ASPECTS AND FAMILY CHARACTERISTICS

Educational aspects and family characteristics help explain why women have trouble advancing in the field of IT. The National Science Foundation reports (NSF96-311) that:

- Women still take fewer high-level math and science courses in high school

- Women earn fewer science and engineering bachelor's, master's, or doctoral degrees
- Women remain less likely than white males to be employed in science and engineering
- There is a $13,200 salary gap between men and women with science and engineering doctorates.

While occupations have become less segregated than in the early 1900s, 71% of the men in this country occupy jobs that are 80% male, while 48% of the women hold jobs that are over 80% female. Only five occupational groups, including household worker, service employee, elementary school teacher, secretarial/clerical worker, and nurses, account for approximately three-quarters of all jobs held by women in the United States. More recent information shows the same pattern and suggests that the overall labour market still shows signs of job segregation by sex.

Covert discrimination may begin many years before a woman enters the career path of technology. For example, parental influence has a great impact. Parents are responsible for role modeling in the division of labour in the household as well as in society. Therefore, many little girls learn to be nurturers and caregivers at the same time that little boys learn to be competitive and tough. As adults, these traditional gender roles may be carried into the workplace.

While some families teach their children that women can have career opportunities equal to men, other parents teach their offspring that women should work only when required by financial necessity. Using interviews, Gerson examined the self-reported life histories of 63 women from a variety of class backgrounds, including homemakers, employed mothers, and childless women. Those employed were in both clerical and professional male- and female-dominated occupations. The purpose of this study was to compare women who became domestically oriented with women who pursued work careers to learn how and why their commitments developed.

First, in the traditional model of female development, Gerson found those who choose motherhood over a work career. These women were reared with the knowledge that a woman's place was in the home. Second, Gerson found women who were taught to think they would marry and be homemakers, but circumstances turned out to be different from what they expected. Due to financial problems, a loss of the sense of self, or divorce, these women returned to the workplace to discover that they enjoyed having a career more than staying at home. Unfortunately, when some of these women reentered the workforce determined to move up the corporate ladder, actions to improve their educational qualifications were ignored by their employers. As one woman in our study stated,

Academic degrees and specific training are used as minimum requirements to apply for some positions, but the humorous thing is they are ONLY check-off boxes. (And sometimes we ignore that the required training classes or required degree level are not met by the candidate we hire or internally transfer into the job.) Also, once you are in a job ladder, getting more course-based training or another college degree is never an input to evaluation for promotion.

The third category of women found by Gerson were women reared with the belief that they could have a career, even when that career was in a predominantly male profession. After choosing not to have children, concentrating instead on years of education and training in pursuit of their career goals, they suddenly began to wonder if they should have had children after all. Finally, this study identified women who grew up believing they would have a good career, but suddenly found themselves married and grudgingly lowering their self expectations to accommodate the plans of their husbands.

These women were sometimes in jobs they disliked; they opted for becoming a mother to escape their unpleasant circumstances at work. Thus, it seems that a "feminine personality" did not lead most of the women in this study into the role of motherhood. Instead, many of those who worked viewed motherhood with ambivalence. In addition, some of the women used motherhood to escape unpleasant or stifling work situations. A 1992 report entitled, How Schools

Shortchange Girls, by the American Association of University Women (AAUW) documents a strong correlation between the confidence of female students and their intent to participate in higher educational levels of math and science. Thus, Durack asks if "technology" is considered a male term? Are females subjected to insinuations that they do not belong in technological fields?

Many males self-select out of these areas due to lack of skills, while females avoid these disciplines regardless of their aptitudes. In the book entitled Does Jane Compute?, Roberta Furger brings to the forefront various ways mothers and teachers discourage girls from entering math, science, and computer fields. Not only are these actions a discouragement to young women but they reinforce the male notion that women do not belong. This belief can be carried over into the workplace, strengthening the male-dominated culture. In the words of one respondent,

I actually have had no problems with technical men ... I have had trouble with female bosses, who have basically been quite sexist. My most recent incident involved the job I just left where I was told I was "not technical enough" for my position ... my position/job description is more analytical (I was a senior systems analyst doing intranet analysis/design/programming) than technical. In addition, I was the only programmer in the department; no one else can do more than create some access queries. I also had the most MS certifications in the department.

(How much more technical did I need to be? I later found out that every woman in the department had at some time been told that women in this department were some of the most impressive women I have met in my career. Although most are not college degreed, all were very impressive in their knowledge and skills and their ability to implement those skills.) I don't know if this manager is projecting her lack of technical ability (she is definitely nontechnical) onto other women, or if she just doesn't like women. This same woman, having the opportunity to "get rid of" the laziest member of the department decided not to because apparently he IS technical enough. I smartly got a new job, and no longer work there, but I was wondering if anyone else had these kinds of experiences with female bosses.

CORPORATE CULTURES

The culture of the organization may be another factor resulting in glass ceilings for women in the IT field. In Rosabeth Moss Kanter's look at women's roles in the workplace, she identified four typical categories in which most women could be found. The four roles, mother, confidante, seductress, and pet, are all based on stereotypical expectations of women in many organizational cultures. When women in the workplace fall outside these four categories, they are considered deviants and ostracized. In some company cultures, merely being labeled as "feminist" holds negative consequences.

Since repeated observation of a phenomenon may cause schemas to change and subschemas to form, continuous exposure to traditional roles or characteristics in gender-segregated departments may create more traditional gender schemas, which strengthen as tenure increases. On the other hand, individuals in desegregated departments should be more aware of egalitarian roles and attitudes and hold more nontraditional gender schemas, with the strength of these schemas also increasing with time. Thus, the length of time individuals spend in a segregated or desegregated department may affect their gender schema content, and, thus, their attitudes.

Rosemary Wright researched the trends of women entering and existing fields of Information Technology. The result of her work, the "Controlled Progress" theory, combines Kanter's Tokenism Theory and Jacob's Social Control Theory. Kanter's theory suggests that women do poorly in male-dominated organizations because they are few in number, or tokens. Wright's research found that as the proportion of women in IT increased, the segregation within the occupation declined and the earnings gap narrowed. The women were no longer tokens. Jacob's Social Control Theory suggests that "women receive lifelong social control messages about male-dominated occupations: They do not belong and should not be in them.

As a result, women decline to enter male-dominated majors and occupations and choose to leave male-dominated majors and occupations." In her study of women entering and exiting computer-related occupations, Wright noted that women leave computer work more than men when controlling for differences in background, education, experience, specialty, and industry. In general, women can more easily enter IT fields and acquire salaries close to that of their male counterparts. However, pressures exerted by the culture found in these occupations result in their leaving.

It is not surprising that researchers have had trouble categorizing the barriers to advancement for women. As evidenced by the following respondent's comment, even the women in IT sometimes have trouble classifying the cause of their situation. In the last promotion I tried for, I didn't get the job even though I was the only candidate with experience and had proven I could to the job by being acting manager. The candidates were a white male, a white female (me), and a Chinese female. I was ranked second by all the interviewers because the inexperienced white male was more enthusiastic than I. The interviewers were all male, all white except for one Hispanic. I am in a group where the males are more comfortable with each other than with women. I find it hard to believe that if the white male had the experience, and I had the enthusiasm, the outcome would have been different.

I had difficulty in trying to define that [experience] and past experiences by the categories in the survey:

1. Educational qualifications (was not an issue, all met the educational requirements)
2. Quality of performance on the job (our ranking in our jobs is not known by the interviewers, only our reputations, and I do not believe this was an issue for any of the candidates)
3. Length of time employees have held their current positions (did not matter to the interview process)
4. Length of time employees have worked for the organization (did not matter to the interview process).

Thus, corporate culture can have an effect on women's ability to advance in IT. One CIO notes that there are a variety of management skills. A willingness to accept a diversity of skills is the single factor that can promote women's success. Consequently, the unwillingness to accept skill diversity results in a much more male-dominated culture. This impediment to advancement may also lead to women exiting the field.

Conversely, one empirical study, suggests factors beyond male culture as contributing to the small proportion of women in IT management. Igbaria and colleagues (1997) suggest that the limited representation of women in managerial jobs is largely a function of their relative youth and limited period of work experience within the profession. Both women and men reported similar perceptions of the likelihood of promotion in the organization. Consider the following response.

... being at the "bottom of the food chain," it's hard for me to have a lot of opinions about promotion at the upper levels. Other people may feel that way as well. Promotions to low-level and midlevel management positions really aren't the issue in the glass ceiling, it's those senior vice presidents. Now we have only one female vice president, but it's hard for me (having only worked here for a few years, and not being interested personally in a vice presidency anyway) to say why (though I do have my opinions).

Note that the women who have succeeded in attaining high-level managerial positions in IT are likely to have had business training and emphasize their business skills over technical expertise. Thus the perception of gender bias in promotion decisions would appear to be nonexistent for some. The following examples are also indicative that not all women perceive a glass ceiling in their organizations.

I work for a small company as a government contractor, and the environment I work in would include the larger Government Agency, where several civil service, contractors, and military [employees] work. I have been with this organization for nine years now, and I have seen the environment change dramatically from a rather female-hostile one to a more neutral one. This is partly due to having more women in the Agency now, but also going through several "field tests" that were difficult, but gained the trust of the "men in charge."

Another female IT employee in our study responded similarly. I'm aware that there is a glass ceiling at some organizations, and I've known women who have encountered obstacles (but who, for whatever reason, are reluctant to mention them), but my own career has suffered no bafflers. It might be because I work at a startup software company that's growing so fast that opportunities for advancement abound for everyone, and because everyone is much more focused on finding quality people than on trying to keep some people down. Recruitment is such a big challenge for us that no one would consider turning away a qualified candidate.

Considering the above statements, small entrepreneurial firms seem less discriminating toward women employees than large corporations. However, when considering the next comment from another woman in our study, one might reconsider. Answering the questions of why more women did not respond to our questionnaire review request, she stated,

Self deception. If they suspect a glass ceiling, they may just pretend it doesn't exist for them or tell them that they'll be an exception. They may try to ignore the entire issue.

It's every depressing to internalize the knowledge that the bottom line is that you're not going anywhere in a particular job regardless of how good you are. I think it's natural to avoid it as long as you possibly can. Your survey probably hit some buttons.

I know of a true story where someone told a group of high school interns (girls) that she had never felt discriminated at work. And I believe that she believed that statement. But I knew that the previous year she had been excluded from a short list because the selection committee refused to consider a woman.

SOCIOLOGICAL FACTORS

Another hindrance to the advancement of women in IT may stem from sociological origins. Igbaria and colleagues conducted a study to develop a profile of IT personnel. They looked at demographics in terms of education and experience, family characteristics, career orientations, job function, and career history and attainments. Their findings suggest a significant relationship between gender and education with a larger number of women in the sample ending their formal education after attaining a bachelor's degree. Their sample also suggested that women were less likely to marry than men, and married women were less likely to have children than were married men. This may be an indication that women in the IT field anticipate difficulties in balancing their career and family responsibilities.

Much of the origin of gender segregation in the U.S. stems from internalized social values and beliefs that foster ideas of unequal access. From early childhood, girls and boys are socialized in different ways, with the socialization of males being closer to management training than that of females. For example, boys are taught to be competitive and aggressive, while girls are taught to be passive and dependent. Thus, individual career choices are influenced by teachers, peers, parents, and counselors who may direct boys and girls toward traditional gender-role jobs.

Nadelson also found that locus of control, fear of success, and sex-role orientation also influence the career choice of women. Women with high internal locus of control are more likely to succeed in nontraditional areas, while androgynous women are less likely to regulate their behaviour according to cultural prescriptions, also making success in nontraditional areas more likely. Igbaria and Baroudi focused their research on gender differences in career advancement prospects and the effects of job performance on those prospects within the IT workplace. They found no association between gender and job performance ratings and attributions. However, they did find that the effect of job performance evaluations on attributions is much stronger among males than females. In other words, supervisors were unlikely to attribute the performance of female IS employees to efforts and skills but rather to luck or lack of task difficulty. Thus, women were seen as less promotable than men.

While some technical wizards are promoted to management and fall, others may not be given the opportunity. There are indications that a glass ceiling does exist in the IT world. Information Week provided a list of the 500 leading IT users in 1996. Women held the highest-ranking IT position at about 7% of these organizations. Another indication of the scarceness of females in high ranking IT positions is the composition of membership in the Society for Information Management (SIM), an organization of senior IT executives, Of SIM's 2,700 members only 195 were women.

A survey conducted by New York research firms of senior women executives reported 52% of the respondents, including IS professionals, found "male stereotyping and preconceptions about women" as the biggest factors holding back their careers. A perfect example of this impediment exists in the following woman's response:

Women don't get promoted because they have to fight to be assigned any projects of "value" and promotion at my company is based on your "results" and the value of those results to the corporation. I actually think being measured on your results is a good thing, but if I can only be assigned low-value projects then by definition my value is low. Hence the evaluation and promotion procedure looks very, very fair. Problem is that without good assignments I can't get the right inputs to put into that very fair process. [Same person in a later response] Many people focus on the evaluation and promotion process itself. Even if this process is good and fair, the process that inputs to that process can be broken. This is what is happening in my company. The process is broken one step earlier! This doesn't really make the situation any better. I now have the (possibly invalid) theory that companies have focused on ensuring fair treatment in:

- Job hiring practice
- Evaluation and promotion practice

But have not fixed the problem in the middle. The hiring and promotion practice is controlled by the Human Resources department and they oversee every little step in those processes. But assigning projects, etc. is a day-to-day process that goes on in individual groups. Corporate Human Resources cannot control all of that behaviour process. Hence, women get assigned less important projects and we get the end result I am seeing. Have you heard others voice this view?

Thus, technical skills are necessary but not sufficient for promotion in some organizations. Business skills and people skills are also required. The technie must be able to relate to nontechnical people as well. McGee reports 40% of recently promoted managers (both male and female) in all industries quit or are demoted within 12 months. The largest factor contributing to failures by technical managers is that they do not possess the people skills needed to manage others effectively (McGee, 1996).

Anecdotal evidence of advancement obstacles is plentiful. Comments from the women in our study, as well as several other female IT executives (DiDio, 1998), reveal potential barriers and provide suggestions for career advancement. Three general categories emerged in our study as potential barriers to the advancement of women in IT fields: educational aspects and family characteristics, corporate cultures, and sociological factors. Suggestions for increasing promotion opportunities include more networking for women, coordinating career and family planning, being confident and aggressive in assignments, as well as being technically competent and avoiding the "woman thing."

From the helpful comments of our respondents, we can conclude that finding a solution to the glass ceiling for women in technology may be more complicated than even our best researchers had concluded in the past. As one participant put it, I have worked outside academia and have worked with computers for about 25 years. How do I separate out the problem in computers from the general corporate problem of overlooking competent women? When I interact with my technical colleagues at the University, never had a problem in terms of recognition of professional competence, but they in turn have nothing to do with my tenure/promotion at my current job. Equally well qualified women do not get to the same opportunities as their male peers. But, how exactly you get to this using quantitative research methodology is, I believe, problematic.

Perhaps, in spite of the fact that computers are viewed as very black and white, those of us who deal with computers and their problems know all too well the ambiguity and workarounds we have to use, and look at forced choice questions as not reflecting our experience in the workplace, i.e., we are used to having to consider many options to solve the questions that confront us daily and are too accustomed to saying, "Well, maybe it's this, but it could be that."

While our study resulted in very insightful and interesting comments, several limitations exist. For example, many of the women contacted removed themselves from the study because they felt their situations were not applicable. Take, for instance, the following comment. I took a look at your survey after this second request. As I'd surmised from your first posting, I don't fit the profile of [the] person you're trying to survey; to wit, I am a consultant, have been for over 8 years, love what I do, and avoid the entire "glass ceiling" issue by not being part of any individual corporate structure. I'm well aware of glass ceiling problems at some of my clients, but I'm not an employee, and can't give a definitive answer for any particular company.

As can be surmised from the proceeding comment, we can learn much from the individuals who do not fit the profile of the original questionnaire. For example, we can see that this particular person elected to leave the corporate environment to avoid the glass ceiling. Questions with a focused qualitative origin may have resulted in more in-depth information. Another limitation concerns the source of the data. As one participant notes:

Systers might not be the best place to look for glass-ceiling experiences. This is pure speculation, but a lot of women I have known who have hit a ceiling aren't on lists like these. Sometimes, they drop out altogether, and sometimes they're just not as connected to organizations like this. It is possible that the women on Systers have had more success in their careers than other women. The fact that they're on this list suggests that they might be more aware of the problems in the workplace with regards to women, and so are more aware of ways to combat it.

The issue of privacy on the Internet also surfaced. As one member noted, most women on the list are currently employed. She states, although this list is supposed to be private, nothing on the Internet can really be made secure. Posting information anywhere that one is dissatisfied with one's job, and especially that one's company is sexist, could have a severe impact on one's career. Even posting such things about a former employer could affect how a person was seen by a potential future employer.

One of the comments we received also suggested an area for future research. Many of our targeted respondents were working as independent contractors. They suggested that we conduct a survey on this category of employees "with questions on how men and women are treated differently by the businesses contracting work with them." Due to the results reported herein, I would also suggest the questions be open-ended and broader than in our original study.

We have yet to determine whether corporate cultures and society's biases will halt the advancement of women in the IT profession or if the severe shortage of IT skills will balance the equation. Until the gender disparities in IT are eliminated, the Internet provides a means of uniting women throughout the industry. Web sites, such as Systers, provide a forum for women to discuss sex discrimination and a multitude of other topics relevant to women in the information technology field. Meanwhile, one thing seems to be certain in the field of IT, at least for some women. As evidenced by one respondent, "Yes - the glass ceiling is real, and my face is pressing against it right now!" No Longer "One of the Boys": Negotiations with Motherhood, as Prospect or Reality, among Women in Engineering.

Women who train and work as professional engineers in Canada and other industrialized countries are women operating on male turf. Unlike professions such as medicine and law, both of which are much closer to gender parity, engineering remains "archetypically masculine". In spite of nearly two decades of "women into engineering" campaigns supported by government and industry, the numbers of women entering engineering have been described as "derisory in most countries". The Canadian Council of Professional Engineers (CCPE) notes that, though the proportion of women in Canadian engineering schools increased annually after 1972, in the last few years it has levelled off at about 20%. While hardly derisory, these numbers fall far short of gender parity.

Retention of women in engineering over the long haul is also likely to be a problem given that the growth in numbers of those actually practising the profession is among women in their late 20s and early 30s. These women are also at the age where family formation becomes salient. The arrival of children seems to be one critical point at which women, but not men, leave the profession, move to part-time work, and in many other ways put their careers "on the back burner".

Motherhood, it seems clear, is a significant watershed, and one that policymakers and others concerned about retaining women in engineering should take seriously. But the reasons why it is such a watershed-and hence what needs to be done to compensate for its effects-may be more complicated than the conventional explanations about work and family balance suggest. A more elaborated explanation is that motherhood, as embodied and material experience, exposes a major fallacy inherent in the liberal discourses of equality and gender neutrality, which establish the terms for women's entry into male-dominated occupations and workplaces in the first place. These terms allow women to enter, not as women, but as conceptual men.

This conceptual cover is blown when they become, or think about becoming, mothers. For many women (especially those who themselves internalize the gender neutrality discourse), actual or prospective motherhood compels them to confront identities as "engineer" and "mother" that may be "mutually incongruous" (Jorgenson, 2000: 7) and require complex negotiation and management. In this chapter I examine this more nuanced explanation, and explore its implications for all women in engineering, whether or not they are or will become mothers.

WOMEN IN A MAN'S WORLD

The experiences of women on male-dominated turf have perhaps been most closely documented in Kanter's landmark study of women salespersons in the formerly all-male sales force of a Fortune 500 company in the United States. This study introduced the concept of tokenism to many researchers in the field of work and organizations. Kanter's research predated the large-scale entry of women into the professions (and, by extension, into many male-dominated workplaces) since the 1970s. Much of this expansion was impelled and facilitated, in the wake of the second wave of the women's movement, by a discourse of liberal feminism whose goals included equality for women and men under the law, and the same employment opportunities for working women as those enjoyed by men.

Unlike Kanter's tokens, more recent women entrants to male-dominated occupations have had more legal, and, increasingly, cultural support for their presence on male turf. But while the terms of their participation have changed somewhat, the difficulties foreshadowed in Kanter's study (difficulties which Kanter herself thought force of numbers would help to eliminate) did not instantly disappear. A 1992 report by the Canadian Committee on Women in Engineering cited many stories of sexism, systemic discrimination and workplace inequality, and a series of "common and difficult" barriers faced by women engineers.

Why should such barriers persist, especially in a discursive climate of gender equality and "family-friendly" workplaces? Acker contends that organizations are not gender-neutral spaces that women may enter on the same footing as men; neither can a "job" be defined as abstract and gender-neutral, performed by an abstract and disembodied "worker" who exists only in relation to the job. Acker's widely cited argument is that in the real world of actual workers, the closest approximation to the disembodied worker who exists only for the job is "the male worker whose life centers on his full-time, life-long job, while his wife or another woman takes care of his personal needs and his children".

Acker's description was until recently a good fit for most engineers. The template of the engineering professional developed out of a history of engineering as a profession with origins in military institutions, and strong links to the symbolically masculine attributes of scientific and technical rationality. Recent initiatives to get women into engineering have usually been predicated on the assumption that "women must be modified to fit into engineering, not the other way round". In ethnographic research on engineering women in a variety of educational and work settings, Eisenhart and Finkel (1998) found that organizational expectations regarding commitment to workplace activities and the worker identity favoured people who were able to put work demands first.

At the same time, these expectations were perceived by everyone concerned, women and men alike, as gender-neutral. The researchers came to view gender neutrality as a socially and culturally constructed discourse that "confers legitimacy on women's professional contribution only when they act like men" and "makes discussion of women's distinctive issues virtually impossible". Recognition of the challenges of "making women fit" links to a broader critique of the liberal feminist position that gender equality means treating women and men the same.

Rothman (1994) points out that, while liberal feminism works well in defending women's right to enter male worlds, and to "work at men's jobs for men's pay," it does little to defend women's rights to be women. In particular, it does not address the equal-treatment dilemma posed by motherhood, which is "the embodied challenge to liberal philosophy", and the rock on which claims of gender neutrality must founder.

MOTHERS IN A MAN'S WORLD

Motherhood as a barrier to women's career progress in engineering is demonstrated in much research through the 1990s. Studies in the United States, Britain and Canada all point to the challenges for women in combining "masculine" professional work and motherhood. They may find themselves, as noted earlier, in workplaces in which a discourse of gender neutrality masks clearly masculinist expectations about work performance and career progress. At the same time, they confront cultural expectations about mothers, framed around a dominant ideology of "intensive mothering" that directly contradicts workplace expectations. In contrast, the men with whom these women work are not subject to the same expectations regarding their family involvement.

These men are much more likely than their women colleagues to have partners who can take on the bulk of family responsibilities. For most men, the prevailing cultural expectation is that they will be responsible for their family's financial provision, whether or not their contribution is supplemented by working partners, and whether or not they are also involved caregivers. Thus, as Evetts comments about her sample of women and men in science and engineering careers, men have ideological support for career development, whereas "women developing careers are pathfinders in an, as yet, relatively unsympathetic and underresourced world".

Organizational responses in the form of "family-friendly" policies and programs would seem to be the way to overcome this underresourcing. But research evidence suggests they are not helping nearly as much as company rhetoric and popular discourse would suggest. While policies like parental leave or flexible work schedules are generally couched in gender-neutral terms, and are purported to be directed to both women and men, in practice their take-up by men has been minimal. This constitutes women as the prime beneficiaries of such policies, and further entrenches the idea that they are special concessions or benefits for women rather than rights to which all workers are entitled.

Lift and Ward (2001) call this a "woman's problems" approach to equality-one that accentuates women's "difference" and seeks to accommodate it. Several British studies of women in male-dominated occupations show that women are aware of the way such "special concessions" may mark them as different, and recognize the consequences of taking them up. Lewis suggests that women's reluctance to do so may stem from a low sense of entitlement (since the programs are seen as "perks"), and the powerful effect of organizational discourses of time, where productivity and commitment tend to be seen in terms of hours spent on the job. Commenting on their study of British women engineers in high technology jobs, Jones and Causer conclude:

[F]or women in technical employment actual or potential motherhood continue to serve as a disqualifying capacity, to be obscured as much as possible. The invisibility of the family remains central to the demands of the high technology workplace.

Managing Gender If women's entry to male occupational turf is largely based on liberal assumptions that women are for practical purposes the same as men, it follows that women themselves will need to "manage gender" in order to fit themselves into existing organizational cultures and structures. As Dryburgh points out, the professional socialization of women in engineering school teaches them to present themselves as competent and non-threatening, and to show solidarity with other members of the profession. This requires "their willingness to identify with, rather than challenge, the macho engineering identity". But there is more at stake here than professional socialization. Whatever their standing as "conceptual men," real-life embodied women must negotiate feminine subjectivity as well.

This is neatly illustrated by one of Miller's (2004) interviewees, a woman engineer working in the same city as the women in this study:

When you go to the field, you don't take a purse because you're really rubbing that female helplessness thing in, and you put all your junk-the female hygiene stuff in your little pockets. Another thing you do when you work downtown is you always wear wide skirts because sometimes you're going to be going to the field in the afternoon. And you can wear high heels to the office but keep a pair of flat loafers there.....

Presumably, a woman's willingness to submerge her feminine subjectivity corresponds to her willingness to see herself as a "conceptual man." Much research on women in engineering indicates that many do indeed position themselves in this way. In the workplace, they work to be accepted as "one of the boys." Those who use this strategy "want to be 'like' their male colleagues and accent this similarity while distancing themselves from 'the majority of women'". Jorgenson notes that this is "a typical adaptive strategy on the part of many women who measure the requirements of success in male terms and attempt to assimilate by disqualifying their femininity and by matching male styles of behaviour". But this suggests a conscious "anti-woman" stance that misrepresents the complexity of the situation.

As the previously cited work of Acker and Eisenhart and Finkel suggest, matching male styles and behaviour may be difficult to avoid when they are presented as organizational expectations and simultaneously proclaimed as gender-neutral. And acting like a man in order to achieve workplace recognition and rewards is not necessarily the same as identifying with men. While some of the women engineers in Kvande's study did indeed, as noted above, strive to be "one of the boys," others drew on other discourses (or, in Kvande's terms, constructed other femininities) that corresponded to a view of themselves as different from, not the same as their male colleagues.

Kvande found that the women who saw themselves in this way were invariably women with children. Jorgenson, whose research focussed particularly on the ways women engineers with children managed the potentially contradictory discourses of motherhood and engineering, found similar complexity. Sometimes the women positioned themselves as competent career-oriented professionals, sometimes as caring mothers, but usually with an awareness of the incompatibility of the mother-engineer identities. As one of her interviewees commented, "I didn't want to try to be the perfect engineer because I knew I wanted a family".

Jorgenson's work summarizes the position outlined at the start of the paper that women enter engineering work as "conceptual men," and that motherhood is, in many cases, a "defining moment," separating mothers from men and presenting women who want to be both mothers and engineers with practical, and discursive, challenges. I now turn to the interview data in order to explore these claims empirically.

The women whose interviews are analysed in this chapter were participants in a larger study of engineers and engineering work conducted between 1997 and 2000. In separate phases, the study first tracked engineers who had graduated from a Western Canadian faculty of engineering between 1980 and 1990, and then surveyed engineers in the upstream division of a major oil company based in Calgary. In phases, extensive work and family history data were collected from a total of 179 women and 211 men. Of these, a total of 48 women and 42 men also participated in semi-structured, face-to-face-interviews.

Of the women's interviews, seven were used to provide quantifiable data, but were not transcribed due to time and resource constraints at the end of the project; four were not used because the women concerned had left engineering for reasons unrelated to family issues. The remaining 37 transcribed interviews provide the empirical basis for this chapter. Of the 37 women, 17 were childless and 20 had children. The age range of the women without children was 27 to 41. Eleven were married or in long-term relationships and all were working full time in engineering-related jobs.

Those with children ranged in age from 32 to 45. All but one was in permanent relationships or married. Two had no paid employment. Five were working a variety of part-time hours, and 13 worked full time-all 18 in engineering-related jobs. My strategy in analysing the interviews is informed by the work of Gubrium and Holstein, who call for a "new language" to talk about the social world-a language that can balance naturalistic "descriptions of reality" with attention to the way such descriptions are constructed. In this approach, individuals are not seen as creating meaning "from scratch," but as working with a variety of institutional and organizational resources. My interest in this chapter is to examine the ways women take up available understandings of engineering and motherhood.

This involves not only viewing interview accounts as links to the social worlds of interviewees, but also as indicators of the ways they present themselves and negotiate their social identities. Harre describes this as "an index of location in a material world, and an index of moral position in a world of discursive values". Another model for my approach is Jorgenson, whose attention to the ways women engineers discursively position themselves with respect to their identities as engineers and as mothers builds on the work of Davies and Harre. As Jorgenson also points out, this approach is similar to that of feminist post-structural theorists who are interested in the way discursive practices generate subjectivities.

Since women without children seem logically to be better placed to work as "conceptual men" than those who are mothers, the empirical analysis first explores this issue among the 17 women who had no children at the time they were interviewed. These women were all working in jobs directly related to their engineering training. Their career paths and daily work routines were generally indistinguishable from those of the men interviewed as part of the larger project, who were their counterparts and colleagues, and who in all cases were numerically dominant in their workplaces.

They were doing the same kinds of engineering work as their male colleagues, and generally experienced the same pleasure and satisfaction in solving the complex technical problems characteristic of that work. To that extent at least, they were indeed working as "conceptual men." But they differed in the extent to which this way of working corresponded to how they discursively positioned themselves in relation to "the boys."

For example, many of the women engineers had encountered overt sexism at work. But in most cases these incidents were framed as minor. Chris laughingly referred to some "interesting experiences," but said she wasn't "the kind of woman that wants to make a statement." Marcie had also had "one or two incidents," but commented:

> It can be irritating sometimes but usually it's just a matter of just getting in and not having any attitude, just go in there and try and get along with all these guys I'm working with, you know? I don't have any attitude of being, well, you guys are out to get me. You've just got to fit in and it seems everything is going to go OK. It usually does.

By diminishing the importance or severity of sexist incidents, both Chris and Marcie were resisting being positioned by others as women and, implicitly, therefore not "one of the boys." For women who want explicitly to align themselves with men, however, even well-meaning efforts to distinguish them as women in order to provide extra career support may also be resisted. So for example, Alice, a senior technical and business specialist with an oil company, spoke disparagingly of her company's efforts to provide new women engineers with women as mentors.

"They tie you up with females," she said. Alice framed this practice as a disservice to women. Paula was even more explicit about the importance of learning, as a woman, how to fit in and play the game by men's rules. Her interview was rich with examples of shifts in discursive positioning, as she alternated between self-presentation as a woman and alliance with men. For example, she spoke of a point early in her career when her shyness and lack of confidence meant that she "interviewed terribly." Then she shifted to the present time:

> Now, after being in the position where I've ... hired engineers to work for me, I know what I'm looking for and I know that I wasn't what I was looking for. I can't afford the time or energy to hire someone who's shy, who can't speak up or if they have a problem is afraid to ask and that kind of thing (emphasis mine).

Paula claimed there were "unspoken rules" for making men feel more comfortable, and that women "get upset about the wrong things." ("If you're going to pick something to stand on, don't get upset about, you know, some purse issue. Men can't handle it ...") Paula's position was that men are "political," while women "can be really, really catty and difficult and emotional."

After telling a story of dealing with a secretary whom she'd upset ("I'm handing her kleenex and I'm like, oh my god, [I've] got to get this bid out at noon"), she then assumed the woman position on the same issue: "I do get quite emotional about things and I try to rein it in because guys don't like it when you cry in the office." Paula's discursive shifts reflected shifts in subjectivity that were often painful, and that were missing in the talk of women less inclined to align themselves with men's workplace style. These women spoke as those who knew what was needed to get the job done (often by working like their male colleagues), without losing sight of the ways they differed from men. So, for example, Colleen said:

I routinely get the comments that, "It's so nice that you're just one of the guys." Now that's supposed to be a compliment. It's because that's how they mean it ... "You're not like a woman, blah blah." Actually, I am like a woman.

Sally, at 41 one of the oldest and most experienced engineers in the group, used her age and experience to contextualize the fluid and shifting subjective alignments already described. She commented: "For the first five or six years I was convinced ... I was being treated no differently and I was doing my very best just to be one of the guys." But this conviction did not last. According to Sally, "You go through the, hey, you know, I'm just your regular Joe, to wait a minute, I'm not a regular Joe, to, OK, not only am I not a regular Joe, but I'm not going to try and be one any more either." In her case, it involved recognizing that she had a "different way of thinking," a "different style of working," a "different interactive style."

In Kvande's (1999) terms, Sally constructed a view of herself as "different from" her male colleagues. Yet seen in another way, Sally-a senior manager in a major oil company-had achieved career success very much in male terms. Her experience provides a useful link to the issue of motherhood because she attributed her career success to the fact that-not from choice-she didn't have children. Sally noted that despite her company's public claims to being "family-friendly," the "day-to-day business environment" included the perception that to get ahead "you've got to put in the long hours" and be "willing to sacrifice."

Asked if she thought more women in the organization would make a difference, she said: "I think that may be the sort of thing that keeps women from making a difference." She was explicit about the difference it had made to her career: "Because I don't have the child connection ... I have been able to, if need be, go the extra mile, every time they've asked." Sally and Alice (the technical and business specialist cited earlier, also 41 and childless) both provided good examples of the sorts of long-term engineering careers available to competent and highly motivated women able to be single-minded about their professional work. They were also the oldest of the women without children, and both seemed likely to remain childless.

This was not the case for the younger women, who still needed to confront the possibility of motherhood. Among these women, particular understandings both of motherhood and engineering work framed talk that was also significantly shaped by age and family or relationship circumstance. The single women's responses to the prospect of motherhood were provisional and speculative, since all saw a permanent relationship as a prerequisite. For example, Rosemary, four years post-graduation, and another woman who tended to align herself uncritically with her male colleagues, commented:

I'm probably indifferent either way, you know. I think it would depend on my spouse. Like, if I met somebody and they wanted kids, then I would be open to having one, maybe two. And hopefully maybe they would like to adopt children rather than (laughter) ... I just can't see myself just, just staying home and being mom. ... So, but if, hey, my previous boyfriend, he was more than happy to be a stay-at-home dad. So that, that's a fit for me as well.

In this way, at the hypothetical level at least, she constructed a family scenario that would allow her to remain "one of the boys." This scenario did not challenge the "intensive" version of mothering that would remove her from the workplace. Instead, Rosemary discursively nominated her hypothetical partner as the full-time caregiver, and gave herself a family role similar to those of her male colleagues. In other words, she positioned herself as a conceptual "father." Like Rosemary, Julia was also 27, and four years past graduation. Though she did not self-identify as "one of the boys" in the way Rosemary did, she was relishing the hands-on, technical, outdoor nature of her field work job. But she also saw this way of working as contingent:

Now I don't have the five-year to ten-year plan. I mean, between you and I, I would love to be a stay-at-home mom. ... But, I'm not married. And I don't have any kids. So until then, I'm going to do the best job that I can, and follow my career, and if it happens, it happens. If it doesn't, it doesn't.

Julia's vision of motherhood included the view that "if you have children ... somebody should be at home"-and she was clear that, in her family, unlike Rosemary's, she would be that somebody. She presented this version of mothering as incompatible with engineering work: "If I could work from home, or if I could work part-time, then that would be my ideal. But in engineering, you don't seem to be able to do that."

Other single, childless women, with more work experience than Julia, took her story to another level: children needed care that mothers should provide and that they, as mothers, would potentially be willing to provide; in the absence of these family obligations, they were devoting their energies to engineering work; this engineering work was getting to be of a kind and at a level that would not easily accommodate maternal responsibilities. Thus for example Sarah, a 34-year-old engineer who had recently been promoted to manage a major energy project for her company, expressed excitement that this project could be "a stepping stone" to "a lot more exciting projects." Asked if she thought she would be able to combine her present job with children and family responsibilities, Sarah said:

> I think I would. I know women that do do that here but they have to have a very understanding spouse that's more flexible. It's very difficult to do this job and have a spouse that's doing exactly the same thing with exactly the same sort of aspirations, I think.

Sarah's immediate qualification of the possibility of a work-family balance in her current job (by positioning herself, like Rosemary, as a father) was qualified still further by her comment later that she "couldn't go on maternity leave in the next two years" even if she wanted to, and that she had "sort of accepted the fact that [having children] might not happen." Sarah had recognized, in Wajcman's (1996) terms, the "domestic basis for the managerial career." But she also identified another problem when women's careers follow a male trajectory-in other words, when women work as "conceptual men" on an ongoing basis:

> It's a really hard situation to be in. ... I have several female friends who are engineers. ... We're all single and I have found that I have this large group of professional women friends who men are I think threatened by and we're all having a real hard time coming to grips with the fact we may not be what men are looking for in a wife. ...

Paula, whose alternating alignments with men and with women were noted earlier, fully subscribed to an intensive view of mothering ("having the woman at home makes the difference to what kind of family you have"). But she also had a particular view of engineering work, based on the demanding, intensive, field-oriented work she herself had been doing. For Paula, motherhood and engineering as she had experienced it were certainly, in Jorgenson's (2000) terms, "mutually incongruous":

> A lot of people say, well, would you recommend engineering for a young woman? And I (say), you know, the

work is really wonderful. If you like problem solving, (if) you like applying your skills, you know, it's great. But if you ever want to have children and have a family, think twice.

Later she conceded that some engineering work ("anything in the office on the computer") was more amendable to part-time or job-sharing arrangements. But though it would be "a small price to pay" because "families should come first," she also linked these arrangements to a "shunting off" of career path. Different versions of the engineering/motherhood balance came from women who were in permanent relationships with men, and who were all anticipating having children sooner or later. These women were in two groups. When interviewed, four were recent graduates, within six years of graduation, and all were in their 20s. Three were a little older and more experienced (all were 34 and had 12 years of engineering experience behind them).

Among the younger four, the ideology of intensive mothering appeared in comments rejecting nannies or day care as strategies enabling full-time work while having young children. But they also rejected the stay-at-home mother option; all planned to work part-time when their children were young. They all assumed that part-time work would be viable-even when, as in Sheila's case, there was some evidence (from a colleague working an 80% schedule) that it might be hard to manage. (Sheila commented, "I honestly think that she's a little bit less organized and that I could probably handle it a little better.")

These women also expressed a strong sense of entitlement with respect to what their employer ought to do for them. And they were united in their conviction that their partners-all of whom were also engineers-would share the child-care responsibilities, likely also moving to part-time work to do so. This conviction was striking, given their collective experience of working in resoundingly masculinist workplace cultures where men, for the most part, were able to delegate their family responsibilities, and where male engineers working less than full time were almost unheard of.

The three older women were characteristic of many women in male-dominated occupations in having deferred childbearing. All three spoke about their work, and their current workplaces, in terms that clearly indicated career success: a raise or stock options whenever she thought about leaving (Marcie); promotion from a junior position to the same grade as her male colleagues (Helen); a senior management position in a company she had helped to grow (Shelley). All three intended to keep working after having children, and all three, in different ways, planned to make their experience and seniority work for them as they thought about accommodating their jobs to family responsibilities. As Shelley said:

I've been with the company for a long time and I've always been a very good employee. As a result I'm paid well now, and I have a lot of responsibility and respect [within] the company. And, you know, that's my money to cash in when I need to negotiate a deal. A position of strength to bargain from is always a good thing. What seems to be the case is that this position of strength is achieved by proof of successful career performance according to male standards-in other words, by women paying their dues as "conceptual men?" This is not to suggest that these women achieved their success by aligning themselves with men. For example, some of the experience that earned Helen her current job was gained in an overtly sexist work environment that she was "not ever going to be a part of."

It is also not to suggest that "male standards" are uniform. For example, most of Shelley's male colleagues and superiors were about her age; she suggested that their relative youth made them less conventional. But in every case, the standards in place were standards established by men. Having met those standards, women felt freer to negotiate as women for changes they needed to accommodate their family responsibilities. To summarize, the 17 women without children produced a number of different scenarios for the way motherhood might combine with engineering: motherhood viewed as incompatible with engineering, and chosen as its alternative; motherhood refused or delegated or privatized to enable the continuation of the engineering career; motherhood and engineering combined by means of modified work arrangements (earned by male-defined career success) and the equal participation of husbands and partners.

Of these scenarios, only the first assumed that motherhood and engineering were truly "mutually incongruous," and this was not a common position. But the "strong" view of intensive mothering it implied appeared in more diluted form in all the accounts. This in turn shaped how women thought they would need to accommodate their work. Unless (as in Rosemary's case) they planned to become "fathers," motherhood was seen as putting an end to business as usual.

For most of the 20 other women in the study, the arrival of children did indeed signal changes in their relationship to their work as engineers. In fact, the choices and accommodations anticipated by the childless women turned out to be a generally accurate summary of the routes the mothers took. As with the mothers in Kvande's study, though, they were generally more likely to position themselves as women, differently situated from their current or former male colleagues.

Five of the women gave up full-time engineering work at or shortly after the arrival of their children. At the time they were interviewed, two were not in paid employment at all, and spoke as if a return to engineering was unlikely. Holly commented: "As soon as I had a baby, my total perspective changed." For Jenny, the other stay-at-home mother, her first baby's arrival signalled not so much a change of perspective as the opportunity to retreat gratefully from a world she had never wholeheartedly embraced. Of all the women in the study, Jenny was the only one whose talk suggested a resolute refusal to join "the boys."

For example, she did not like field work, and when obliged to do it, got "the field guys" to come with her, adding, "They always liked tagging along with a woman. It was easy." She discursively framed women as having "a lot to offer in their feminine side and their skills and their own things that they shine in." And she found it unfair that the women who did appear to be "climbing the ladder" were "very aggressive."

Rather than succeeding as women, "they were maleizing themselves, and having to, to get anywhere." Not surprisingly, Jenny's choice was motherhood over engineering:

> It's not a door that I've closed and I don't have bad memories. Although what I hear about engineering now ... I think, oh, man, I don't want to get into that any more. I really don't.

The others had had longer, and more conventionally successful, careers as engineers before having children. All undertook intermittent consulting contracts, but at the time they were interviewed none were working more than a day or so a week. Kate, at home with her first child, aged nine months at the time of the interview, framed her stay-at-home-mom status as "a wonderful break" after having worked in engineering for 15 years. The baby was long-awaited.

She commented: "I didn't sort of have huge expectations of it but when we finally did [have] him, I just thought, oh, why wouldn't I just kind of stay and enjoy him?" Kate had worked long enough, and recently enough, that the engineer identity was still strong ("even though I'm not working I'll always be an engineer"). But asked whether she would be an engineer ten years down the road, she replied, "Probably not." Kate had worked in engineering much longer than Jenny, but she too was framing motherhood as the opportunity to re-evaluate. Without adopting Jenny's more essentialist version of femininity, she distanced herself from many of "the men" who, unlike herself, would enjoy just sitting "in one room" doing detailed engineering work. She also distinguished herself from some other women engineers who were "really quite driven." Asked how these "driven women" would manage in engineering when they had children, Kate spoke of women she knew in just this position:

> They have a really high energy level, they probably don't get as much sleep as I do. ... Their husband has a less pressured job and he does more. I mean they make it work, they really do, and they seem to be hanging on and some of them have done just fabulously for themselves ... I'm tired watching them.

They are really energetic, driven people and they always have been.

Lisa's work history was similar to Kate's. She had worked full time for 10 years for one company, then switched to part-time with the birth of her first child. But half-time work with a second child heightened the tension between work and family responsibilities:

I wasn't doing a good job with anything. ... If it had gone on any longer I would have regretted it and you can't live your life like that. You've just got to do what you know you can.

Lisa's decision to end her part-time work arrangement occurred at a time when her husband's career was taking off, so it "made sense" for her to be the one to pull back and devote time to the family. But like Julia, cited earlier, Lisa had broader aspirations about family and motherhood, to which this decision conformed:

I really wanted to be the one with the babies. I wanted to nurse them, I wanted to raise them. ... It would have been a sacrifice to not be home with them, to me. I really wanted to do that. It was the life experience I wanted to have...

While for all four women, the commitment to motherhood rather than engineering could be construed as voluntary, for Ellie, the fifth woman in the group, it was not. At the time she was interviewed she was recovering from two very difficult pregnancies, residual physical problems following childbirth, and an extremely demanding second baby. ("I think I literally lost my mind", she commented.) In Rothman's (1994) terms, she was experiencing the "embodied challenges" to working like man-challenges she resisted as much as she could.

Echoes of the energetic and driven women engineers described by Kate appeared in her talk of working while pregnant and sick, or doing from her hospital bed the work her (female) replacement was supposed to be doing. Ellie spoke optimistically about returning to work: "I do want to work. I really enjoy working. I never wanted really to be a stay-at-home." The clear implication was that when she was physically able, she would pick up her working life. Six of the women with children continued to work full time, or close to full time, in engineering jobs.

But the conscious downplaying of career goals in order to accommodate family responsibilities expressed by Lisa was evident in the talk of these women as well. It was also reflected in their practices-a shift in the kind of work being done to something perceived to be less stressful (Linda), a refusal of promotion in order to remain in a familiar and manageable work environment (Joanne), a move from permanent employment to consulting as a means to achieve flexibility (Kelly), the use of a pregnancy to signal a shifting of gears after a successful corporate career (Hilary), cutting back to four instead of five days a week (Shauna).

These work arrangements were accompanied by talk that linked them to family benefits. In all cases but Joanne's, the family accommodation represented some form of job shift from a prior high-gear career path in male-dominated workplaces. In Joanne's case, it was more a matter of consciously slowing her progress. In none of these cases could the focus on motherhood be construed as legitimating a failure to succeed in male terms. The third group of mothers is those whose careers appeared on the surface to have been less affected by motherhood.

Given the way these women were working, and the jobs they were doing, they could be described as mothers in careers more often associated with men. The nine women in this group had all reached senior levels of management and/or technical specialty. But in this group also, the balance of motherhood and career was complicated and fluid. It was also in this group that the most vivid images of "conceptual men" becoming mothers emerged. Cassie was one example.

As a woman who had always been able to work as "one of the boys," Cassie downplayed issues of gender in the workplace, noting that she had never experienced "discrimination, or anything like that," and was "not a supporter of affirmative action-type programs." She said she thought "opportunities go to those people who are willing to work for them." But this perspective was challenged by an unplanned pregnancy at a time when she was making dramatic career progress.

> My manager and I had [pause] had some issues, when I first told him that I was pregnant. We went back and forth quite a bit. The first thing he said to me was, when I told him, was not, "Congratulations," it was, "Well, who's going to do the annual plan?" Because he started, he goes, "Well, how long [a maternity leave] would you be taking? How much are you entitled to? Would you consider coming back early?" And we went back and forth for four or five months. And I was just miserable. ... It put a real strain on our relationship. ... It's probably taken us a good year to get back to where we were before (emphasis mine).

"Where they were before" positioned Cassie as "one of the boys" again. This was possible because she was able, like many fathers, to privatize her family responsibilities. Her partner, like many mothers, was willing to allow hers to be the privileged career, and they also hired a nanny. She spoke about increasing her family involvement some time in the future, when she would have "accomplished quite a bit-unless, I mean, I have an opportunity for moving further." Carla's case is worth noting because it is such a good example of the discursive positioning of the "professional engineer" and the (very much embodied) mother. When Carla returned to work after her first maternity leave, she tried to breast-feed her baby during her lunch break as a way to continue nursing. She said:

> Well, I tried it for two weeks, but then my milk supply was so big, it was just like ... you know, here I am a professional engineer and my boobs are leaking all over the place and I just couldn't, couldn't do that.

Asked if those around her at work were supportive, she replied, "Well, I didn't really talk about it with anybody. It was kind of a private thing." Carla's acknowledgement of the incongruity of "professional engineers" breastfeeding, and of breast-feeding itself as belonging in the private domain, hinted at the subjective shifts she also negotiated. Carla's career choices were constrained by her family's need for her income. Like many men also, she was the family breadwinner, in a position to delegate family work to her partner. Unlike most men, however, she expressed unease about this arrangement. Her interview was interspersed with comments that clearly indicated what Smith (1987) would call a bifurcated consciousness, divided between a focus on her work (which she enjoyed), and preoccupation with a domestic life over which she had reluctantly surrendered control.

"There are really times that I long to be the stay-at-home parent," she commented. For other women, there was a more conscious crossing over from a family focus to a more explicit career orientation. Zoe responded to an appeal by a friend to leave her flexible consulting arrangement and lead a small company; Ingrid's long-time male mentor asked her to return to work part time two months after her second child was born. Ingrid spoke of having planned not to return to work till the children were in school. But the part-time work quickly turned to full-time, then a partnership. Her account combined expressions of her enjoyment of her job with regrets about its costs.

> I think once a woman works, it's hard not to work. It's hard to stay home and not have that challenge. ... Knowing that other people are advancing, advancing, advancing. ... The downside is the time. You don't know (if you raised) your kids yourself. I don't consider, myself, that I've raised my kids ... I consider that they spend more time with their babysitter than they do with me, right? I consider that and now it's more time at school than with me, right? So I consider myself kind of the secondary raiser, kind of in their lives, my husband and I.

But in this group of mothers there were also those whose accounts were much less conflicted. For example, Denise had her first, and only child, at 35. She took 20 weeks of maternity leave, the maximum her company allowed-"and honestly, I was dying to get back to work." She commented:

> It didn't change much in my life. I still worked the same hours. I was still the same person at work as I was before. Just because I have a full-time nanny during the day, I was pretty uninterrupted, having a child, compared to what it could be.

The accounts of the other mothers in this group fell somewhere between Ingrid's and Carla's regret at their time away from their children, and Denise's apparently more successful privatizing of her family life. But if there were differences in the ways these women discursively framed their career and family experiences, there were striking similarities in the material circumstances out of which their careers emerged. Six of the nine had partners in less stressful, more predictable jobs who were able to pick up the family slack, and/or considerable support from extended family.

Nina's mother was the primary caregiver for her children, and her trades-employed partner had the "second" job. Ingrid's sister-in-law cared for her children, and her parents were available as back-up. Rosie's partner held the regular-hours second job, and her child-care arrangements were further supplemented by a devoted network of parents and siblings. In other words, these women's successful engineering careers were made possible by a substantial private infrastructure similar to that available to many career-oriented men. In two of the three cases (Zoe and Hannah) where partners' careers did not take second place, both women noted that having to share top billing meant husbands making some career sacrifices of their own.

To summarize, the 20 women with children followed fairly closely the paths anticipated by the childless women engineers described earlier with respect to the combination of engineering and motherhood. A very few, like Holly and Jenny, voluntarily "chose" motherhood. All the others negotiated a balance between being an engineer and being a mother that was both discursive and practical. For some of these negotiators, the balance was achieved by a conscious gearing down on the work side-but usually only after careers had been established and dues paid. For the others, it was achieved (as just noted) by means of privatizing and delegating family responsibilities in order to maintain career progress.

This study has proceeded from the assumption that motherhood is a watershed for women in engineering, and has explored what was described at the start of the paper as a more nuanced explanation for why this might be the case:

that women enter engineering jobs as "conceptual men," and that problems arise because mothers can't be conceptual men.

What it means to work as a "conceptual man" is not self-evident. In this chapter I chose to see women engineers working in this way if they were doing the same kind of work, in the same conditions, for the same hours, and with the same general expectations about quality of performance as their male colleagues. Another part of the definition was that this work was done in workplaces dominated by men-a condition that was more than met in every case. I also tried to distinguish between working as a conceptual man, and aligning onself, and discursively positioning oneself, with men.

On the basis of this definition, all of the women without children were working as conceptual men. Often, though not invariably, they also positioned themselves as "one of the boys"-though this positioning was seldom sustained and consistent. Nine of the 20 women with children were also working as conceptual men-though they were much less likely to position themselves with "the boys." In my discussion of these nine, and in comments about the plans of some of the childless women also proposing to delegate to partners or otherwise privatize their family responsibilities, I have suggested that these women were or would become "fathers."

This proposition is not entirely theoretical. In a separate study I explored the ways the men with children interviewed for the same engineering project balanced work and family responsibilities. Serious accommodation to family responsibilities generally took two forms: a choice of work (generally office- rather that field-based, with predictable hours); or downshifting from an intensive work focus to a more relaxed pace-usually the choice of men who had achieved considerable career success first. But for all of these men, the balance of work and family still typically involved working days of eight to 10 hours, and in almost every case, also involved a partner working part-time or not in paid employment, and available to pick up the slack.

Access to this private infrastructure of support characterized almost all the fathers. For those mothers who have access to something similar, the "father" analogy has some merit. For the mothers, "downshifting" to accommodate children went much further: an opting out of engineering, temporarily or permanently, or a reduction in work hours. Fathers never employed these strategies; indeed, men with young families working less than full time never emerged in the larger study. This is why such strategies come to be identified with women, and why so-called "family-friendly" organizational policies purporting to help employees balance work and family responsibilities come to be perceived as helping women fit in to men's workplaces.

As noted by researchers cited earlier, these policies may become another organizational device for differentiating women from "the boys"-and mothers from fathers. The foregoing of course assumes that "family-friendly" policies and programs are available at all. Commenting on ten years of research on work-family issues in Canada, Higgins and Duxbury (2002) identified a lag between the emergence of work-family issues as a concern for employees, and employers' sensitivity to the issues. Economic and industrial factors are also relevant.

Many of the engineers in the present study worked in the energy industry, which was undergoing major restructuring during the economic turbulence of the 1990s in Canada. As McKee et al. also concluded from their study of "family-friendly" policies in the U.K. oil and gas industry, such policies have a low priority-and employees are unlikely to press their demands-in times of economic uncertainty. Women, for the reasons noted above, may be even more reluctant to do so. If this is the case, and if they also lack access to the private infrastructure of family support available to most men in engineering, then engineering as a profession will continue to be difficult for women with children.

Bibliography

Anker, R. and C. Hein, 'Why Third World Urban Employers Usually Prefer Men', *International Labour Review*, Vol. 124, No. I, Geneva, 1985.

Beech, C., *Women and Women into Information Technology*, a report by the British Computer Society, 1990.

Byrne, E., *Women in Science and Technology: The Institutional Ecology Approach*, Interim Research Report, Department of Education, University of Queensland, 1988.

Chew. S.B. and R. Chew, 'Information Technology as a Strategy Human Resource Development', in E.C.Y. Kuo, C.M. Loh and K.S. Raman, *Information Technology in Singapore Society: Trends, Policies and Applications*, Singapore University Press, 1990.

Davidson, M.J. and C.L. Cooper (eds), *Women and Information Technology*, Psychology and Productivity at Work Series, London, John Wiley and Sons, 1987.

Deakin, R., *Women and Computing: The Golden Opportunity*, London, Macmillan Press, 1984.

Eriksson, I.V., B.A. Kitchenham and K.G. Tijdens (eds), *Women, Work and Computerization: Understanding and Overcoming Bias in Work and Education*, Amsterdam, North Holland, 1991.

Faruqui, A.M., M.H.A. Hassan and G. Sandri (eds), *The Role of Women in the Development of Science and Technology in the Third World*, proceedings of the conference organized by CIDA and the Third World Academy of Sciences, Trieste, Italy, October, 1988.

Harrison, P. (1983), *The Third World Tomorrow*, NY, Pilgrim Press and Harmondsworth, Penguin

Irvine, J., 'Women into Information Technology', *Information Technology and Public Policy*, Vol. 8, No. 3, Summer, 1990.

Kluzer, S., *Computer Diffusion in Black Africa: A Preliminary Assessment*, unpublished paper, SPRU, University of Sussex, Brighton, UK, 1988.

Lim, G.K., 'Women's Participation in the Computer Industry in Singapore', in Ken Tijdens *et al.* (eds), *Women, Work and Computing: Forming New Alliances*, Amsterdam, North Holland, 1989.

Lovegrove, G. and B. Segal (eds), *Women into Computing: Selected Papers*, 1988-1990, London, Springer, 1991.

Mitter, S., 'Computer Aided Manufacturing and Women's Employment: a Global Critique of Post Fordism', in I.V. Eriksson, B.A. Kitchenham and K.G. Tijdens (eds). *Women, Work and Computerisation: Understanding and Overcoming Bias in Work and Education*, Amsterdam, North Holland, 1991.

Mumford, E., *Where are Tomorrow's Top Women Executives ?*, Manchester Business School Review, Vol. 4, No. 3, 1980.

Ng, C. (ed.), *Technology and Gender: Women's Work in Asia*, Women's Studies Unit, UPM and Malaysian Social Science Association, 1987.

Ng, C. and J. Othman, 'Information Technology, Gender and Employment in Malaysia', in S.C. Bhatnagar and M. Odedra (eds) *Social Implications of Computers in Developing Countries*, New Delhi, Tata-McGraw Hill, 1992.

Odedra, M., *Information Technology Transfer to Developing Countries: Case Studies from Kenya, Zambia and Zimbabwe*, unpublished Ph.D. thesis, London School of Economics, 1990a.

Odedra, M., 'Poor Management leads to Gross Under-utilization', *Computer in Africa*, Vol. 4, No. 5, July, 1990b.

Parikh, I., *Women in Management: an Annotated Bibliography with Emphasis on Commonwealth Sources*, London, Commonwealth Secretariat, 1987.

Stamp, P., *Technology, Gender and Power in Africa*, Ottawa, international Development Research Centre, 1989.

Subramaniam, P.R., *The Future for Women in Information Technology*, M. Sc. dissertation, London School of Economics, 1991.

Tijdens, K., M. Jennings, I. Wagner and M. Weggelaar (eds), *Women Work and Computing: Forming New Alliances*, Amsterdam, North Holland, 1989.

Virgo, P., 'The Case for Women into Information Technology Campaign', *Information Technology and Public Policy*, Vol. 6, No. 3, Summer, 1988.

World Bank, *Sub-Saharan Africa: From Crisis to Sustainable Growth*, Washington DC, World Bank, 1989.

Wright, B.D. (ed.), *Women, Work and Technology: Transformations*, Chicago, University of Michigan Press, 1987.

Index

I

L

M

N

P

R

S